BILLY, ERIC & ADOLF

One War, Two Brothers

To Maureen.

Enjoy the
read

Chris
White

The Author

Chris Whitfield lives on the Wirral in the UK with his wife Gill, Tilly the Border Terrier, and Lola the Cockapoo. He has three grown up children, Oliver, Hannah, and Charlie.

Billy, Eric & Adolf is his fifth book. His previous work includes a humorous series on disappearing things, *Chimpanzees in Dungarees* and *Hitchhikers & Scary Bikers*, a novel, *The Drummer's Tale*, and a history of Football World Cup Nations, *Big Balls!*, which reached number one on the Amazon Kindle charts.

BILLY, ERIC & ADOLF

One War, Two Brothers

Chris Whitfield

Sedbergh
Publishing

First published in 2015 by Sedbergh Publishing

The right of Chris Whitfield to be identified as the author of this work has been asserted by him in accordance with the Copyright, Designs and Patents Act 1988.

A catalogue record for this book is available from the British Library.

Sedbergh Publishing Ltd Reg No. 7794755

Printed in the UK by ImprintDigital.

ISBN 978-0-9571193-2-1

www.chimpsindung.co.uk

This is a dramatised story based on real events and the lives of Eric Norman Whitfield and William Edgar Whitfield during the Second World War and its aftermath. Some names and identifying details have been changed to protect the privacy of individuals.

**Billy dedicates this book to Joyce,
his beloved wife for more than sixty years.**

*Once upon a lakeside
There lived a lonely swan
Underneath the one cloud in the sky
That covered up the sun
Then one day his true love
Flew in from the mere
And the only cloud up in the sky
Began to disappear
So then upon a lakeside
There were no lonely swans
Only best of friends
And love embarked upon.*

CONTENTS

Foreword

The newspaper headline read more like a plot line from an episode of *Dad's Army*.

'Hitler wanted sleepy Bridgnorth to be Nazi HQ after the invasion of Britain.'

I laughed out loud... surely not? Innocently searching the internet for wartime photographs of the Shropshire town, I had inadvertently uncovered one of life's unexpected ironies. The article, from the Daily Telegraph 21st April 2005, explained that newly-discovered secret papers had revealed Bridgnorth as Adolf Hitler's preferred choice for the headquarters of Nazi GB after a successful invasion of the British mainland. The town's central location, the nearby RAF base, the fortification possibilities from its unusual 'town on a hill' geography, all contributed to earmark the place as ideal. The documents proved that German invasion plans were still up and running one year after the Luftwaffe's Battle of Britain setback. They were dated 1941, the same year that my dad was evacuated away from the dangers of the Liverpool Blitz... and yes, he was sent to Bridgnorth. The absurdity of the young, twelve-year-old Billy Whitfield escaping the bombings by relocating to the town Adolf had chosen to make his home from home appealed to my sense of fun.

The idea for a book about my dad's wartime experiences arose from conversations with him that were increasingly veering in the direction of Bridgnorth. My mum would ask about a family matter, while my old man talked at the same time about catching rabbits or fruit-picking in the Shropshire countryside as a lad. He asked me one day if I would write up his reminiscences, and I agreed.

We set up a routine of visiting the local Wetherspoons every Monday evening - yes I know that sounds more like Community Service - my dad drinking mild and dredging his memory for anything he could recall from nearly seventy five years ago, while I downed Diet Pepsi and scribbled frantic notes. I had expected to compile a few anecdotal recollections of times gone by, something nostalgic to its core, but nothing much else. However, both my dad and I were about to be taken by surprise.

One name kept cropping up during our discussions, his brother Eric. He was five years older than my dad and therefore lived a very different war. While Billy enjoyed the war years growing up and learning to be independent, not least of all when living in the peace and tranquillity of the Shropshire town Adolf failed to conquer, Eric was a Royal Air Force volunteer in Bomber Command, the most dangerous place for a serviceman to be in the Second World War. The more I discovered about my uncle, the more compelling the need to tell his story as well. *Billy, Eric & Adolf* was born.

Piecing together Eric's tale was greatly helped by the personnel and casualty records my dad obtained from the RAF as next of kin, the BBC's 'WW2 People's War Project', and by a number of Bomber Command enthusiasts and aficionados out there, including Andrew Macdonald, Alan Wells, and Frank Powley. I remain grateful for their valuable contributions. And I would also like to thank my daughter Hannah for her help in editing the text.

At the time of writing, more than a year has passed since the original idea to write the book, and it has been quite a journey, hard work, yet a labour of love. My dad is now well into his eighties and not in the best of health, but it has been truly heartening to see how much help and comfort this endeavour has afforded him. As I narrated draft pages to him, he would sometimes laugh, sometimes cry, and sometimes drift off to another time and place. Together, we had somehow achieved the impossible, reuniting the young Billy with his mum, his dad, and most movingly of all, his brother Eric. It has been more than a pleasure to play my part.

Chris Whitfield
April 2015

Introduction

I am an old man now. This back and these legs, so important for the heavy lifting when I made propellers for a living, are not what they used to be. These arms, once routinely outstretched as I dived to turn the centre forward's shot around the post, are now emaciated and frail to the eyes. And this brain, the receptacle that stores a lifetime of flashbacks, memories and reminiscences, has inevitably lost its sharpest of edges. Yet beneath the withered, thinning skin, the bones that creak, the breath that labours, the mental pauses; there is the child. They say that boys never grow up. Even as adults we want to play with train sets and dinky cars, and our unrealistic dreams of playing football or cricket for England remain strong, vivid, and unaffected by the long passage of time. The child within me is certainly alive and well, as energetic as if flesh and blood, habitually full of hope, optimism and naivety in the pictures that play in my mind as I lay back, close my eyes, and drift. The young Billy, however, lives in another age, an age of innocence, an age of danger, an age of uncertainty. The time has come for me to share some time with him and his brother Eric, my brother Eric. It has been a while. I hope you will join me.

Billy

PART ONE

BRIDGNORTH

CHAPTER 1

The air was a thick composite of steam and coal dust. Through it permeated the sound of a thousand voices and the industrial clatter of locomotives, far from resplendent with their grimy windows and tarnished nameplates. Adjacent to the maritime corridor of the River Mersey, the Chester bound platform of Woodside Station was filled with hordes of orderly children, some unable to hide the fear and apprehension of what was happening in their young lives but most acting as though ready for the annual charabanc to Blackpool. To Billy's right, hanging from intricate, Victorian ironmongery, the station clock with its large, black Roman numerals against a faded sepia background, struck nine o'clock. He counted the chimes. On the ninth, he heard his name, the tone shrill and piercing.

'Billy Whitfield?'

'Yes Miss.'

He held up a right hand. His left was holding a pillowcase, packed last night by his mum with all the worldly possessions he needed for the indeterminate time ahead, socks, underpants, a couple of shirts, a spare pair of trousers, gas mask, and small piece of shrapnel for luck. He compared the gabardine mackintosh hanging from his own shoulders to the thick, woollen overcoat of the teacher allocated to look after his group, the result inducing a pang of envy on his part.

'Here you are Billy,' said Miss McDonnell, her breath vaporising in the cold air of the January morning as she passed him a luggage label.

'Thank you,' he murmured.

The tag, no more than 4" x 2", displayed a heading of 'WALLASEY' printed in blue capitals across its width. Beneath it was stamped 'Gorsedale Secondary School', a large number '17' scrawled in crayon, and the name 'Billy Whitfield' written in a small, spidery longhand.

'Use the safety pin to attach it to your coat,' said the teacher.

In his efforts to close the pin, Billy pricked his thumb and a tiny drop of blood appeared, which he quickly dispersed by rubbing against the tips of his other fingers before finishing the task.

The train was the 9.25am to Bridgnorth, and four carriages stretched out before his eyes. He was escorted to the first one. On the rattling door he read the letters 'THIRD' spelled out in faded, flaking gold. One joker at the back claimed he was Little Lord Fauntleroy and demanded a first class seat but was given short shrift. Miss McDonnell led the group to their compartment, a confined space of polished wood and stale cigarette smoke, and helped place the luggage and pillowcases on to the racks above. Billy sat down closest to the window. Next to him was Roy Stubbs, a pal from school, with another four lads from their year at Gorsedale packed on to the bench seat. They felt like sardines in a tin. On the opposite side of the compartment sat Miss McDonnell and a further five children, but with two younger family members within their throng, they seemed to have more room. He recognised three of them as the Kirkbride family, Joan at thirteen a year older than Billy, her brother Kenny about eleven, and Ronnie nearer seven. Young Ronnie was silently sobbing, his eyes bloodshot red, his dripping nose held in check by a woollen glove, and his mouth locked in the shape of an inverted 'U'. He was a sorry sight.

Through the window, Billy observed the hustle and bustle of the station as more children were marched to board the train. Beyond this and cordoned off behind a rope, anxious parents waved to their little ones. When the last child from the platform had been dispatched, he heard the guard's whistle, a signal for most in the compartment to get up and look out of the window. One of the taller boys stretched and pulled down the sash through which half a dozen severed heads began shouting their final goodbyes. Billy waved lifelessly from his seat to no one in particular. He searched for his mum but failed to spot her. His dad was not there. He had said goodbye about an hour ago in a matter-of-fact manner, as though off fishing for the day. The carriage shuddered as the train moved forward, and he finally caught a glimpse of his mother on the platform. She was expressionless, though dabbing her eyes with a screwed-up, white handkerchief. The engine quickly gathered speed, and she gradually became a small dot that finally disappeared when the train snaked its way along the track and left the station behind.

Green fields and hills replaced the terraced houses and factories, and Billy Whitfield, aged twelve, glanced down at the 'Wallasey No.17' luggage label bouncing up and down against his breast pocket. He was no longer a name. He was a number. A darkening shadow abruptly shrouded his thinking, and his mind drifted back a few weeks to the event that had precipitated today's journey.

****

It was the last Friday before Christmas 1940, and Billy was celebrating the warm glow that greeted the end of school term. He had not especially enjoyed his second year at Gorsedale Secondary, the masters to a man, strict disciplinarians who tolerated neither dissension nor tardiness, the latter Billy's Achilles heel, a natural inability to get out of bed in the morning costing him dear. His palm had already felt the thrash of more than one rattan cane, and he had written enough lines in detention to fill a book. It was evening, and Billy had settled down to listen to the wireless with his mum and dad when the now familiar sound of the air raid siren invaded their peace.

15

'Bloody Germans,' groaned his dad.

'Ted!'

Even when the prospect of danger presented itself, his mum continued to admonish her husband for his colourful language.

'Are we going in the shelter?' enquired Billy, getting up from his chair, unable to hide an element of excitement in his voice.

'No, it's too cold and damp,' said his mum. 'We'll go under the stairs,' the Corporation's brick-built refuge in the yard evidently far from welcoming to her sensibilities at this time of year.

Their rented house in Chepstow Avenue was a larger than average, four bedroom affair, and the space under the stairwell was big enough to accommodate a bed. In complete darkness, the three family members were shortly huddled together lying on the mattress, acutely aware their position offered almost worthless protection in the event of a strike. There was then silence, except for the sound of ARP wardens mobilising other residents to take cover, until the dreaded hum of Luftwaffe aircraft colonised the air. The anti-aircraft guns responded by blasting shells and ammunition into the night sky, each rhythmic sequence of fire illuminating the house and shaking its foundations. Bizarrely, these defences provided the most unsettling noise of all.

As he became accustomed to the dark, Billy could see his mum and dad, neither especially religious, praying with their eyes closed. His was a mixture of fright and thrill. In the distance, he heard the descending scream of a German bomb that climaxed with a thunderous explosion… then another, this time a little closer… and then…

Surprisingly, the bomb when it landed made more of a thud than a bang. No.12 Chepstow Avenue briefly shook, as though struck by an earthquake, followed quickly by the accompaniment of breaking glass, clanging metal and falling masonry. The flashes and terrifying acoustics of the bombing raid continued for a few more minutes, until the skies were empty again and the drone of the enemy aircraft had faded, replaced by the sirens, bells and whistles of the emergency services.

'What about the budgie Ted?' whispered Billy's mum, as they all sat up tentatively on the bed.

'What's that?'

'The budgie… is the budgie alright?'

'Bloody hell Eva…'

'Go and look Ted.'

Billy's dad rolled off the bed and walked across the hall to the front room. He was back in less than half a minute.

'He's gone,' he said, brushing a layer of plaster and dust from his shoulders.

'Oh no...'

'And so are the bloody doors and the bloody windows.'

Billy stretched his head from under the stairs to see the front door missing, ushering in cold air infiltrated by acrid smoke. Wrapped in blankets, Ted, Eva and Billy went out on to the street to be confronted by the horrors of war. No.2 on the corner had taken the direct hit. The scene was one of twisted metal and wooden beams protruding from a base of bricks and rubble where half an hour before the twenty-first birthday of George Preston had been in full swing.

'Oh Ted, Eric wasn't…'

The words of Eva trailed off in dread.

'No,' he replied firmly, 'he's at Scouts tonight.'

'Oh yes, thank goodness.'

She breathed easy again. Billy's elder brother Eric was seventeen and friendly with the younger Bob Preston. His mother's initial panic that he may have been at the party subsided, displaced by a growing disbelief at the sight before her eyes. The adjacent house in Serpentine Road was ablaze, hoses from the arriving fire engines ready to be unravelled. One glimpse at the burning red sky indicated this to be no isolated incident.

Billy spotted a fragment of shrapnel from the impact next to his tattered slipper. He picked up the metal object. It looked like part of an anti-aircraft shell, not quite as impressive as the nose cone with fuse rings he found last week but one for his growing collection nonetheless. The piece was still warm when placed in his pocket.

As he went to move across the road to find more, an ARP man shouted, 'Hey! You! Get back!'

Billy sheepishly took shelter behind his mum and in doing so overheard his old man murmur.

'That's it Eva. Your mother's right. He's got to go away.'

'Who's he?' thought Billy.

****

The stations came and went, Miss McDonnell answering the regular question of 'Are we nearly there Miss?' each time with a firm rebuttal in her Scottish accent. The only toilets on the train were in the end carriage, and so at Shrewsbury there was a mass evacuation of those desperate to go, Billy included. A few minutes later he was back in the compartment, this time by the door rather than the window. He now had to strain his neck to catch the names of the stations, the only thing to differentiate one stop from the other. Fighting the tedium, he challenged Roy to a game of who could remember the most stops since Shrewsbury.

'Berrington, Cressage, Buildwas Junction, Ironbridge & Brosely, Jackfield Halt, Coalport, Linley Halt,' said Roy, a note of triumph carried by his words.

'You missed Cound.'

'Eh?'

A confused Roy picked his nose then rubbed the prize into his ginger hair, glistening with Vaseline.

'You missed Cound,' repeated Billy, 'Berrington, COUND, Cressage, Buildwas Junction, Ironbridge & Brosely, Jackfield Halt, Coalport and Linley Halt.'

It was his turn to be triumphant.

'Bugger,' said Roy, under his breath so that the teacher could not hear.

The train began to slow, Billy's heart correspondingly quickening when he saw the black lettering on the unkempt, white sign at the next station. It read 'Bridgnorth', journey's end.

'Come on boys and girls, we've arrived,' said Miss McDonnell, standing up to retrieve the authentic and improvised suitcases from the luggage rack. 'Now remember to stay close to me as we leave the train.'

Her words were stern but delivered with kindness.

The eleven children from the compartment dutifully followed their new guardian as though walking out at Wembley for the FA Cup Final. They alighted on to the platform, Billy gulping the Shropshire air, so much fresher than that left behind by the banks of the River Mersey. The station seemed even busier than Woodside, although there was surprising calm and quiet. The sound of winter birdsong was clearly audible to his young ears, suggesting his fellow junior passengers were as tired as he was after the long and arduous journey, their energy and excitement from earlier in the day having ebbed away like the evening tide. Miss McDonnell led the group through the crowds and the sandstone main station buildings to the roads outside, where they were confronted by a steep climb up a hill. There appeared to be steep hills everywhere. Breathless, feeling cold, tired and hungry, they finally made their way into a school hall in Listley Street, where they were directed to sit down on a highly polished parquet floor.

Miss McDonnell said her goodbyes, and after a short wait as more children joined them, Billy's group were called to stand in front of a large desk manned by two smartly dressed, busy, efficient women. One by one, the youngsters filed past the ladies showing the luggage label hanging from their clothes which was then matched to a name on a list. In return, they were handed a brown paper bag before returning to the wood floor, Billy delighted to find inside his a packet of biscuits and a chocolate bar. He ate them hungrily in one sitting.

A long, tedious wait ensued, the boredom only interrupted by a medical inspection and glass of milk, until the shorter of the women behind the desk guided Billy, Roy, and the three Kirkbrides towards a formidable looking lady dressed in a thick tweed skirt suit with a matching hat that framed her face. It was the face of a bulldog, her lower jaw jutting forward determinedly. The canine menace, however, unravelled when she smiled, a row of pristine bottom teeth displayed as a benign expression took over. When she spoke, her voice moved up and down an octave with the uniformity of a metronome.

'Good afternoon, my name is Miss Lawson from the WVS. I'm going to find a nice home for you here in Bridgnorth.'

She looked at Billy.

'And there's no need to look so frightened young man, I won't bite.'

Knowing the bulldog's reputation for ferociousness, he was not totally convinced.

'Now come along everyone,' she continued cheerfully, 'follow me.'

They left the building and trotted towards a van parked on the opposite side of the street, the young visitors trying to keep up with her brisk pace. The vehicle was a dark grey Bedford with painted out sign, although the words 'Ice Cream' remained detectable. The children piled into the back. It had no seats, just a few blankets on the floor, and when Miss Lawson closed the rear doors, the only light came from its two half-moon windows. Rapidly acquainting her passengers with the shortcomings of her double de-clutching technique, Miss Lawson jerked the van into motion to provide the evacuees with a ride akin to cowboys at the rodeo. As Billy's head knocked against the side of the van like a woodpecker in slow motion, he glanced at Roy, nervously picking his nose again, and at the Kirkbrides, now huddled together as one. He took a deep breath and sighed. The Bridgnorth adventure had begun.

A few minutes later, the Bedford manoeuvred past two imposing metal gates into a driveway flanked by a sizeable, well-kept lawn, the centre of which housed an impressive bronze statue, its fountain dribbling a spurt of water. Stepping out on to the gravel, Billy stared at the detached house before him. They didn't have dwellings like this in Wallasey, even in Warren Drive. He counted nine windows, a door, and a small board declaring 'Chatham House', the property's front façade dominated by ivy clinging doggedly to slate grey pebble-dashing that climbed towards the guttering. He gave Roy the thumbs up. They had unequivocally fallen on their feet. But when Miss Lawson signalled for the pair to wait while she approached with the Kirkbrides, his spirits plummeted. This mansion was not for them after all.

The guardian rang the bell, revealing a slow, patient chime, and in keeping with the theme, a minute or so passed before it was answered. Standing in the doorway was an old man, dressed in formal attire that even from a distance away, Billy could see was shabby. If Miss Lawson was a bull dog, this chap was a bloodhound, his sagging jowls resolutely slumped either side of an unsmiling mouth from which laughter had probably not been heard since the reign of Queen Victoria.

'May I help you?' he drawled.

'I am calling about the evacuees,' replied Miss Lawson, her manner full of good cheer.

The old man glanced up and regarded the youngsters with mild disdain.

'Round the back,' he said rudely, jabbing his forefinger to the right.

'Shall I say who sent us?'

Miss Lawson was doing her best to remain civil.

'Jarvis the butler,' he announced solemnly before closing the door without any further acknowledgement.

'Come now children, follow me.'

Billy and Roy lagged behind as the party plodded towards the tradesmen's entrance at the rear, noticeably lacking the refinement of the front. This time a parlour maid answered. Subdued, she listened to Miss Lawson while staring at the ground before closing the door and disappearing inside, re-emerging after a short delay with a shake of the head. It was a no and a return to bobbing up and down again in the back of the van.

After the screech of another gearbox change and the sound of the tired engine labouring up the latest hill, the vehicle stopped outside a smart semi-detached house in Hightown, the elevated part of Bridgnorth. Miss Lawson instructed Billy and Roy to stay put, while she took the Kirkbrides with her, but they were all back in no time.

'No luck there, I'm afraid,' she shouted, opening the rear doors. 'And so on to the next we go.'

Miss Lawson appeared indefatigable, her zeal impervious to the refusals, but after a succession of 'no thank you' responses, Billy detected a drop in her natural enthusiasm. She opened the back door of the van and talked directly to the children.

'Look, it's a bit late now, so I've decided you can sleep in mine tonight, and we can set out first thing in the morning afresh.'

The unwanted evacuees accepted their fate and somewhat disconsolately endured one final bucking bronco ride to Miss Lawson's cottage. The rest of the day was a combination of battleships, hangman, jam sandwiches, and cocoa before slouching off to their beds. As the moon struggled to shine its light through low clouds in the evening sky, Billy's head embraced the pillow hoping that fatigue was about to bestow a night of sweet dreams. But it was not to be, the memory of the day's rejections difficult to shake off. He suddenly felt very alone, very unwanted, an orphan, and he began to sob, silently, his arms held tightly against his chest, his body curled up like a baby in the womb.

Billy awoke the next morning to a hearty breakfast cooked by Miss Lawson's housekeeper. He was just swilling down a cup of tea, when he heard the growl of a vehicle outside the cottage.

Miss Lawson bounded in to exclaim, 'Good news children, I have found places for you all.'

She looked towards the Kirkbrides.

'Now you three will be staying with Mr Johnston the solicitor and his lovely family in a nice big house in Hightown.'

Joan reassured her brothers by taking hold of young Ronnie's hand and smiling warmly at Kenny. The moment confirmed in Billy's mind that the Kirkbrides would be alright. Miss Lawson then turned to Billy and Roy.

'And you boys are going to live on a farm.'

A farm? Billy was unsure whether this was good news or not but decided to remain optimistic.

'Right... on with your coats and follow me,' said the WVS lady, making some strange arm movements that pointed in the direction of the front door.

Quickly gathering their belongings, Billy and the others were soon ready to go and meet their new families. On leaving the cottage he breathed in the fresh Shropshire morning air, noticing a milder edge to the weather, although overnight rain had dampened the ground underfoot. As he walked through the front garden, his outstretched palm patted the sodden bark of an apple tree, Billy drying the hand on his backside before getting into the van.

After depositing the Kirkbrides at a nicely appointed residence in what seemed a 'posh' part of town, Miss Lawson invited the two remaining boys to share the front seat for the remainder of the journey. Billy sat closest to the door and gazed out into the winter gloom. He had never seen a road with such a sharp gradient and was slightly unnerved by his driver's tendency to treat the task as an audition for the Keystone Kops, the vehicle's engine screaming in protest at the demands being made. He readied himself for the crunch of gears and a likely careering off the road, but the ride eased when they reached Lowtown, the relatively flat part of Bridgnorth that straddled the River Severn. The scenery changed from houses and shops to fields, trees, the occasional building, and after a long curve in the road, a few wheat barns on the right with two vast carthorses grazing outside. The van then turned left and halted in front of two wooden gates, as dilapidated and decrepit as those at Chatham House had been elegant and pristine. Billy and Roy jumped out to open them, permitting Miss Lawson to steer the Bedford to the end of a small driveway, the boys following behind. Billy took in the sights.

Attached to a tree was a rectangular sign drooped at an odd angle, its 'Potseething Farm' lettering carved into the rotting wood. A number of hens and chickens weaved random patterns as they strutted across the clay ground, beyond which thirty or forty sheep grazed on a grassy expanse bordering wheat fields that stretched out to the distant horizon. Behind the modest-sized, red brick farmhouse, a cow shed emitted a powerful aroma of manure, although Billy wondered if the adjacent outside lavatory was the culprit.

'Ow bist?' said an older man, presumably the farmer, emerging from the toilet.

Billy's theory about the smell had taken a new twist. The farmer's appearance bore the marks of a lifetime in the outdoors, his ruddy face smudged in crimson, an arrangement of blood vessels vying for attention with the deep lines etched into his leathered skin. His eyes narrowed as if staring into bright sunshine, whitened tufts of hair sprouted from his chin like daffodil bulbs in early bloom, and his open mouth revealed a solitary, yellowing front tooth. As for his apparel, an old sackcloth coat held in place by binder twine swirled above scuffed hobnail boots, the look topped off with a battered old flat cap. Billy had never seen anything like it before in his life.

'Good day Mr. Stoneycroft,' said Miss Lawson, 'is your wife about?'

'She be in the 'ouse,' he replied, his voice gruff, his manner short but not hostile.

'Thank you.'

Before the WVS guardian could reach the front door, it was opened by the farmer's wife. Billy was still only twelve but would later look back and consider this the moment that puberty kicked in. Here was a full-figured woman, probably in her forties, who instinctively emphasised her feminine curves by straightening out her dress with palms that followed the outline of waist and hips. This was Shropshire's answer to Betty Boop.

'Hello Rose,' said Miss Lawson, 'here are those two strapping boys I told you about earlier.'

Mrs Stoneycroft appraised Roy and then Billy, her reaction impassive. She followed this with a simple statement.

'The camp beds from the RAF base have just arrived.'

'Excellent,' gushed the WVS lady, 'so that's that.'

The news meant that the deal was done. Miss Lawson shook their hands and said farewell, Billy silently grateful for her efforts and her kindness. Now he knew. Potseething Farm was his new home... with Betty Boop and Old Macdonald.

Entering the farmhouse, he and Roy were accosted by a divergent blast of warm air from the living room and cold air from a store room opposite, the two boys surprised to see a cow standing patiently inside next to a wooden bucket. Rose introduced the lads to her eight-year-old daughter Patricia before escorting the pair up a dark staircase, turning right at the top into a bedroom, their bedroom. It was bereft of anything other than a small window, two camp beds, whitewashed walls, and a few damp stains. It was no Chatham House. And it was freezing cold.

A few hours later in candlelit darkness, Billy shivered as he made a mattress out of blankets for his camp bed. He heard footsteps coming up the stairs, Rose appearing at the door carrying two objects wrapped in towels.

'Here you are boys; these will keep you warm tonight.'

She placed a hot, covered brick under the covers of each bed, and wished her new tenants a good night. Their shivering gradually subsided until sleep beckoned.

'Billy?' whispered Roy.

'Yes...'

'Are they really married?'

'I think so'

Both boys were young but still old enough to feel incredulity at the mismatch of the one-toothed farmer and his glamorous wife.

Roy yawned, 'Goodnight Bill.'

'Goodnight Roy.'

Billy turned on his side and stared at the wall. Last night he had cried himself to sleep in a warm, cosy, comfortable cottage. Potseething Farm was none of these things. It didn't even have running water or electricity. Yet this was his home, one where he had been accepted. He was not an orphan tonight, and there were no signs of tears. His thoughts turned to his mum, dad, Eric, Wallasey, the bombings, and the novelty of the Shropshire countryside. He closed his eyes and drifted into a long and deserved sleep.

CHAPTER 2

'I'm going to bible class on Sunday.'

Eric's quietly spoken words stopped his dad from taking a mouthful of food wrapped around the end of his fork.

'Bible class?' said Ted, putting down his knife and stretching the elastic of his braces. 'Bloody hell son, what for? To become a bloody vicar?'

'Less of the bloodies Ted,' said Eric's mum, fighting her customary losing battle to keep bad language away from the house.

'I don't think the Reverend E.N.Whitfield has a particular ring to it,' said Eric, prior to consuming a mouthful of fried bread.

'Oh, I don't know,' she said, 'sounds rather grand to me.'

Eric was aware that his mum's breezy manner belied an underlying apprehension for the year ahead. Father and son continued eating, but Eva lifelessly pushed food around the plate with her cutlery.

'Is a vicar one of those reserved occupations?' she suddenly asked.

'Yes mum, but I've no intention of becoming a man of the cloth.'

'Oh.'

Eva failed to hide her disappointment.

Eric looked up at his mother. Life had dealt Eva Whitfield a hand that meant she lacked conventional beauty, her everyday looks not helped by plain, horn-rimmed glasses and a drab hairstyle, yet she possessed a warmth and sincerity to which the goddess could only aspire. Today, however, she looked tired with dark lines under her eyes, her sallow complexion a fitting canvas. Her younger son Billy had left for Bridgnorth a few days ago, and she was already missing him. The thought of her other child going off to serve in the forces was not one to countenance. He suspected the uncle he never met was also looming heavy in her thoughts. Her brother, Private William Beecroft, aged eighteen and brimming with naïve patriotism, had answered Lord Kitchener's Great War call in 1915, proudly marching off to deal with the Hun in Europe. His fate, as with so many of his peers, was to be scattered over the muddied fields of the Somme, an unknown soldier's grave his final resting place.

'I suppose your job at GEC might be reserved?' she suggested, already hinting that the hope was forlorn.

'Mum,' said Eric, 'a purchase order clerk for a company making light bulbs is not quite as essential for the war effort as a doctor or a teacher.'

'I suppose not.'

Eva pushed back her chair and took her unfinished breakfast to the kitchen, returning shortly to pour three cups of tea, all with milk and two sugars. The clink of a teaspoon on china competed for attention with the ticking clock on the mantelpiece and a dog's bark from somewhere outside.

Eric took his first sip, announcing, 'Actually, I did want to tell you something.'

His eighteenth birthday loomed in a few months' time, the decision point for countless young men up and down the land to consider their options, military or otherwise. His mum sat down, while his dad wiped the grease from his mouth with a crumpled handkerchief pulled from his trouser pocket.

'I want to volunteer for the Royal Air Force.'

The declaration was greeted with a loud farting noise.

'Deary me…' exhaled his dad, searching in vain for a dog to blame.

'Ted!'

For once, his unsociable habit of wind at the breakfast table was timely, providing a welcome diversion from the likely impact of Eric's news.

'Isn't that Brylcreem Boy paraphernalia for posh lads son?'

'Not these days Dad.'

'Why the RAF?' said his mum, a hint of resignation already in her voice.

He gave a non-committal response, although it was a question already answered in his head. There was no single reason. Whilst he found the prospects of serving in either the Navy or the Army distinctly unappealing, the recent Luftwaffe raids on his home town had stoked a strong desire to exact retribution in a like-for-like way. Furthermore, the bombings had revealed another side to the RAF's allure with the sheer adventure and excitement of taking to the skies in armed combat the stuff of *Biggles*. But if he had to choose one factor above all as to his preferred path, it was a desire to better himself.

A glance at his dad reinforced the point, now pulling his trousers out from the crack of his backside. Beneath the swept-back, receding grey hair, the owl-like features, the crotchety exterior, and the swear words, beat the heart of a good man. Edgar Whitfield had served with the Merchant Navy for many years before moving on to a variety of different jobs including travelling salesmen, newsagent, and his current position at the Co-op laundry. He worked hard to feed and house his family, but it was a struggle. Yet he was one of the lucky ones. He was from 'good stock', his stepfather George Russell, an Alderman who had recently run for Mayor. On more than one occasion, George had stepped in to help out his stepson financially, times that left Ted Whitfield appreciative but dispirited by the damage to his pride. Eric had matured to recognise he wanted something different. The Royal Air Force, the most prestigious of the services, would provide the opportunity, one that he would grab with both hands. For Eric Whitfield was going to become a pilot.

He thanked his mum for breakfast and then left their latest rented house, this one in Barrington Road, to catch the number three bus to the ferry. It was time to go to work in Liverpool.

****

The following Sunday was a pleasant day, winter sunshine casting long shadows, a mild breeze gently wafting the honeysuckle shrubs, pink blossom and evergreen foliage as Eric and best friend Len McCabe strolled through Central Park towards the Oakdale Road Mission. The pair might have been twins, each attired in a belted, double-breasted raincoat, shirt, tie, pressed trousers, and highly polished shoes. A dark grey trilby hat, under which greased and centre-parted hair resided, finished off the sober look, more than apt for what lay ahead today.

The bible class in the church annexe began at two o'clock, and the friends arrived just in time. Len led the way, opening the door to reveal an area set out like a school classroom, the turnout impressive with nearly all desks full. An elderly lady with a kind face was waiting patiently at the front, and after depositing their hats and coats on a stand by the door, the newcomers were steered to a desk with two empty seats towards the back. She then addressed the group, her voice frail but clear.

'Hello everyone… for those who have not met me, my name is Miss Finch, and I am here to welcome you all to another lesson in God's teachings. And I'm delighted to say we have two new pupils this week. At the back over there we have Derek and Len.'

Len held up his hand.

'Yes?'

'It's Eric actually.'

'My apologies young man… a very warm welcome to Derek and Eric.'

The newcomers exchanged a look. They would let it pass.

'Right everyone,' Miss Finch continued, 'in these very difficult times, I thought it only right and proper that today we examine the 23rd Psalm of David from the Old Testament.'

'Yea, though I walk through the valley of the shadow of death, I will fear no evil:

30

for thou art with me; thy rod and thy staff they comfort me.'

'Never have such words been more appropriate and more needed. So let us start by taking the opening line, *The Lord's my shepherd.* Does anyone feel brave enough to offer an interpretation of these words?'

A few hands went up, Eric unnerved to see Miss Finch pointing at him, until he realised Len was ready to make his bow as an ecclesiastical scholar.

'Yes Eric?'

Len did not correct her and answered, 'Is Jesus working for a hill farmer?'

Eric grimaced at his partner's literal analysis and heard a few minor sniggers. The tutor, although tolerance personified, quickly moved on to another, more worthy contributor. The voice was gentle, feminine, with little hint of an accent.

'Is the Psalm using the shepherd as a metaphor... that God provides food, shelter and protection for believers in the same way a shepherd does for his flock?'

'Excellent Vera... very good indeed,' cooed Miss Finch.

Eric glanced across but through the heads failed to get a clear view of the respondent, other than she was brunette and her friend next to her, blonde.

'Now,' continued the teacher, 'how about *I'll not want?* What might this mean?'

Although relieved his pal sat this one out, over the next three quarters of an hour, Eric witnessed Len unashamedly offer more pearls of biblical wisdom. Miss Finch, slightly worn down by his woeful lack of insight, eventually indicated they should break for tea.

'OK, Eric lad, now's our chance,' said Len, running a right hand through the undulations of his wavy hair

'What's that?'

'Time to meet Vera and her friend.'

Quick as a whip and leaving Eric trailing in his wake, Len marched off to intercept the two young, keen participants from the far side of the room. By the time Eric caught up, the trio were by the long trestle table with its array of china cups and saucers sitting on a pristine, white tablecloth. His friend had made an immediate impact, the girls seemingly laughing at his every word.

'Ah, and this is my best chum Eric,' said Len, gurning as though proudly showing off a prize-winning marrow.

Each girl offered a hand, which he dutifully shook. This not being aristocratic circles meant there was no need to lower his head, purse his lips, and kiss.

'You've answered a lot of questions haven't you,' said the blonde girl.

Eric's worst nightmare had come true. Due to the mix up of their names by Miss Finch, these pretty young things believed he had given all the hapless answers uttered from Len's mouth. He winced at the recall of his friend's interpretation of *Thou preparest a table before me in the presence of mine enemies* as a Nazi-British joinery collaboration. After putting the record straight, he heard some minor small talk in the recesses of his mind, 'I'm Margaret and this is Vera', 'Nice to meet you,' but Eric's attention was one dimensional. He was rather taken with Vera.

She was a pretty girl with little make-up, her dark, lustrous hair brushed back from her forehead yet long enough to cascade down past both shoulders, her almond-shaped eyes, a striking violet that contrasted sharply with his undefined shade of blue and grey. She had more than a passing resemblance to Vivien Leigh playing Scarlet O'Hara in *Gone with the Wind*, and for a fleeting moment he wished he had the matinee idol looks of Clark Gable. The thought was a little harsh. An attractive and arresting child, Eric had grown into a handsome young man, with even features, thick dark hair, and a broad mouth that always returned a warm smile. But for now, the attentions of Vera and Margaret were largely focussed upon

Len.

Behind the trestle, an older lady with hunched shoulders and unsteady hands was struggling with a large, metal teapot. As she poured tea for the young students, her spectacles kept falling off her face, just missing the cups. With as much beverage in the saucer as the cup, Eric had to concentrate hard when drinking to avoid ruining his Sunday best clothes.

All too soon, tea break was over, and it was back to the bible class for the second session. Len had been right. It was a great place to meet girls. Eric was nearly eighteen yet still awaited his first kiss, and his friend's suggestion to attend these meetings seemed worthy of a try. It was a good idea anyway, Sundays in winter never much to write home about at the best of times. But regardless of such motives, after the horrors of what happened to the Preston family in Chepstow Avenue, a dip into spiritual waters had to be a soothing balm. Returning to his seat, Eric was again unable to get a clear view of Vera, but no matter. The image in his head was crystal clear, and he liked the portrait. Unfortunately, there was a problem. She evidently did not feel the same about him. For the first time in his life and without knowing, Eric was experiencing the start of a dull ache that had inspired composers, poets and novelists over the years.

On cue, Miss Finch ended the lesson with a promise that at the next class, they would study Corinthians 13:4-8, *Love suffereth long…*

CHAPTER 3

Billy was getting used to this walk. St Mary's was a few miles from the farm, a hike that took at least half an hour every week day morning. As he made his way along the Oldbury Road into town, he clapped his gloved hands together to generate warmth. It had not been a severe winter, but the dawn chill and piercing wind still had the wherewithal to catch the breath of a young man in a hurry. He gazed through the gaps in the passing hedgerows awaiting the white blooms of blackthorn and saw barren pastures dusted with rime from the dawn frost.

The familiar rumble of a car's engine came into earshot, he and Roy automatically easing to the side of the road to allow the vehicle past. The sleek, black Jaguar SS 21 saloon, with its five headlights organised in front of the radiator grill like a constellation of stars around a sun, contained the usual occupants. There was young Patricia from the farm sitting in the back as regal as Princess Margaret and staring ahead at an imaginary fixed point, keen as ever not to acknowledge the young lodgers trudging down the road. And there was the mystery man in the driver's seat, his tilted hat only partly obscuring his film star looks. Billy knew nothing about this Dick Tracy figure, nor why he gave Rose's 'little girl' a lift to school every day. Despite a lack of natural curiosity in such matters, he was intrigued by the routine, a routine that reinforced Potseething's natural order. Even if there was a hurricane outside, the two evacuees would still be expected to pound the lanes and streets on foot, while Patricia was chauffeured in the warmth and comfort of a luxury car. Billy and Roy, those two rascals from Wallasey, were definitely not welcome inside the Jaguar.

Crossing the River Severn, the now familiar bell tower, stained-glass windows, and half-pillared turrets of St Mary's came into view. Billy had been in Bridgnorth for over a month and to his surprise had found great solace and comfort in attending this school. Gorsedale Secondary Modern back in Wallasey had conditioned the young William Whitfield to associate a place of learning with strict discipline and obedience. It was a place to get a strap across your back rather than a hand upon your shoulder, a perception quashed by his experiences within this former church hall now functioning as a school for evacuees.

Billy and Roy were hugely thankful for the warmth of the building as they strolled through the front archway and into the large open plan area divided into three sections, each with a cluster of desks arranged to face a blackboard. They crossed the polished floor to join their classmates sitting on the uncomfortable wooden chairs. Billy, elbows resting on the drawer-less desk, counted eleven pupils in his class today, all boys. The numbers were down one from last week.

His tallying was interrupted by the familiar Scots brogue of Miss McDonnell. Billy really liked his teacher. He had been surprised and delighted to discover on his first day of Shropshire schooling that his guardian from the train journey to Bridgnorth was also in charge of the older pupils at St Mary's. She was kind, friendly and enthusiastic. Yet there was a downside... her strongly held Caledonian roots. He had noticed that the class spent a disproportionate amount of time studying things Scottish. In history, it was Robert the Bruce, poetry meant Rabbie Burns, and music was all bagpipes and traditional Celtic singing... without the bagpipes. Following a geography lesson studying the workings of a blast furnace, this February morning was proving to be no different.

'Right boys, we're now going to sing,' she burred.

There was a collective groan and an inward equivalent from the other two classes across the room. They were not about to perform 'Jerusalem'.

'Today's song is 'Doon by a Wee Bit Wimplin' Burn', a lovely song with a dark ending.'

The groans lessened as the pupils resigned themselves to the tongue twister that lay ahead.

'I'll sing it first,' she said, clearing her throat and taking a deep breath.

Her vocal was tuneful but possessing of a reedy treble, piercing to normal ears, but deadly to dogs or anyone with earache.

Doon by a wee bit wimplin' burn,
I met my lassie fair yestreen,
A lassie wha's baith young an' braw
A lassie wi' twa bonnie een…

Billy and his classmates listened, their attention hanging by a thread, thanks solely to the promise of the ditty's gruesome finish.

…nae matter what should e'er befa',
  Till grim death should us sever, O.

Whatever it meant, the ending was a disappointment to this group of boys, perhaps hoping for something more worthy of a Bela Lugosi film. It was now their turn, and following a myriad of unsuccessful attempts, Billy was not alone in welcoming the sound of twelve chimes from a nearby clock tower to signify dinner time. He and Roy stayed at their desks while the others filed out to the canteen area for a sit down meal.

The boys from the farm reached into their bags and pulled out the jam sandwiches prepared earlier by Rose. They began to eat, just as the delicious odour of a roast beef dinner assailed their nostrils. Billy had noted Miss McDonnell's tendency to watch this ritual with a slight frown. The same happened today, until she smiled and left to enjoy her own

36

lunch.

'Roy… you've got jam all over your chin,' said Billy.

His friend wiped it with the back of his hand and licked it clean.

'Hey Bill, have you heard about the hermit?'

'The what?'

'The hermit on the hill.'

'Can't say I have.'

'Arbuckle was telling me… lives up in the caves apparently,' said Roy, biting a chunk from his second sandwich.

'What caves?'

'Up in the hills… the Hermitage Caves.'

As Roy spoke, he provided his friend with a bird's eye view of chewed bread and jam.

'Never heard of them,' said Billy, now looking a trifle unsure at his own food.

Cut into the red sandstone hills of the Wolverhampton Road overlooking Lowtown, a series of cave dwellings, centuries old, still survived in a landscape of deadwood shrubbery and old oak trees.

'Apparently, he wears a big smelly coat and hat made from rabbit fur, and…' Roy's eyes widened, 'Arbuckle says he's a cannibal.'

'Don't be daft,' said Billy.

'He is!' insisted Roy.

'Why would he eat humans when there's a load of rabbits running round?'

The reasoning stumped Roy who conceded the point with a shrug.

The afternoon's lesson was mathematics, hardly Billy's strongest subject, but at least Scotland was not the central theme. Eventually, three o'clock arrived, and it was time to endure the thirty minute journey back to the farm. The halfway point on this daily trek was close to St Nicholas' Church on Oldbury Road where the lane veered sharply to the left. Today, the driver of the sleek, Jaguar SS 21 chauffeuring Patricia home was travelling too fast and failed to see the two schoolboys just around the corner. The young pedestrians had to take quick, evasive action, jumping into a hedge to prevent being splattered across the carriageway like a couple of sedentary hedgehogs.

'Bloody hell,' exclaimed Billy, instinctively calling upon his dad's favoured vocabulary as he picked himself up and dusted off a small covering of foliage.

Roy's reaction was a tad more extreme.

'Aaaaarrrggggghhhhh!' he screamed, sprinting away like a cheetah at a speed likely to get him to Potseething Farm before Patricia and her chauffeur.

Billy was momentarily perplexed, until he felt a tap on his shoulder. He turned around, his stomach lurching at what he saw.

'Who is ye?'

The sound was a gravelly, countryside drawl, the sight, a hermit whose sartorial inelegance made Farmer Stoneycroft look like royalty. He was wearing a patchwork fur coat tailored from a selection of rabbit furs, its stench the other extreme to the pleasantry of freshly baked bread. This was the vagrant from the Hermitage Caves, the cannibal. Poor Roy was clearly on his way back to change his underpants.

'I say who is ye?' persisted the tramp.

Billy looked into the small, hazel-coloured eyes set in the blood red face.

'I is Billy.'

The young evacuee had no idea why he had adopted a rural accent.

'Billy w'at?'

'Billy Whitfield.'

'You're not from 'ere is ye?'

'No, I've been evacuated… from near Liverpool.'

The tramp glanced up as though trying to dredge some distant memory.

'Liverpool? ...used t'work there, when on ships... the Merchant Navy ye knows,' he muttered, before coughing up a ball of phlegm that he spat on to the steel cap of a dishevelled right boot.

'My dad was in the Merchant Navy,' said Billy, pride a natural accompaniment.

'Was 'e? W'at was 'is name?'

'Ted.'

'Just Ted.'

'No, Ted Whitfield.'

'Ted Whitfield? No... rings no bells.'

'What's your name?' Billy asked, the eye contact easier to maintain than the holding of his breath.

Even on this cold February afternoon, the coat was giving off a pungent scent capable of mild asphyxiation.

'Don't 'ave one really... people just calls me Trampy.'

'Right... Trampy.'

'Where is ye stayin' Billy boy?'

'Potseething Farm.'

'Well bugger me with 'pitchfork. That's where I doos work in summer. Looks like ye'll be seein' more o'me then.'

This news about the 'cannibal' was not great for Roy, the youngster soon to be haunted by images of sitting in a giant saucepan of boiling stock with only vegetables for company. Trampy held out his hand in a friendly gesture that the evacuee shook in return before parting and heading home. He was going to a farmhouse both frugal and primitive, yet compared with the tramp heading up to his cave in the hills; Billy was staying in a palace.

CHAPTER 4

Patricia, Billy and Roy were sat around a large oak table finishing their breakfasts in the farm's kitchen. This was the room in which they spent most of their time, an imperative in January and February when the convection heat from the wood burning stove provided the only effective warmth in the house, but equally welcoming in the relative mild of spring when the other rooms retained their chill.

The cast iron stove with its firebox, oven, hot water tank, and tall stove-pipe dominated the living area. A flat iron sat perched above the range next to shelves that kept food warm, the culinary centrepiece adorned with a collection of different-sized copper pans, pots and kettles hanging from a wooden mantel attached to a stone wall. In the far corner, a well-stocked pantry featured a variety of foodstuffs including a selection of cured pork, while two armchairs and a long settee faced a wireless positioned on a sturdy sideboard. In the other corner, a door led to the bedroom of the farmer and his wife, a section of the house unequivocally out of bounds for the young lodgers.

Billy sniffed the buff-coloured envelope hoping to discover a mild aroma of soap, the scent of his mother. He could only smell paper. This was his favourite moment of the week. Every Saturday morning, a letter would arrive from home containing a postal order for sixpence, which he would cash in Hightown Post Office to buy a giant vanilla slice from the cake shop next door. Today's correspondence also contained some unexpected news. His parents were due to visit Potseething Farm on Easter Monday, now only two days away.

'Mrs Stoneycroft,' said Billy in a surprised tone, 'my mum and dad are coming here on Monday.'

'Yes I know,' said the farmer's wife, pouring tea for the breakfasters. 'I invited them.'

Billy had mixed emotions. He wanted to see them, but he had been away for three months now and had developed a level of independence that might sit a little uncomfortably with them.

'What about, erm..?' Roy nervously twisted a few strands from his fringe around a forefinger.

Rose picked up on his apprehension.

'Yours are coming too,' she said, reassuringly. 'And suffice to say, you will both need to have a bath. I don't want them thinking you've turned into something from *Oliver Twist*.'

Bathing was not such a dreadful notion now it was April and a milder climate had taken hold. The memory of sitting inside a galvanised iron tub in the animal food store during the chill of the winter months remained a shuddering thought.

'Ow bist?'

Farmer Stoneycroft walked into the kitchen. It was 9.30am, and he had already been up for more than four hours. Billy had quickly learnt that farming was not for the faint-hearted.

'Roight lads, 'ere t'is.'

The farmer placed the radio's accumulator on to the table with a thud. This was another task 'not for the faint-hearted'. The Ever Ready glass container with its tar-sealed hard rubber top measured only 6" x 5" but possessed the weight of a baby elephant. It was the job of Billy and Roy each week to carry the unit to an electrical store in Hightown and exchange it for a fully charged one.

After a few deep breaths and the appropriate mental preparation, the evacuees set off for town, Billy winning the coin toss and opting for the first leg of the journey. Faced with the steep inclines up to the town centre, Roy predictably reached the electrical shop, breathless, aching, and with the arms of an Orang-utan. Agreeing to collect the recharged unit after their regular game of Saturday football, the pair headed off via the post office to enjoy their pastry treats at the cake shop before, with a fresh cream residue brushing the sides of their mouths, the two walked through the Northgate Arch and took to the nearby playing field to join nine other team mates already limbering up for the encounter in store.

Billy was the goalkeeper, blessed with fine agility and a safe pair of hands, though he was a little on the short side. Today's opposition brought an extra edge to proceedings. St Mary's School for Evacuees were playing Bridgnorth Grammar School. St Mary's comprised a rag bag of shapes and sizes, from the impressive bulk of 'Arbuckle' at right back, a big lad unaffected by the strictures of food shortages, to 'Tiny Tom' at outside left, so small he warranted a tag stating 'Handle with Care'. Nobody had a football kit and only one of the players, proper boots.

The contrast with the Grammar School First XI was glaring. Appearing from the pathway of a neighbouring building, eleven strapping athletes strode confidently on to the playing surface, each outfield player draped in a clean white shirt, black shorts, and white socks sat comfortably within dubbin-soaked, brown football boots. The team's immaculate hair accompanied good looks and strong physiques, and they displayed a single-minded, steely determination that permeated their facial expressions. This could have been Wembley 1939.

The ages within the St Mary's team ranged from about eight to fourteen, whereas the Bridgnorth players to a man looked about twenty six. Billy watched in mild consternation as the team in white limbered up, performing star jumps in two neat rows. In stark contrast, he turned his head to see a distracted Roy vigorously picking his nose. The game's referee was the sports master from the Grammar School whose main objective was not so much to uphold the rules of the game but to ensure his team emerged victorious. It did not augur well.

Yet with only one minute of the match remaining Billy had the chance to become the hero of the hour. Bridgnorth Grammar's centre forward ran into the penalty area and fell over a stray lace from his left boot. The ref had no doubts and awarded a penalty. The same player would take it, retreating about ten yards for a long run up and blast towards the goal. Billy noticed the kicker eyeing the left of the goal, and assuming big frame did not mean big brains, he chose to dive the same way. It was a sweet hit and seemed destined for the top corner, until the young keeper flung himself towards the upright and miraculously tipped the shot around the post. The referee blew for full time just as ecstatic team-mates mobbed Billy. Thanks to his last minute heroics, the team had only lost 9-0.

After the match, the two friends picked up the accumulator and journeyed back to the farm, embracing another battle of endurance. To vary the route, they chose a different way home and were surprised to come across a partly demolished shop. They stood there wondering as to the cause, when a policeman approached.

'Good afternoon lads,' he said, exuding authority. 'Have you not seen this before?'

They shook their heads.

'That's where the bomb dropped,' he said gravely.

'The bomb?' said Billy.

'German plane, 29th August 1940, hit the shop and the Squirrel Hotel over the road there. There was also a direct hit in Church Street and by St Leonards. Two women killed... poor beggars...'

The bobby's gaze turned to the heavens, his thoughts now lost in reminiscence about the fateful night. The irony was not lost on Billy that to escape the Luftwaffe, he had been evacuated to a town recently bombed by the Nazis.

'Anyhow, must move on, so you look after yourselves boys,' said the PC, giving a half-hearted salute before continuing his beat.

When he was at a safe distance, Roy turned to Billy.

'I'm fed up,' he said, placing the accumulator by his feet.

'What do you mean?'

'I'm fed up living on a bloomin' farm with no water and no electricity. And why are we here? To escape the bombs? And yet the bombs have fallen here as well. It's daft. I want to go home.'

'Come on Roy, it's got to be safer here than Wallasey.'

'Maybe, but I'll take the chance.'

Roy's outburst was not a complete surprise. His friend had become increasingly withdrawn in the last few weeks, a trickle of homesickness threatening to become a torrent. He was contributing less and less in school and had resented helping out on the farm. This was in sharp contrast to Billy's disposition. After a shaky start, he felt at home in this rural backwater, relishing the freedom and independence that the arrangement offered. Admittedly, the Farmer and Mrs Stoneycroft were not replacement parents, clearly having more time and giving greater consideration to their daughter, but they were not unkind people. He was also enjoying school, Miss McDonnell increasingly maternal with her pupils, something that he valued. Unlike Roy, Billy didn't want to go home.

On Easter Monday shortly before noon, the two evacuees were sitting on top of the gates to Potseething Farm looking down Oldbury Road anticipating the day's visitors.

'What car do you think they'll be driving,' said Roy, swinging his legs.

'Hopefully not the Co-op Laundry van,' said Billy, 'though if you see a giant gas bag floating round the corner, you'll know it is.'

'I reckon it'll be a Ford Model Y, a 1932 version with a short radiator grill, straight bumpers, and nine openings on either side of the bonnet.'

There was no conceit in Roy's informed remark.

'Blimey, you know about your cars don't you?'

'I suppose so.'

'Tell you what... I'll make one prediction.'

'And what's that?'

'It'll be black.'

Roy laughed.

In the distance they heard the growl of a car engine. The boys looked at one another, nodding their heads in affirmation.

'Here they come,' said Billy, sliding down from the gate.

Roy stepped out into the road to get a better view.

'It looks like a Rover 10, maybe a convertible.'

Bill joined him, 'seems I was right.'

'You never mentioned a Rover.'

'It's black.'

'Oh, fair point.'

The lads waved their arms as if guiding the pilot of a Tiger Moth to the runway. Billy spotted his dad at the wheel and his mum in the front passenger seat, Roy's parents presumably in the rear. He waved. They waved back as the vehicle made its way through the gates and came to a halt next to the farmhouse. The visitors were all dressed in their Sunday best, but it was a bad start for Billy's dad when he stepped out of the car. Ted Whitfield had to suppress a 'bloody hell' as his shoe made a perfect imprint in a dollop of manure.

'Hello Billy... how are you?' said his mum.

'Fine thanks.'

He was struck by the kindness showing in his mum's face, something he had almost forgotten, but he kept the thought to himself. There were no hugs or embraces. These were not tactile times, and whilst emotions and feelings ran deep, the norm was to suppress them, keep them in check.

Rose came out of the house, and Billy noticed his dad perk up. With Eva's attention diverted to matters of chickens, hens and sheep, Ted quickly appraised the feminine curves of the farmer's wife. Roy's dad, loosening his tie from the starched collar of a white shirt, attempted a corresponding ogle but was spotted by his wife, an unsmiling woman at the other end of the pole as regards glamour and voluptuousness.

'Let me show you round,' said Rose.

The farmer's wife gave her guests a brief guided tour of Potseething, after which it was inside to the farmhouse kitchen for tea and biscuits. Billy said nothing as the adults talked about the war, something never discussed in his mum's letters that tended to specialise in the ordinary. He would know about a good old sing song with Eric at the piano but not about the bomb dropped on the Manor Lodge Old People's Home that killed all its residents.

'Mind you,' said Roy's mum, grinding her teeth as she placed her white lily patterned china cup on to its saucer, 'it's been quiet on the air raid front for the last month or so... which is why...'

She hesitated, everywhere suddenly quiet, at least until Farmer Stoneycroft burst into the farmhouse to puncture the silence.

'Ow bist?'

He had made no compromises for his guests, dressed in something more suitable for packing potatoes. He coughed, cleared his throat with an exaggerated 'kkkk' sound, and spat the contents on to the hearth.

Cupping his groin he complained, 'Bludy 'aud ewe, lambin' up thure... kicked me roight in the Tommy Handleys.'

Billy caught his mum's eye, and underneath her benign, unmoved exterior, she was amused, this playful side to her something he loved and wished he saw more often. Rose, unlike her husband, was blessed with a normal level of social awareness and moved hurriedly to take control.

'George, this is Billy's mother and father, Eva and Ted, and this is May and John, Roy's parents.'

'Ow bist, won't shake yer' ands... covered in sheep muck.'

Rose struggled not to roll her eyes in exasperation. May looked on disparagingly, the back of her hand covering her nose, her facial expression contorting as though she had tasted a portion of said animal droppings. Recovering her poise, she nodded towards Roy who started to gather one or two small things before disappearing upstairs. He returned a few minutes later carrying the pillowcase used on the Woodside to Bridgnorth journey three months ago. As he stood there, nervously picking his nose, the truth dawned on Billy. His pal was going home. He had not been bluffing.

Roy's mum took her cue. 'As I was saying, erm, the bombs have been quiet the last few weeks and, what with Roy missing home, and, much as we really appreciate all that you've done for him, we both feel the time's right for him to leave here.'

May squirmed a little on her chair. Roy's dad just stared into his tea.

'Oh, right, well, if that's what you want,' said Rose.

'Yes well, we do,' said May.

'Of course... of course...'

Rose turned to Billy. 'And what about you, young man, do you want to go home.'

'No.'

Billy's response was quick, and there was probably part of his mum saddened by its swiftness. His willingness to stay had nothing to do with any concerns over the Mersey bombings. He remained too young to have any vivid sense of mortality. It was more a case of finishing the adventure that had begun in this previously unknown world of agriculture and countryside. He had given an honest answer to Rose's question, and the fact he was about to be left on his own didn't seem to matter. In fairness, since Eric started work at GEC, Billy had become used to occupying himself, the five year gap between the brothers too wide to bridge. While the elder matured into young adulthood, the boy Billy still messed about with conkers, catapults and marbles.

Outside in the Rover convertible, Roy, looking more sheepish than the flock grazing on the pastures in the distance, squeezed between his parents on to the cramped back seat. Billy gave him a quick nod of the head. And that was that. Eva and Ted thanked Rose, said goodbye to their younger son, and stepped into the car, Billy's mum at the last moment remembering to pass him the gumboots she had brought him from home. With the help of a starting handle, the ignition brought life to the grumbling engine of the vehicle that began its long drive home along the A483 towards the Wirral peninsula.

The motor had only left a few yards of tyre tracks on the road, when Farmer Stoneycroft inexplicably walked out straight into the path of the oncoming car. Ted slammed on his brakes and, for once, a succession of 'bloodies' was warranted and not subject to Eva's reprimand.

'Ow bist,' he said nonchalantly, before resuming his walk across to the barns.

It was clear that Old George remembered the era when the automobile was simply a drawing on an engineer's desk. Moreover, he still acted as though it was. The car moved off for the second time, Billy watching from the gate to see the Rover disappear around the far bend and out of view. He knew he ought to be feeling lonely. But he didn't. He felt at home.

CHAPTER 5

'Luncheon meat'... two words to affirm that life goes on. The quiet in the office was such that Eric could hear the scrape of nib on manuscript as he made a posting in the Purchase Order Ledger for catering supplies, an immaculate entry assured by his flawless handwriting and judicious use of blotting paper. The requisitioned food had no impact on his hunger, although best boiled ham, caviar and champagne would have produced the same indifference today.

Diagonally opposite him, partially obscured by a marble pillar, the polished wood-framed chair was empty, the mahogany desk neat, orderly, the same way Mr Leadbetter left it every day at 5.00pm before journeying back to his Liverpool home. After the relative calm of the previous few months, May 1941 had seen a renewal of the Luftwaffe's attack on the area. For a number of consecutive nights, German bombers had blitzed the city, and the shelter in which the office manager took cover yesterday evening with his family had suffered a direct hit, all occupants lost. His quiet, 'Goodnight young man' from the day before would be the last words he heard from this mild, thoughtful gentleman.

Eric's mind wandered back to the journey into the office earlier that morning. Walking through the city centre, it had seemed only a matter of when his job at GEC would be affected by the ongoing devastation. For the time being, the building had evaded any shelling, and it was business as usual, but the same could not be said for the sights encountered as he travelled from the Pier Head to the office. The overhead railway at the junction of James Street and the Strand was a mass of twisted, distorted metal, its tracks yielding in a meandering, downward incline to street level from the loss of the support girders, all very different from that warm summer's day in August 1938, when the young Eric had sauntered the same way towards his first day of work at GEC. The most common sight today was an ARP warden in a tin hat patrolling danger spots and pavements swathed in ash-covered bricks from nearby, blasted properties. He mused this was fast becoming a variant on Dante's *Inferno*.

Resuming his work, it was a weary Eric who stood up from his chair to move across the office floor and file away the leather-bound ledger on the second shelf of its metal cupboard. About to return to his desk, he hesitated, retrieved the large book, and opened it to flick through its pages. Mr Leadbetter's intricate script stared back at him in the guise of inane entries such as 'Liverpool Corporation', 'Paid' and 'Cancelled'. The unfairness of this good man's plight surged through the young clerk. But for Adolf Hitler, his manager would be here today offering his usual careful instructions and guidance, his brother Billy would not be away in Bridgnorth, and his mum would not be scared out of her wits every night at the wail of air raid sirens. He looked at his watch. It was 11.30am, time to do something about it. He approached the deputy manager, a conservative man, a stickler for the rules, fully expecting a refusal when requesting the afternoon off. To his surprise, the stand-in duly agreed. It seemed everything around him was changing.

Forty-five minutes later, Eric walked into the Labour Exchange in Seacombe. It started well. Compared with the other men in view, he was smartly dressed, something apparently spotted by a staff member.

'Are you here to volunteer for the RAF?'

'Yes I am.'

Eric felt a surge of pride, until he realised he was standing next to a poster, its white-edged red capitals against blue background inviting him to

Join the RAF Volunteer Reserve.

'Down there pal, first on the right.'

'Thanks.'

He had a second look at the notice and immediately disregarded the requests for navigators, gunners, wireless operators and ground crew. It was the first line that seized his attention, *Pilots Age 18-25.* He corrected his posture by straightening his back and then walked confidently into the room, empty except for a few chairs and a sandy-haired man with thin moustache and slight twitch sitting upright behind a desk.

'Yes?' he barked.

'I'm here to volunteer for the RAF.'

'I see.'

The representative looked Eric up and down, displaying neither approval nor disapproval.

'Here, fill this in,' he grumbled.

He passed Eric a pen and 'Form 1866 Royal Air Force Volunteer Reserve'. There were no difficult questions, and so when completed, he handed it back.

'This seems to be in order,' said the official scanning the document. 'However, as you are seventeen, you will need to get one of your parents to countersign.'

Eric wasted no time in rushing home where his father was happy to sign the required form, his mum accepting unfolding events with reluctant grace. He immediately returned to the Labour Exchange to hand over the document to the serious man with moustache and twitch.

'We will contact you shortly about attending a Selection Board,' he said, his face maintaining its ever-present scowl.

They shook hands before the man snarled a 'goodbye'.

He had done it. He was joining the Royal Air Force. It was a fateful moment.

****

Eric was on his way to bible class with Len, the first such visit since January, events having conspired to cancel further meetings until today. Miss Finch the tutor had been ill for a number of weeks, and then the 'Hun' intervened with sustained bombing raids that damaged, amongst many other things, the Oakdale Mission. And so almost four months since their last get together, bible studies were finally resuming.

The most recent blitz from the Luftwaffe had been kinder to the Wirral side of the Mersey than to Liverpool, but its impact was still central to Miss Finch's thinking when she addressed the group, all sitting dutifully in neat rows of desks and chairs.

'You may recall,' said the teacher, 'at our last meeting I promised to discuss Corinthians, a part of the scriptures that has love as its central theme.'

Eric involuntarily glanced to his left in the direction of Vera and Margaret, both giving the tutor their full attention.

'And in these dark days of our history,' she continued, 'when we all rightly have questions, doubts, and misgivings, when our faith is truly put to the sternest of tests, the need for love is at its most potent and most vital. So let us open our bibles and turn to the New Testament and Corinthians 13:4-8 to see what the good book teaches us about love.'

A few people fidgeted in their seats. This was not the most comfortable subject for those here today, Eric included. Miss Finch read out the first line.

'And though I have the gift of prophecy, and understand all mysteries and all knowledge; and though I have all faith, so that I could remove mountains, and have not love, I am nothing.'

A discussion ensued with class members making notes, some more assiduous than others. Miss Finch invited class members to read a passage.

'Vera?' she said, 'would you mind reciting the next few lines?'

The dark-haired attendee put down her fountain pen, gently stroked her dark hair, and read.

'Love suffereth long, and is kind; love envieth not; love vaunteth not itself, is not puffed up, doth not behave itself unseemly, seeketh not her own, is not easily provoked, thinketh no evil; rejoiceth not in iniquity, but rejoice in the truth.'

Eric's bible had a generous margin in which he was able to record his own thoughts and interpretations, his blue-black longhand almost perfectly symmetrical. But after Vera's contribution, his mind was elsewhere. It was an exaggeration to say he was transfixed, but he had been struck anew by her attractiveness. Without thinking, he had recorded one word on his page... 'love'. Sensing that Len might be glancing over his shoulder, he quickly added 'envieth not'.

The lesson continued, Eric experiencing an increasing sense of detachment, especially when the class discussed Matthew 5:44, Miss Finch reading the text.

'But I say unto you, love your enemies, bless them that curse you, do good to them that hate you, and pray for them which despitefully use you, and persecute you...'

He stopped listening. The country was at war, the enemy bombing the heart out of cities and towns, with friends and work colleagues paying the ultimate price, conditions that surely could only generate anger and disgust. Loving your enemy appeared to be a distant ideal. He was sure he was not alone in having such thoughts, but he, like the rest, kept his counsel. The only solace from today's session was the chance to meet with Vera again, and after the class had finished, Eric kept up this time behind Len to rendezvous with the girls at the exit.

'Hey Margaret, Vera...' said Len, mercifully silent during today's class, 'would you like to be walked home?'

The two friends exchanged a glance that suggested approval.

It was Margaret who spoke, 'Go on then,' she said, linking arms with Len, 'I live off Rake Lane and Vera off Seaview Road.'

Vera looked at Eric. He wanted to offer his arm, but it seemed temporarily glued to his body. After an unnecessary delay, they began the walk home, shuffling side by side. They passed a drab shop window displaying a drab poster for the Grosvenor Ballroom, one of the main venues for couples in the town to enjoy an evening out. He looked down at his brogues, one right and one left, both polished to produce the shine of a royal silver goblet. In dancing parlance, however, he was the possessor of two left feet. He needed dance lessons in the waltz or foxtrot before plucking up the courage to ask this young lady to an evening of ballroom.

In front of them, Len regaled Margaret with a few tales; the blonde hair on her head lurching back as she laughed out loud. Eric could not compete. He was not a naturally funny man. Not that he was overly serious. He enjoyed a joke and a bit of banter as much as the next man, but he was some way from being the next Arthur Askey. Instead, he and Vera talked. She had recently turned seventeen and was one of three siblings, her sisters Betty aged twelve and Sylvia aged fourteen. She also mentioned that she worked at a bakery on Seaview Road and offered a few other background details as to her life. Eric did the same. It was hardly romantic stuff, but it helped occupy the time.

They passed the scene of a devastating bomb attack in which many residents had perished, the only indication of normality a child skipping, albeit against a backdrop of buildings nothing more than brick shells.

'It was terrible what happened here...' said Vera, her words drifting away as she put a hand over her mouth and fought to extinguish the images forming in her mind.

'I know,' said Eric.

'I hope they don't come back tonight.'

Eric glanced at the sky. It was worryingly clear, ideal conditions for the

Luftwaffe to continue their relentless attack on the Mersey docks. He fully expected another raid and so failed to find any words of reassurance. He tried another tack.

'I should be able to do something about it soon,' he said, locking his eyes on to the cracks in the paving stones.

He sensed Vera turn her head in his direction.

'What do you mean?'

'I volunteered to join the RAF this week as a pilot. I want to go and give the Germans a taste of their own medicine.'

There was a slight hesitation before she said, 'Good for you.'

The response to Eric's ears lacked a little conviction, and he thought back to the bible class and wondered if Vera shared the ideals of Miss Finch. He doubted it.

They continued to walk, their partnership sobering by the second in sharp contrast to Len and Margaret, the latter animated by an endless stream of amusing comments from Len's treasure chest of anecdotes and funny things to say. Eric heard himself talking about purchase orders and the death of poor Mr Leadbetter. He was glad when they reached Margaret's house and said goodbye to Vera's friend, Len joining the pair for the last few streets. The walk that had started promisingly with thoughts of dancing had fizzled out to nothing much more than a thank you and goodbye. It was time to head home for Sunday roast followed by another testing time under the stairs or inside the brick shelter out in the yard.

CHAPTER 6

Billy surreptitiously stared over the shoulder of Farmer Stoneycroft and scrutinised the photograph of HMS Hood spread across the full width of the newspaper's front page. He was intrigued by battleships and U-boats, telling himself that one day he would join the Royal Navy. The main headline ran 'Bismarck Sinks HMS Hood' with 'Few Survivors' in smaller print underneath. The farmer was sat in his armchair, shaking his head and muttering as he absorbed the shocking news.

Billy's attention returned to his brother's letter from the day before. It contained the exciting news that Eric and his friend Len planned to cycle the hundred and eighty mile round trip to Bridgnorth at the end of June, giving him something different to look forward to. He wasn't lonely as such but had missed Roy a little. Having said that, his friend's departure had not all been bad news. There had been a definite shift in how the family at Potseething treated him. Rose was a little more attentive, Patricia now said the odd word to him, but it was the Farmer who had shown the greatest change, involving him more and more in the agricultural chores. He had cleaned out the livestock buildings, assisted with the muck-spreading, and when the sheep flock became afflicted with blowfly, he helped apply bottles of white liquid over the infected areas. He was settling into the rural way of life, so much so he was occasionally tempted to check his reflection in the mirror to ensure he had more than one tooth in his smile.

Old George folded and put down his newspaper. He had shaved, greased his hair, and dressed in a loose-fitting, but pressed, dark grey double-breasted suit, finished off with shoes that shone like patent leather. There were only two times in the week that the old man looked presentable, Saturday evenings when having a pint with his wife at the Halfway House, and Sunday mornings when going to church. Rose and Patricia appeared from upstairs. They were both wearing smart, navy raincoats, the elder's unsurprisingly tapered below the bust to accentuate her female charms. Billy, however, was in everyday clothes. Unlike the others, he had work to do. It was time for the Stoneycroft family and their young lodger to go to the Sunday Service.

The walk along Oldbury Road that morning was a challenging one. It had been an unseasonably cold month, and Sunday 25th May was a particularly unpleasant day with heavy rain and the occasional thunderstorm, young Patricia no doubt bemoaning the absence of Dick Tracy and his luxury car. Everyone was relieved when St Nicholas' came into view. On a sunny day, Billy might have noticed the yew trees that lined the perimeter of the church grounds, their flaking, red-brown bark contrasting sharply with their small leaves pointing to the sky in the flush of mid-spring bloom. But on this occasion, he kept his head bowed until reaching the welcome shelter of the main building.

The church was early Victorian, its quaint, diminutive appearance reflective of the sparse scattering of homes and farmhouses within the Oldbury Parish. The most arresting aspect of the structure to Billy's eyes was the chimney stack on the church roof. According to his over eager imagination, it bore a striking resemblance to the rocket in Jules Verne's *From the Earth to the Moon*.

The Potseething group walked from the vestibule and into the nave to be faced by an almost full congregation for the 10.30am service. George, Rose and Patricia chose to sit down in an aisle towards the back, leaving Billy to carry on towards the altar, where he received the usual warm smile and welcome from the Reverend Kirke, standing behind the pulpit, bible in hand. The same could not be said of Mr Ogden who scowled at Billy and jerked his head towards the right hand side of the pipe organ. The young helper took his place out of view of the worshippers, though regrettably in full view of the cantankerous organist.

'Air young man, I need air,' barked Ogden, his face reddening to the colour of a cherry.

It was Billy's task to compress the foot bellows and pump wind to the pipes of the organ. This was not St Paul's Cathedral, the instrument compact enough not to require the stamina of a cross country runner, yet it was still an arduous job. The apparatus was wooden and had a tendency to creak, and so when the Vicar gave his greeting and his 'pause for reflection', a rhythmic squeak could be heard from the side of the nave. To the ears of some, it sounded mildly obscene, as though an act of sexual depravity was taking place under God's roof, these same people visibly thankful when the singing began.

The first hymn was 'I know that my redeemer lives', the organ behaving well until the pitch began to drop during the last verse. Billy knew the expression 'eyes out like organ stops', but it was never more apt than today when appraising Mr Ogden's complexion His face had intensified from cherry to beetroot, silently shrieking for the evacuee to pump the bellows. He responded, the organist just about managing to get to the end of the hymn without having to stop.

After a reading from Psalm 24 and a lesson from John, it was time for another hymn, which thankfully went without incident. The sermon of the Reverend Kirke referenced the HMS Hood tragedy and called upon his flock to pray for all those affected by the incident. Billy thought of the photograph in the Sunday newspaper and then remembered the forthcoming Art Competition in school. He vowed to paint the vessel.

His mind continued to drift, gazing around the insides of St Nicholas' from his hiding place. He spotted a long rectangular wooden plaque on the wall, its appearance redolent of an upturned coffin lid. The engraving read 'THIS WINDOW IS DEDICATED TO THE HONOURED MEMORY OF...' and was followed by a list of names. Billy counted thirteen, unlucky thirteen. The tribute finished with the words '... WHO GAVE THEIR LIVES FOR THEIR COUNTRY IN THE GREAT WAR 1914-1919.' Billy knew from history lessons that the war ended in 1918 and so was surprised at this date. Above the plaque, and despite the grey rain clouds darkening the skies outside, daylight shone through the memorial window, illuminating the saints pictured in each of the two, long narrow leaded-glass arches.

'Wind, I need wind!'

Unfortunately, Billy had floated into a dream world unaware that another hymn was underway. The words of panic and disquiet from Mr Ogden were soon joined by his instrument's deep groaning. The young assistant's attempt to pump the bellows was too little too late, and the hymn ground to a halt. The look on the face of the organ player certainly lacked the tolerance preached by Jesus to his disciples, Billy fully expecting the sack after this debacle. Sounding even more like the bed frame from a house of ill-repute, further creaking was painfully audible during the lesson from Genesis, but happily the final hymn passed by without incident, and the service concluded with the Lord's Prayer and a Blessing.

Billy picked up his jacket and slithered out from behind the organ. Mr Ogden was standing up ready to rebuke him when the vicar came across hurriedly from the pulpit.

'Splendid work today Billy, splendid indeed...'

His kind intervention had saved the young helper, now able to collect his sixpence in return for a promise to be back in time for the 6.30pm service. He still had a job, although no thanks to Oggie the Organist.

****

59

Over the next few days the weather improved, and it was a hot sunny morning that greeted Billy for his long walk to school on the day of the Art Competition. Armed with the newspaper cutting of HMS Hood, he planned to do a watercolour of the battlecruiser, partly as a tribute but also as a celebration. Barely a week or so after its sinking, the Royal Navy had exercised the sweetest kind of military retribution by destroying the Bismarck, the German destroyer that had downed the Hood.

A bead of sweat trickled its way from temple to chin as the thirteen-year-old rolled up his sleeves and ambled along the country lane, newly aware of the bright colours that peppered his view. The blues, greens and oranges of the Kingfishers gliding between trees complemented the many shades of pastures, hedgerows and wild flowers already blossoming.

By the time he reached school, his socks almost squelched inside his shoes. The old building, ordinarily so expert at retaining the cold, was today hot and stuffy, not the best conditions for giving free rein to creativity, but Billy was ready to do his best. He thought it a shame that Roy was not there for the competition. They would have had a laugh. Roy was not the best with a paintbrush, readily admitting he was no Turner or Constable. Indeed, the only valid mention of Constable in the context of a painting by Roy was his likely arrest for crimes against the Art World. In contrast, Billy had a good eye for drawing. He had natural perspective and was especially good at copying an image. With a palette of twelve colours, a couple of brushes, and a blank piece of paper, he readied himself for a military masterpiece.

Of course, he was too young and naïve to paint HMS Hood in the way historians would now demand. Forty two thousand tons of Clydebank metal hit by a salvo of German shells and exploding in a column of flame that climbed six hundred feet into Scandinavian skies until the cruel, gravitational forces of nature returned its molten, twisted, distorted remains to a sea of burning oil before sinking to the ocean floor, the vessel's watery grave shared with all but three of its one and a half thousand crew.

By way of stark contrast, Billy's watercolour of the Hood was serene, the sea pure, still, blue, the sky reflecting the magnificence of the ocean below, and the battlecruiser pristine, sleek, and proud. It carried none of the scars of war or damage from the brutal world, in many ways a reflection of Billy the evacuee in Bridgnorth. The final flourish at the foot of the painting was a piece of wordplay that the master of British propaganda, Lord Beaverbrook would have endorsed.

'*A Battleship a Day Keeps the Hun at Bay.*'

He handed his competition entry to Miss McDonnell.

'Well done Billy, that's beautiful,' she enthused, holding the paper at different angles.

'It's HMS Hood,' he replied.

'Well, that's very fitting… and such a good slogan… well done again.'

'Thank you.'

'… and did you know the Hood was built on the Clyde in Scotland?'

There was always a link back to the land of porridge and heather.

Dinnertime arrived, Billy staying at his desk to eat the usual jam sandwiches while the others left the hall for the canteen. Miss McDonnell, as she always did, watched him with a slight frown, though today she elected to speak.

'Billy?'

'Yes Miss?'

'Why don't you go and have a meal with the others?'

'I haven't got any money.'

Dinner was beyond the funds of the evacuee. Children such as the Kirkbrides staying with the solicitor were given an allowance to pay for school meals, but Billy had to settle for a couple of slices of thick bread smothered in jam.

'Here, take this,' said Miss McDonnell, rummaging through her purse and placing on his desk a few pennies with the bearded face of King George V.

He hesitated before the scent of rabbit pie proved too much of a temptation. Picking up the coins, he thanked her, stored away the half-eaten jam butties to eat later, and rushed out to revel in the thrill of pastry, meat and gravy. It was an act of kindness that Billy truly appreciated, and an indication that although a long way from home, he had good people like Miss McDonnell looking after his welfare.

The dinner was weighing leaden in his stomach as the satisfied diner returned in the afternoon for a history class about the Tudors and the Stuarts, learning why rebellion and war endured with the Irish and, more predictably, the Scots. The lesson ended early to permit the announcement of the Art Competition winner, and the presence of a few butterflies in his guts proved he was serious about winning. The contest had been open to all ages, and some of the younger pupils had produced work of a dubious quality, Billy fearing they may get marked up for effort. He need not have worried. After the runners-up position was awarded to little Peter Smith's 'Oak Tree Field', that to Billy's eyes should have been renamed 'Cow Pat Field', he heard Miss McDonnell's proclamation.

'And so the winner of the St Mary's Art Competition for 1941 is Billy Whitfield for his delightful watercolour of the Royal Navy's HMS Hood.'

The victor was invited to stand at the front of the class and acknowledge the generous applause from teachers and fellow pupils. He drank it in. But in all the excitement of the contest, he had forgotten about the prize. For a brief moment he had visions of a tin of toffees, a fountain pen, or if he was really lucky, a book token. When the clapping subsided, he was handed something by Miss McDonnell. In truth, it was a bit of a disappointment, the painting of the Hood. That was the prize. It was a like getting eight draws on the football pools and winning back the original coupon. The artwork was not even going to be displayed on the school wall alongside little Peter's magnum opus of farmyard muck. Nonetheless, he quickly adopted a philosophical mind-set, rolling up his watercolour and securing it with an elastic band. He would at least now be able to show Rose and Farmer George at Potseething.

The next morning, Billy improvised with string to hook the rolled up picture over his shoulder prior to heading into town. Rose had been really impressed with the prize-winning effort and suggested contacting the Bridgnorth Journal for inclusion in the 'Let's Talk It Over' section with 'Candidus'. As it was a Saturday, his hands were otherwise occupied with the radio accumulator, a solo chore to which he was now truly conditioned, although the intense heat and humidity of the day was going to make the task even more of a trial than usual.

He was just making his way out of the farmhouse, when he saw Trampy closing the gate to the main road. The rabbit fur coat and hat had been replaced with his summer clothes. Basically he was wearing a sack. If this was the post office, the smell would have warned him in advance, but amongst the litany of farmyard whiffs and pongs, the stench of the vagrant was not out of place.

'Billy Boy!' shouted Trampy.

He was impressed that the vagabond had remembered his name.

'Hi Trampy, what are you doing here?'

'Workin' lad, workin. Summer 'elp for Farmer George.'

'That's good...' said Billy, sensibly dropping the heavy accumulator to the floor.

'And where's ye goin' on a bootiful day like t'day?'

He explained about the Ever Ready chore and the painting. Trampy asked to see the watercolour, which the young artist unrolled and spread out before him.

The vagrant puffed out his cheeks, 'Tell ye w'at Billy boy, ye's got some talent with those brushes, I'm tellin' ye.'

His explanation about the painting left Trampy utterly perplexed. In his world, there was no such thing as a World War or naval battles in the North Atlantic. He might live in a cave and stink like a back yard lavatory with blocked drains, but he lived a peaceful existence, one for many to envy at this time in history.

Billy repackaged the artwork, bid Trampy farewell, and continued on his way out of the farm and along the Oldbury Road. Ahead of the usual routine of cashing the postal order, wolfing down the cream slice, and losing yet another game of football, he located the offices of the Bridgnorth Journal to post the rolled-up artwork through a generous-sized letterbox. He crossed his fingers it would feature in the next issue.

The local newspaper was delivered regularly to Potseething Farm, and Billy waited anxiously for the paperboy to bring the latest edition. When he heard the familiar smack of newsprint hitting the stone floor behind the front door, and with nobody else in the house, he ran hurriedly to retrieve the paper. It was surprisingly slight, no more than four pages in length, and his spirits sank when he saw there were no photographs in the issue, presumably another consequence of the war. He found the 'Candidus' section on the inside front page, thumbing down the comments and observations to read a slightly disturbing note about prayers and wishes being with the family of the Reverend Kirke who was seriously ill in Bridgnorth Infirmary. But he quickly forgot about this on seeing the next entry, *A Battleship a Day Keeps the Hun at Bay'*.

The article explained that an evacuee from Wallasey, William Edgar Whitfield, aged 13, had won an Art Competition held at St Mary's School for painting HMS Hood, the journalist taking the opportunity to glory in the recent sinking of the Bismarck. Billy experienced a swell of pride and vowed to keep the cutting to show Eric.

He checked the calendar. His brother was going to be here in three weeks time. They had not seen each other for nearly six months, and Billy wondered if Eric would see any change in him. He felt different, more adult, more independent, and for a second or so contemplated growing a moustache to further emphasise his progress to adulthood. Unfortunately, he still had a face like a baby's bottom and had already suffered traumas in this regard as an eight year old. He recalled the holiday in Granddad Russell's Welsh Cottage when his attempt to shave had ended with streams of blood pouring down his savaged face, creating a scene from *Dracula*.

Although tempted to try Farmer George's chair, Billy played safe and sat at the table. He picked up a pencil and began to draw 10 x 10 grids on blank paper with letters across the top and numbers down the side, the alternating grids headed 'Billy' and 'Eric'. To continue the HMS Hood theme, he was preparing for a few games of 'Battleships' with his brother. But he checked himself, screwing up the paper and throwing it in the bin. He had just remembered. He was almost a grown up now... and games were for children.

CHAPTER 7

Len's hair was plastered to his skull, looking every inch as though someone had thrown a bucket of water over his head. The rolling up of his shirt sleeves and trousers was a pitiable adaptation to the searing heat, his feet inside sockless boots already saturated in perspiration. Eric fared slightly better, his thicker hair lacking the ridiculous appearance of his friend, and his light-coloured clothing more suited to the conditions. It was the start of the Summer Solstice and only 10.30am, but the sun was already high in a cloudless sky, its rays burning the scorched earth and tarmac below. The two friends were about an hour and a half into their marathon cycling journey to Bridgnorth and were taking a first rest at the side of the road.

'Crikey,' gasped Len, gulping generous mouthfuls of water from a flask, 'you picked a right day for this.'

'I know,' said Eric, wiping a brow with his forearm.

'I think I've lost half a stone in weight already. By the time we get to Bridgnorth, I'll look like Stan Laurel.'

Eric checked his own light khaki outfit and looked at his friend's less appropriate attire.

'What made you wear a black shirt?' he said.

'Oswald Mosley.'

'The Blackshirts!'

They laughed as Len gave a fascist salute; though the mirth died quickly when an open-top car sped past, its occupants looking on contemptuously.

'Bugger me Eric; I might get locked up for treason now.'

They laughed again before resuming their journey, the escalating high temperature an increasingly stern test of endurance. On one stretch of open road, the heat created a mirage-type effect of haze and shimmer that almost sent Eric off into a dream world. The bikes did not help with their heavy frames and single gears, but at least the terrain was gentle, the riders thankful this was Shropshire and not neighbouring Montgomeryshire with its peaks and mountains.

The evidence of the natural world flourishing in its summer prime was everywhere, the country lanes flanked with red poppy coated pastures, yellow rapeseed fields, and lush green meadows, nature's own traffic light display. The dairy livestock were sitting down, and considering the clear, blue skies and benign outlook, this clearly had nothing to do with rainstorms on the way. The cattle were just a bit knackered. It all seemed a million miles from the over-familiar sight of bombed-out buildings in Liverpool and Wallasey, and for a brief while it was easy for Eric to consider the war as a figment of the imagination.

The travellers made it to Whitchurch, the half-way point, around noon. The Horse & Jockey on the A41 had rarely welcomed two more grateful visitors, a sentiment reinforced when accosted by the cool of its stone floor and wooden furniture. The first pint of best bitter was downed in one, both young men exhaling in deep deference to the thirst-quenching qualities of the brew. The pace for drinking the second was a tad more leisurely, permitting some light conversation.

'Do you want sit down?' said Eric, the edge of his tongue skilfully travelling the rim of his upper lip to clear the beer froth.

'You must be joking,' replied Len, wincing as he caressed the seat of his pants. 'It feels like someone's shoved a poker up this backside. Why can't they make a bike seat that doesn't tear your behind into shreds?'

'Fair point, I suppose.'

For an eighteen-year-old, Len sipped expertly from the glass before saying in wistful tones, 'You know Eric, instead of another forty five mile bike run in weather only fit for 'Mad Dogs and Englishmen', I could now be walking through Vale Park hand in hand with Margaret whispering sweet nothings in her ear.'

'Yes, but you don't get views like this back home,' said Eric, immediately spotting his mistake, the window to the bar looking out on to a terraced house in front of which a terrier crossbreed was crouching and doing his business on the pavement. 'Anyhow... you know what I mean.'

Len finished off his second pint and said, 'Not only that, but you could be walking awkwardly next to Vera struggling to find anything to say.'

'Come on Len, that's a bit harsh.'

'Well, it would be if it wasn't true.'

'You're fine with Margaret. She's taken with you. But Vera... I don't think she's too keen on me.'

'Of course she is. You can see it in her eyes, the way she looks at you. Listen pal, I know about these things. They didn't call me Casanova at school for nothing.'

According to Eric's recollections, they called him Little Len, but he chose not to contradict. He liked Vera, and relations with her had remained cordial during bible classes, but he did not share Casanova's viewpoint. With a shrug, he drank the last dregs of his ale before leaving for the second leg of their marathon bike ride.

The scenery, although enduringly quaint, became rather repetitive, all winding country lanes, farms, and small villages with a post office, pub, and black dog panting in the shade. When, after nearly six hours of laborious travelling in sweltering heat along the roads of Cheshire and Shropshire, the cycling journeymen finally rode past the sign that proclaimed 'Bridgnorth', they experienced more than a sentiment of relief. A quick, last survey of the map and it was up and down the Oldbury Road towards Potseething Farm.

'There it is,' shouted Eric, now setting the pace.

Len was labouring behind, the handkerchief on his head sodden.

'Thank the Lord,' he wheezed, perhaps experiencing the most religious moment of his life to date, bible study notwithstanding.

'Here on the left,' said Eric, cocking his leg to climb off.

He opened the gate and propped his bike up against the brick wall of the outbuildings.

Meanwhile, Len's bike was laid out flat, as was its rider who started muttering, *'Yea, though I walk through the valley of the shadow of death, I will fear no evil...'*

He was reciting David from the Old Testament.

'I think you'll live Len.'

The answer was part moan, part whimper.

They were then greeted by the sight of an older and younger man riding into the farm on the barrel seat of a double-axel cart packed with bales of hay. Pulling the wagon was the biggest carthorse Eric had ever seen, its roughened hide casing vast skeletal muscles, tendons and bones, its substantial front and hind legs coated liberally in thick, off-white hair.

'Ow bist.'

The horse stopped.

The farmer looked precisely as Eric expected, a man of the outdoors who might have lived in 1841. But next to him was someone more surprising. It was Bill. Admittedly, six months had passed since they had seen one another, but his younger brother seemed much older, and there was more to the change than him growing up physically. There was the same black hair with its familiar side part, the generous-sized Whitfield ears, and the slightly narrow eyes that had some cruel kids in his school class asking if he was Chinese. But in a collarless shirt with a bronzed complexion and air of countryside-infused health, he looked more Spanish. Billy Whitfield was now Guillermo Whitfield.

'Eric,' said Billy, jumping off the cart.

'How are you Bill?' said the elder brother, stretching a few leg muscles.

'Great thanks… and you?'

'Recovering from a six hour bike ride but otherwise fine.'

Len was just getting to his feet.

'At least...' said Eric with a wry smile, 'a lot better than him.'

Billy grinned.

'Ow bist.'

Eric hoped the old man's vocabulary stretched beyond these two nonsensical words.

'Good afternoon, I'm Eric, Bill's brother, and this is my pal Len.'

'Ow bist.'

'Mr Stoneycroft,' said Billy, 'do you know where they're pitching the tent?'

It had been agreed that the lads could stay for the night.

'Put it far end o' meadow by brook an' on slope...' said the farmer, itching his ear with a little finger and squinting as he gazed up at the pure turquoise sky, '...cos it looks like rain t' me... water 'll drain downstream.'

Eric exchanged a quick, incredulous stare with his fellow biker. Rain?

As the farmer unloaded his cart, Eric turned to his brother.

'Bill, is there any chance of getting water from the house for these flasks?'

'We have to get it from the pump,' he replied, 'the farm doesn't have running water.'

Eric was taken aback at this revelation and impressed at the same time with Bill's matter-of-fact acceptance of the harsh reality. The evacuee retrieved a galvanised pale hanging from a wall and meandered past the hens and chickens to an area of rough, strewn grass, speckled with buttercups, which housed a rusted, fresh water pump, its scythe-shaped lever and general decrepit appearance more akin to something found in a torture chamber. Billy hooked the handle of the bucket over the tap and pulled the lever, the screech of metal on metal greeting the action, before a crystal clear gush gradually filled the container. Eric and Len, the latter now on the way to recovery, greedily dipped their flasks into the pale and swigged the surprisingly cool liquid. Refreshed, they returned to their bikes for the camping gear.

'Ow bist lads, I'll take ye to brook.'

The farmer fancied a break from his hard work, and so the campers followed him across the fields and past the grazing sheep, Billy in tow.

'Is there a pub you'd recommend for a pint?' enquired Len, his hand comforting an ailing posterior as he walked.

"Alfway 'ouse,' muttered Farmer Stoneycroft.

'And where's that?'

'Out gates, turn lef, keep lef, and it's on lef.'

'Right.'

'No… lef.'

Eric had only spent a few minutes in the company of the farmer, but he already knew this exchange with Len was not an attempt at a joke.

The farmer guided them towards a small coppice in front of a narrow brook that threaded its way through grass-covered banks fashioning a scenic, picturesque border. It was here they were to camp for the night. Billy returned with the farmer to finish the afternoon's chores, leaving Eric and Len to erect their tent. It was thirsty work, and although quenched by the fresh water from the pump, they both relished the thought of a beer or two later on. In the meantime, it was time to eat, although unfortunately like campers and not kings. The primer stove lit, it was time to cook the wild mushrooms.

For most of the week, the Halfway House was a quiet establishment; its customers noiselessly supping pints, the predominant sound the clink of glass on glass. However, Saturday evenings were different, the one night when everyone within the vicinity made an appearance, even those sentenced to work around the clock to satisfy the demands of the government. Farmer Stoneycroft was a prime example.

The 1930s had been tough on the farming community. Cheap imports of wheat from USA and Canada had made the arable farm unsustainable and so most switched to livestock husbandry. Potseething had housed beef cattle, a dairy herd, pigs, sheep, hens and chickens, enabling George to scratch a decent enough living. But emergency measures introduced by the Ministries of Agriculture and Food at the outbreak of war mandated a switch to crop growing, and so the beef cattle, pigs, and most of the milkers had to go. He had retained his sheep and was fortunate to do so, but for a man in his later years, the physical demands placed on him to produce wheat for the war effort was already taking its toll. However, Saturday was his chance to relax, go to the pub for a pint, and enjoy a sing-a-long to a few ditties. Sat in his usual seat close to the bar, George had scrubbed up and donned his Sunday best, yet the attempt to wash away the odour of farmyard manure had manifestly failed, and compared with his wife, he was an aged version of a Victorian street urchin.

Rose Stoneycroft exuded glamour, even when needing dough, burying hot stews in hay boxes, or sewing patchwork quilts. Sipping her glass of sherry, although not adorned in pearls, diamonds, or the latest Parisian fashions, she was as far removed from the traditional image of a farmer's wife as could be imagined. The imposition of clothes rationing introduced at the beginning of the month was yet to impact on her wardrobe, something demonstrated by her elegant two-piece skirt suit in air force blue. The mismatched couple sat next to one another, wordlessly staring at their drinks, both awaiting the singing.

By the time Eric and Len had made their way from the outside humidity and into the bar, the Halfway House was bustling with drinkers. Len immediately spotted the farmer.

'Let me get you a beer,' he said to the old man. 'What are you drinking?'

'Mild.'

'Pint of mild coming up.'

'Wife'll 'ave sherry.'

The visitors looked at one another. What wife? Surely not the attractive lady next to him?

'Sherry would be nice,' the woman said in a slightly sultry tone.

'Sherry it is…' muttered a bemused Len, marginally reprising the look on his face from the end of the bike ride. 'I'm Len by the way.'

She nodded in acknowledgement and then turned to Eric.

'You must be Billy's brother.'

'Yes, I'm Eric, pleased to meet you.'

'I'm Rose.'

It seemed that after helping the farmer in the fields under the afternoon sun, Billy was now on babysitting duties. A pang of guilt flashed across Eric's mind.

Len was soon passing across the drinks, his tongue close to hanging out of his mouth as he continued to appraise Old George's wife.

'Bloody hell Eric,' he whispered, 'the old farmer's done alright for himself.'

Eric had to agree. She appeared to be a good twenty years younger and about twenty times better looking.

Barely had the first sip been downed, when the landlord announced to his customers the bad news that Gertie was ill. There was a deep groan and the odd 'bugger' and 'blast'. Gertie was the piano player. Tonight's sing-song was off.

'This man plays the piano,' shouted Len.

Before Eric had time to protest, he was being back-slapped and welcomed as a hero by the punters and ushered to an upright in the corner.

Being the eldest child, he had learnt to play from a young age and was always called upon at family get-togethers to provide the musical accompaniment.

A woman's voice bawled, 'Can you play 'With My Little Ukulele'?'

'Behave... just let the lad play the piano,' said Len.

The place erupted with laughter, Eric's momentary fear that his friend had misjudged the mood and acceptabilities of the locals proving unfounded. The spirit of Miss Marie Lloyd was obviously alive and well in Bridgnorth, Shropshire 1941... at least when the drink was flowing.

'How about this one?' suggested Eric.

He tinkled the slightly out of tune keys and began to play another George Formby number, 'Leaning on a Lamp-post.' Soon, everyone in the pub was singing along, his versatile musical repertoire paying dividends, aided by the progressively wayward conducting of Len. Flanagan & Allen's 'Run Rabbit Run' and a few Vera Lynne songs were given an enthusiastic airing, before the piano player subjected the regulars to something new, boogie-woogie, greeted with fervour and ending with an ovation and a pint on the house. Len McCabe and Eric Whitfield were now indisputably honorary Salopians.

At about eleven o'clock, the campers said goodbye to an inebriated Farmer Stoneycroft, a man who patently worked hard and drank hard, but his wife was nowhere to be seen. Saying farewell to the rest of their new friends from the countryside, Eric was handed a brown paper package by a furtive looking regular before swapping the stifling heat inside the pub for the outside fresh air.

Despite the late hour, it was still very warm as they strolled past an old hay barn and down Halfway House Lane. They had been walking for less than a minute, when the silhouette of a man and a woman appeared in the distance coming towards them. As the image became clearer, Eric saw Rose Stoneycroft with a tall, smartly-dressed man. The stranger tipped his

74

hat in acknowledgement, and Rose smiled a comfortable smile. Whoever he was, the farmer's wife displayed a distinct lack of self-reproach. Len was a bit merry, and so Eric mentioned nothing further as they travelled back to the camping ground.

On his return to the tent by the brook, he glanced up to the evening sky, dark enough for the flicker of stars to emerge in their set formations but light enough to witness the onset of shadowy cloud which threatened to overwhelm the clear of night. Perhaps rain was on its way after all. It seemed he had learnt a lesson today. If you want to know the weather, ask a farmer.

Eric awoke the following morning to the stillness of another day in England's green and pleasant land, the only sound a young man's voice.

'Eric? Are you up? Eric'

It was a murmur, softly spoken.

He sat up, rubbed his eyes and popped his head out of the tent flap to see his younger brother. It had not rained overnight, but the conditions were now overcast, though still humid.

'Sorry to wake you,' said Billy 'but my Sundays are quite busy, and I wanted to catch you before you went home.'

'That's alright Bill. Let's make some breakfast.'

Eric retrieved the brown package handed to him last night and stepped outside into the fresh air, stretching and yawning as he moved forward. He unwrapped the paper to reveal three large eggs and some bacon, lighting the stove on which he placed a frying pan with the rashers laid out. As he tilted the pan over the heat at different angles, he heard Len stretch, yawn and blaspheme from inside the tent. Cracking the eggs, he dropped them into the hot fat that sizzled and spat back with venom. This was going to be a treat and a half.

'By the way Bill, has mum mentioned anything in her letters about my plans?'

'No... what plans?'

'To join the RAF.'

'And become a pilot?'

'Hopefully, yes.'

'Hey... that's great.'

Eric lent back and shouted to his friend in the tent. 'Len, can you bring three plates out?'

A muffled response could be heard.

'When do you start?' asked Billy.

'I've got to get through a panel interview and a medical, but I've been told they're not too strict.'

'So you'll be giving up the scouts now.'

'Yes,' he laughed, 'it looks like I'll be swapping the woggle and the Gang Show for the controls of a Mosquito.'

'What does mum think?'

'She'd rather me be a vicar!'

It was Billy's turn to laugh.

'What about Len?'

'He's starting an apprenticeship with Lairds, which is likely to be a reserved occupation. He's opted for the Royal Navy on his forms, but he'll probably never have to join up.'

A dishevelled Len appeared from his canvas home into the daylight.

'My bloomin' head,' he croaked, passing the tin plates.

'Thanks.'

Len was the proverbial death warmed up.

'I tell you something Billy,' he said.

'What's that?'

'Stay away from the demon drink,' he groaned.

'Time for a feast,' said Eric, plating up the bacon and egg treat for the breakfasters.

They all ate hungrily, as though their first meal in a while, and in no time were sitting back satisfied and content with three empty plates for company. Billy mentioned he had to go to church in about an hour, and so the brothers took the opportunity to go for a Sunday morning stroll, Len staying behind to rest after yesterday's exertions.

Using rocks and small boulders as footholds, they followed the brook and meandered in the direction of the river, Billy telling Eric about the Severn Bore he had witnessed early one morning a few months ago when the natural tidal phenomenon had created waves as tall as fifty feet. Today's conditions were markedly different from the extremes required by the Bore, the water still, calm, a mirror of their respective moods. The tranquillity of the scene was in sharp contrast to the pictures playing in Eric's mind of Liverpool's bomb-damaged streets, and he made a special effort to absorb the serenity of the sight and images before him for future recall.

Spears of purple loosestrife flowers rose up from the nearby shallows as they reached the banks of the main river. Here the pair found a place to sit with the town's bridge as the backdrop. Eric picked up a small pebble, which he threw into the water, the stone skimming across the service and bouncing twice.

'How's it going here then Bill?'

'Great.'

'And you're not homesick?'

'I was at first, but I've grown to like it, especially the farming.'

'And do they feed you well?'

Eric knew this was their mum's greatest concern.

Billy shrugged, 'Yes... I'm never hungry.'

'Good... that's good.'

Both were now taking turns apiece at skimming the stones.

'How are Mum and Dad?' said Billy.

'They're fine... Dad's still moaning about everything, and Mum obviously worries about you, but she knows you're better off here.'

'What about the bombings?'

'There was a bad spell at the beginning of May, but Liverpool got it worse...there wasn't that much damage on our side of the water. It's all been pretty quiet since.'

'There was a bomb here you know?'

'A bomb?'

'Last August... two people killed in Hightown.

'Probably a German crew dropping their bomb load in the wrong place... I don't think you'll get anymore.

'Oh, I'm not bothered about it... Roy was though.'

'He came home didn't he?'

'Yes, at Easter... but I've managed. In fact, it's a bit easier now in some ways.'

'How do you get on with the family?'

'Fine… I think the farmer likes to have a young man around and about. He likes to show me things.... oh and I've been meaning to show you this.'

Billy pulled from his back pocket the Bridgnorth Journal newspaper cutting about the HMS Hood painting. Eric was duly impressed. The pair then stood up and threw one last pebble prior to retracing their steps back to the camping site.

To Eric's surprise, Len had packed most things away, his friend anxious to start the journey home, understandable given the six hours of toil that lay ahead in weather conditions looking increasingly humid and hostile. The sky had turned into a particularly sinister mix of browns and dark greys. With packed rucksacks and laden bikes, they wheeled their way across the field towards the Oldbury Road.

'Right Bill, we'll be off now,' said Eric. 'Can you thank the farmer and his wife for letting us pitch here?'

'Alright.'

'And you be good,' he said as he began to pedal.

'I always am.'

Eric suspected this was true. Back in Wallasey, although far from being a troublemaker, his brother had had his moments. Here, a new maturity was setting in, and he genuinely seemed settled.

'Have a safe journey,' shouted Billy, watching the cyclists getting smaller as they moved away.

Eric managed one last wave before disappearing from view, a moment that coincided with the first drop of rain leaping from the edge of his nose to the ground. Saturday's conditions with the dry, searing sun had been challenging enough, but the Sabbath was shaping up to make the day before seem like a picnic. Heavy rain greeted the first few hours of their ride, and by the time they had reached the outskirts of Chester, thunderstorms had taken hold. The deep rumbles and crashes, normally a disquieting experience, provided a strange source of comfort for Eric. These were noises without serious danger, and in that regard, it was going to be one evening when the Luftwaffe would stay at home and not visit Liverpool Bay.

There was plenty of time on the return journey for Eric to reflect upon things. With his limbs and muscles complaining, he pondered as to the value of this grind. It had to be good preparation for the RAF training that lay ahead, doubting they would be subjected to anything as testing as this. He thought of his brother. Bill had obviously settled well at the farm and was happy. Moreover, he had spotted a change in him, a change for the better. In short, Bill was growing up. Eric would definitely be able to put his mum's mind at ease.

But the thought plaguing his mind more than any other was Vera. Taking his lead from Len, currently struggling ten yards behind with an expression close to suicidal, he had replayed some of the meetings with the attractive brunette at bible class and their now regular walk home. Perhaps he had been too dismissive about her disinterest. He resolved to take the bull by the horns and do something about it... inviting her to the cinema or to a dance. The latter, however, was a problem. He therefore made another decision. He would speak to Aunt Hilda. She would help him. Eric Whitfield was going to learn to dance.

CHAPTER 8

School summer holidays for Billy had always meant long, lazy days filled with visits to the beach at Egremont Shore, games of cricket in the side street, or swimming at the open air bathing pool in New Brighton. The big event was the annual gala held in Central Park with Rose Queen parades, marching bands, pony rides, a fat lady with legs like pin cushions, rowing boats on the lake, cycle races, fairground stalls, candy floss, toffee apples, and firework displays. He could never manage to win the coconut prize he coveted so much but was glad to have an elder brother on hand, Eric effortlessly throwing a ball into three buckets to win the tropical fruit for his sibling. Billy would always try and persuade Eric to have a go at the Boxing Booth challenge, where in a proper ring with an official referee, members of the public were invited to fight a professional, those lasting the requisite three rounds winning a cash prize. Suffice to say, nobody made the distance, and Eric had more sense than to give in to his younger brother's demands. The summer of 1941, however, was going to be very different, work rather than play dominating the months of July and August. It began with potato harvesting.

The day after school finished for the summer, Farmer Stoneycroft tipped off Billy about the opportunity to earn some money by gathering potatoes for a local crop grower. The Salop War Agricultural Executive Committee had earlier in the year appealed to local farmers to grow more spuds, and many dutifully demurred. However, the manpower demands for harvesting the crop were difficult to fulfil, hence the chance for Billy to earn a bob or two. On the last Monday in July, he was picked up outside

Potseething by a farm assistant driving an Albion flatbed lorry. Climbing on the back, he sat down next to a couple of Man Mountain Dean types, their shirt sleeves rolled up to the armpits, revealing biceps like Popeye after extra portions of spinach. They grunted in acknowledgement, Billy's breaking voice returning a squeak.

The radiator of the truck bore a striking resemblance to that of a Rolls Royce, but there the comparisons ended. Every pothole and every crevice in the road generated a shudder which vibrated his body like a tuning fork and induced a jack-in-the-box vault that ended unwaveringly with a painful landing on his backside. The adjacent wrestlers seemed completely unaffected by the journey and watched in mild amusement as Billy pitched and rolled across the flatbed, gripping the wooden rail edge on a couple of occasions when turning a corner at speed. He was not displeased on seeing the vehicle eventually turn into a good-sized farm off the Wolverhampton Road.

But the relief soon turned to foreboding. This was not going to be easy money. They were given an apron to wear containing a pouch on its front and told to follow behind a carthorse and plough churning up the soil in a field the size of Lords Cricket Ground. Billy's job was to rummage around the agitated earth, pick out the potatoes, and collect them in his pouch. When full, he was to empty the contents into a bigger bag at the side. The wage was regardless of the quantity amassed, and so it was the farm assistant's job to make sure nobody slacked.

Billy found it easiest to do the job on his hands and knees and was quickly into the task, crawling along and grabbing a regular clump of soil. For every potato found, there was a beetle and a few earthworms, and the size of the vegetables varied a great deal, but it was not too long before his apron pocket was full. He stood up, or at least tried to, falling over due to the weight of the King Edwards. After a deep breath and moment of sustained concentration, he summonsed the strength to get to his feet, only to discover he had inherited the posture of Quasimodo, his torso involuntarily crouched forward. The only thing missing from the trek to empty his collection was an anguished cry about the bells and Esmeralda. The Man Mountain Deans seemed pleased with the entertainment on offer.

He was grateful when granted a lunch break, collapsing to the floor with his arms splayed at ten to two and his legs at twenty past eight. A giant tray of bread and jam appeared from somewhere, the wrestlers using their burly hands to scoop up gargantuan portions, which they swallowed in no time at all. Billy managed a couple of normal-sized pieces before resting again on the ground until the progressively harsh tones of the farm assistant informed the potato pickers it was back to work.

The afternoon shift was an even greater toil, the cumulative effort challenging even the endurance of the two apes disguised as farm helpers. By the end of the day, Billy had earned the princely sum of one shilling, the hardest day's graft in his brief working life. And later there was insult added to injury when back at Potseething and called for his tea.

'Come on Billy,' said Rose, 'your food's ready... it's a nice potato casserole.

****

August 12th was not glorious in terms of weather, the temperature fresh, the rain persistent, but it remained the Glorious 12th in reference to the start of the grouse season whose occurrence gave Billy another opportunity to earn some cash during the summer holidays. The shooting parties required beaters, and the young evacuee got the job.

On the day itself, gathering at nearby moorland, Billy was handed a stick by the gamekeeper and told to stand with his fellow recruits, all lithe and agile specimens, something that would prove valuable during the shoot.

The party began their walk across open land until the ground underfoot became dense undergrowth. The gamekeeper told everyone to stop, instructing the beaters to stand a few yards apart from one another in a straight line.

The lead man then barked at them, 'When I shout "Take it on", I want you to strike the ground with your sticks and make as much noise as you can. If I say "Take it steady", you have to slow down. And most important of all, when I say "Duck", you need to fall to the ground, and quickly. I've no wish to carry a corpse back home with the game.'

A few people laughed at this point, but Billy failed to see the funny side, more concerned with the paucity of detail in the instructions.

The gamekeeper turned his attention to his fellow rifle holders and bawled, 'RIGHT, LOAD YOUR GUNS!'

Billy glanced over his shoulder, disconcerted to see one elderly farmer in a bowler hat struggling with his weapon, the barrel of the firearm becoming fixed on him for a few unnerving seconds.

'TAKE IT ON!'

The beaters took their cue and started thrashing the ground with their sticks. It took very little time before a fluttering was heard from the branches of the trees, and a large bird escaped from the woods into the open canvas of the sky.

'DUCK!'

Gunfire filled the air. Billy dropped as though hit, crashing to the floor with the same speed and haste as his fellow beaters, though not before a few stray shots whizzed over his head. It was another irony, evacuated to the peace and quiet of the Shropshire countryside where old farmers fired ammunition with a healthy disregard for the safety and welfare of children.

'GET IT BOY!'

Misinterpreting the gamekeeper's shout for the dogs to fetch the fallen birds, one of the more anxious beaters resumed hitting the ground, thereby distracting the hounds who attacked his stick rather than retrieve the game. A few grouse reacted to the commotion by flying out of the woods, which in turn resulted in the old man with the bowler hat firing wildly into the sky, everybody having to duck including the gamekeeper. It was mayhem but could have been much worse, carnage narrowly avoided. The party cut their losses and moved on to another location, where they swiftly corrected the mistakes of the first effort and established a safe and effective method for subsequent shoots, Billy making sure he maintained one eye on the loose cannon in the bowler hat. He finished the day having earned less than a shilling for his efforts, inadequate recompense for such a hazardous job.

On his way back to the farm with rainclouds darkening the early evening skies, he realised he had built up quite an appetite and rewarded his labours with a fish and chip supper from his regular chippy in Bridgnorth, wolfing down the deep fried delight. With a full stomach, he began the long walk to Potseething Farm trying to wipe away the memory of standing in front of a short-sighted old man in a bowler hat carrying a loaded rifle. But when he jumped out of his skin on hearing a passing car backfire, he knew his efforts had been in vain.

Twenty four hours later, Billy was alone in the farmhouse, when there was a knock at the door. It was Trampy.

'Ello Billy Boy.'

'Trampy.'

The vagrant had a package in his hand, Billy recognising its smell, strong enough to mask the pungency of the man himself.

'Anybody in?'

'Only me.'

'Well, bought these for farmer's daughter... can ye give 'em when she's back?'

Trampy passed him chips wrapped in newspaper, the same treat as after yesterday's beating.

'Alright,' said Billy, taking the packet.

'I'm in barn tonight, so I'll go n'get comfortable like.'

Billy said goodbye and closed the door. He stared at the parcel in his hands, the wonderful aroma assailing his senses. He unwrapped a little of the vinegar-soaked newspaper to sample a chip... then a second one... then another. A thought occurred to him. Young Patricia knew nothing about the food, and if he ate it, she would be none the wiser. He made a quick decision, almost as quick as the speed with which he polished off the chippy treat. He was just digesting the last mouthful when the front door opened, Rose and her daughter entering.

'I can smell chips,' said young Patricia excitedly.

'Can you?' said Billy, guilt daubed in broad brush strokes all over his face.

'I've just seen Trampy by the barn,' said Rose. 'He tells me he's bought chips for Patricia.'

'Erm...'

'Where are they Billy? Where are the chips?'

Rose's demeanour was now stern. He had no answer.

'I erm...'

'You don't need to say anything Billy. Go to your room now.'

'Where are my chips mummy?' said Patricia, tears on the verge of making an appearance.

The evacuee slouched away, keen to get out of this uncomfortable situation. He was halfway up the stairs, when he heard a shriek, followed by 'He's ate my chips, he's ate my chips,' and then the sound of sobbing. His relationship with the farmer's daughter was not the best. She continued to show some resentment for him being there, but his actions tonight with the chips had sealed things. Billy Whitfield was not a Nazi, but in the eyes of young Patricia Stoneycroft, he was certainly the enemy.

****

Entertainment had become an inevitable casualty of war, playing second fiddle to the necessities of the time, a good example being the popular Bertram Mills' Circus that had previously toured the country to perform under the big top in front of packed houses. Lions, tigers, and elephants were the main attractions, ably supported by trapeze artists and clowns, but following the events of September 1939, the travelling show had been forced to close. Nonetheless, smaller circuses continued to tour the provinces, visiting towns deemed safe from the Luftwaffe, one make-do affair arriving somewhat ironically in Bridgnorth a year to the day that the Germans had bombed the Shropshire town.

Billy and his friends from school had been amongst the first to buy tickets and were also at the front of the queue for the afternoon of their chosen performance. The marquee was set up close to the River Severn, the warm weather and animal manure combining to create a welcoming odour that cleared Billy's congested head and almost knocked him over. He half expected to turn around and see Trampy next to a dozen of his vagrant pals.

'I can't wait to see the elephants,' said Arbuckle, the heavily-built youngster with a laboured gait not a million miles from that of the African beast.

'They're not in it,' said Billy.

'No elephants?'

'No.'

'Bugger... well at least there's the lions.'

'No lions either.'

'Tigers?'

87

'No.'

Arbuckle let out a big sigh.

'I just want to see the clowns,' said Tiny Tom, blowing a raspberry.

Arbuckle wiped his face dry from the little chap's unsolicited spray of saliva.

'I want someone to fall off the high wire,' said Kenny Kirkbride, licking his lips.

This was the last thing Billy wanted to see. Clearly, Kenny's idea of a great day out was a public execution of sorts.

A bad tempered man in tight, white trousers arrived to scowl, collect tickets, and let the customers into the marquee. The crunch of straw beneath Billy's gumboots echoed as he followed the others to their position on the grass at the front. They had the best 'seats' in the house... or the worst depending on your point of view, given the likelihood of selection for audience participation. The tent continued to fill, and when the last punter was in place, a fanfare of trumpets and trombones signalled the start of the show. The ticket collector, now red jacketed with a transformed disposition of joy, walked to the centre of the ring and began shouting something incomprehensible to which everyone cheered. More trumpet noises ushered in a white stallion with a glamorous assistant standing on its saddle followed by two small black ponies pulling a Cinderella carriage, the elegance undermined by a strong smell of poo. Billy hoped this was something to do with the animals and not the lady on the horse. And despite a couple of wobbly moments, to Kenny's acute disappointment, the trapeze and high wire acts survived their acrobatics.

In the absence of the big game animals, the undoubted stars of the show were the clowns, and three trotted into the ring to another blast from the brass section. One was tall and bald with orange hair sticking out either side of his head at ninety degree angles, another was short and podgy with an ill-fitting suit and hat, and the last one was a dwarf. They fell over, picked themselves up, fell over, hit one another with a variety of comedy objects, fell over, picked themselves up, fell over and so on. The crowd loved it, including Billy who hadn't giggled so much since the football game when Arbuckle tried to kick the ball out for a throw in and fell down face first in the mud. The dwarf clown briefly disappeared before returning in a small car for a routine where the little driver ended on top of the roof rack being bombarded by suitcases thrown by the other two. It was very funny, and a great release for the audience.

The podgy one then picked up a bucket, seemingly full to the brim with water, and rushed towards Billy, tripping up and emptying the pale all over him, the contents, thankfully, paper cuttings rather than liquid. Then, to the evacuee's surprise, the clown held out a hand and dragged him into the ring, the crowd roaring their endorsement at the pending entertainment.

The 'volunteer' was immediately hoisted on to a long, rectangular trampoline, straightaway finding it impossible to stand up. His gumboots, ideal for the everyday terrain of Oldbury and Bridgnorth, were the least suitable footwear for bouncing up and down on a piece of canvas made taut using metal frame and springs. The clown gave him the hat to wear and pushed him over, Billy each time rebounding to a temporary standing position, until pushed back down again and back up, back down and back up. The audience roared with laughter, Billy ending his turn in the spotlight by leaping off the trampoline with the clown to make a perfect landing on to the sawdust. He bowed and drank in the applause, returning to his place the envy of his pals.

He was still basking in the adulation when he left the big top at the end of the performance. A few people pointed in his direction, others still laughing at his gumboots. He would have returned to Potseething Farm that day happy, if not for the conversation he overheard by the exit.

A young boy, no older than five or six was with his mum, holding her hand.

'There's the boy who was on the trampoline,' he said.

Billy flushed on the inside.

'Which boy?' said his mum.

As she asked the question, the lady and her white stallion passed behind them.

'That one over there who smells of poo.'

****

It had been two days ago when cashing his weekly postal order, that Billy had spotted a small postcard on the Post Office notice board.

'Bickton Grange
Fruit Pickers Wanted
3d a basket
Monday 1st September 1941
9.00am start'

Fruit picking? 3d a basket? Unlike the potato harvesting, this really did sound like easy money, especially since he was already a dab hand at taking apples from the trees in the orchard behind school. He had decided to give it a go.

Bickton Grange was part of a large farm undertaking situated within a relatively short distance of Potseething. Billy arrived with time to spare, pleased to discover he was not alone, four young men gathering just inside the gate to await instructions. He joined the group and exchanged a cordial but reserved welcome, recognising them as members of the Bridgnorth Grammar football team, regular vanquishers of St Mary's. With these lads all towering close to six foot, he was indisputably the shortest and chose not to lean back against the gate. He wanted to look as tall as humanly possible.

A few minutes later Bickton's farmer appeared alongside a sturdy looking grey pony attached to a cart. He drew near to the helpers and began counting them with an extended forefinger.

'One, two, three, four…'

He stared at Billy.

There was a short delay before he added, '… and a half.'

Billy feared he may have to fill two baskets for his threepence.

'Right boys, you know the drill,' continued the farmer, his manner drenched in militaristic authority. 'Fill your baskets, bring them to me for weighing, and then drop the fruit into one of those barrels. Ladders are over in that barn. Off you go…'

The other pickers walked purposefully across a small pasture and disappeared through a door-less arch into the brick building, re-emerging shortly each hauling good-sized wooden ladders. Billy edged past and entered the same barn to be overtaken by disquiet. There was one remaining pair of step ladders with a measly three rungs, not much bigger than a milking stool. The farmer's 'half' jibe was biting even harder.

Carrying his little steps and empty basket, Billy trod his way through the residual mulch of rotted manure towards the rows of compact Shropshire prune trees whose white blossom from spring had been replaced by fruit, a rich, deep purple in colour and ripe for picking. He chose the first tree because of its helpful low-hanging specimens and in less than ten minutes had filled half a basket. But his progress slowed when needing to access the higher branches. Standing on tiptoes at the top of the stepladder, he grasped a few leaves to bring the damsons closer but then fell off. The drop of three feet was never going to cause much physical damage, but a face full of putrefied animal muck was deeply unpleasant to say the least.

By the end of the morning, he had just about managed to fill one basket, the four giants having achieved around a dozen, a familiar result of Bridgnorth Grammar 12 St Mary's 1. The afternoon brought a similar outcome, though Billy might have done better if he had not eaten so many.

Used mainly to make preserves, these damsons nonetheless had a sweet taste he found irresistible. Burping for the umpteenth time, he vowed to give the grammar school lads a better run for their money the following day.

As he was leaving the farm, Billy noticed the farmer's grey pony grazing in the middle of a large field. It gave him an idea. He returned to Potseething for his tea and then made his way back to Bickton Grange, where he was pleased to see the pony still outside enjoying an occasional chew on the grass. The farm was quiet, the field shadowed by a clump of birch trees. Nobody was going to spot an intruder. He climbed over the wooden stile and jumped to the ground, walking slowly towards the pony. He whistled quietly to get its attention, the animal eventually turning round with an almost disappointed, disinterested stare. Billy drew near to the animal at a slow pace, all the time whispering encouraging words. As it turned out, he could have sprinted like a puma and shouted in the style of Adolf Hitler at a Nazi rally. The pony was a benevolent sort and certainly wasn't going to object violently to his plan.

Billy jumped on its surprisingly wide back and immediately christened him after the Cheltenham Gold Cup and Grand National winner.

'Come on Golden Miller, one lap to go and we've won the National again,' he said, grabbing imaginary reins and applying an imaginary whip.

The pony turned around as if to say, 'Listen pal, I've been hauling milk churns around all day. All I want to do is have a bit of a rest, so if you don't mind, could you just bugger off?'

Billy wasn't listening.

'... over Becher's Brook, round the Canal Turn, this could be our year again...'

Golden Millar obliged by trotting forward a little, Billy all of a sudden struggling to cling on.

'... two more fences to go, and here comes the second to last... and we're over... now just one from home.'

And yet... the final jump never materialised. Without a saddle, the roughness of the pony's back was already proving too much for Billy's complaining bottom, but when Golden Miller unseated its rider with a sudden shrug of its rump, the landing on the hardened and baked soil, arse first, finished off the job. Billy raised himself from the ground and patted the pony's neck to begin the shuffle back to Potseething, clutching his behind. The Grand National would have to wait for another day.

Unfortunately, the groans and moans from his bum had something else in store that day in a very different kind of race... the race to the toilet. During a fitful night's sleep, the overeating of the damsons from the fruit picking caught up with the evacuee, resulting in a regular sprint to the outside lavatory at the farm. Billy Whitfield had the trots... the Shropshire prune trots.

After a memorable month of potato harvesting, grouse beating, clowning around, fruit picking and pony riding, the school summer holidays, like some more unpleasant things, had disappeared down the pan.

CHAPTER 9

Eric had made an extra effort for today's bible class, an additional shine to his shoes, his whitest shirt, his hair combed with precision, and as he walked alongside Vera on the way home, he surmised that she had done likewise. It was a pleasant late summer afternoon, and despite the limitations of 'Make Do & Mend', she was dressed very smartly in a blue flowered, silk dress tapered at the waist. He had an urge to feel the texture of the fabric, and an ever greater one to touch the smooth skin of her bare arms, but they remained thoughts, Eric briefly cursing the scriptures for their impositions of chasteness and purity.

Today was to be the day. However, fifteen minutes into the journey and his courage had deserted him. He heard the normality of their everyday conversation but was detached, searching for the practised words now elusive, inaccessible. It jarred that Len had such an easy, natural way with the opposite sex, while he was so uncomfortable. It was looking hopeless until, for the briefest of moments, the pair looked in one another's eyes and held the gaze for longer than normal. From somewhere within, he heard his own voice speaking.

'Would you like to go to the pictures?'

He had said it… hardly prose from a Jane Austen novel, but by some distance the most romantic words he had uttered to date.

They were both standing still, and there was silence, unnerving him for a split second before she smiled and replied, 'I'd love to… that would be nice. What's on?'

'There's a spy film called *Cottage to Let* showing at the Liscard Palace.

I'm told it's worth seeing.'

'When do you want to go?'

'Saturday night? The 6.30 performance?'

'You've done your homework, haven't you?'

Eric blushed and mumbled, 'I had a quick look yes…'

'Well that's a date then.'

The day was transformed. She had said yes. He should have listened to Len earlier. Vera linked her arm through his, and they resumed their walk home. Eric was not a man able to read with ease the inner thoughts of a female partner, but Vera's demeanour was conveying a transparent message.

She was definitely thinking, 'About time too!'

Waiting nervously at the top of Valkyrie Road, Eric kicked a discarded cigarette stub into the gutter. The doubts of last Sunday were returning. Had she forgotten? Had she changed her mind? Was there somebody else? The latter possibility sent a shudder through him. He had never given that prospect a second's thought. The tap of high heels on paving stones interrupted this destructive introspection, and he glanced up to see Vera walking towards him, looking wonderful. The war effort may have overlaid a constraint on glamour, but Eric's date was confounding such restrictions. She was dressed in a light-coloured raincoat, the sheen of her black hair all the more striking against the fabric. She wore some make-up, but its application was discreet, the notable exception her mouth with the red of her lipstick, bright and vivid.

'Vera!' he almost shouted, unable to hide the relief that she had arrived on time.

'Hello Eric.'

'You look…' he said, distractedly searching for the right word, but the adjective never came, and he stood there vacant, cursing this display of wanton ineptitude.

But he was in luck. Vera laughed, and carried on laughing, 'Oh Eric, you are funny.'

She kissed him, rescuing him from the embarrassment. It was only a peck on the cheek, but it was his first kiss, and it felt good. The lipstick had evidently left a mark because she rubbed his skin with a handkerchief before linking arms and heading down Seaview Road towards the cinema.

The Liscard Electric Palace had a fibrous plaster façade that resembled a wedding cake prepared by a chef with too many bags of icing. Its interior, however, was more impressive with an expansive marble floor in the entrance hall and two staircases leading up to a Grand Circle. Eric bought two tickets from the box office for the stalls and escorted Vera inside the auditorium, the usherette directing them to their seats on the third to back row. There was just time for Eric to look up and see the blue ceiling panels, the decorative ventilation grilles, and the gold curtains, before the lights dimmed and the sound of a cockerel indicated the start of the Pathé newsreel.

The bulletin included details of heavy raids on Berlin carried out by the RAF with Wellington and Hampden bombers and referred to the bravery of one particular pilot who had made the six hundred mile journey home at low altitude in a flak-damaged plane with only one working engine. The piece served to reaffirm his decision to join the flying corps. After a rather dull magazine feature on wildlife migration, it was the interval.

Eric said to his date, 'Do you want an ice cream?'

'Oh, yes please. Can I have a tub?'

He was back shortly with two tubs and two wooden spoons.

'How's your RAF application going?'

A small piece of ice cream fell from his spoon on to his trousers, which he quickly removed. Vera hadn't noticed. The Pathé story about the Berlin raid had presumably triggered the question. Eric recalled the last time they talked about this subject, when a certain tension had arisen. He spoke a little hesitantly.

'Erm… I'm due to attend a panel interview and medical in the near future… I'm just waiting to hear.'

'What are your chances of getting in?'

'Quite good I reckon… I don't think they can afford to be too choosy at the moment.'

'You'll be fine.'

She appeared genuine in her responses, although he did notice her nervously playing with an earring. In fairness, he could understand her unease about a potential boyfriend swanning off to join the forces after only a few weeks. But in these difficult times, this was far from unusual.

The auditorium filled again in readiness for the main feature. *Cottage to Let* proved to be a decent film with a couple of poignant elements, the story incorporating an evacuee and an RAF traitor. He thought of Billy and himself. His brother fitted the part, but Eric Norman Whitfield would never fail King and Country like the John Mills character. The national anthem at the end of the showing resonated stronger than ever with him.

The young couple left the picture house. Outside, it was dark, the blackout preventing the gaudy lights from illuminating the cake façade, but the night was mild and the sky clear. As they strolled along Seaview Road arm in arm, Vera's words had a wistful edge.

'It's so peaceful up there isn't it?' she said.

'Yes… it certainly is…'

The same skies that presented a combustible backdrop to the terrors of German night bombers and anti-aircraft shells were tonight a calm indigo infused with the haze of a thousand flickering stars. The film at the Liscard Palace was a reminder that the country was at war, but as Vera rested her head on his shoulder, any worries or concerns about the future seemed as far away as the most distant moon.

They reached the top of her road.

'I'll be alright from here,' she said.

'Are you sure?'

'Yes thanks.'

She looked him in the eyes.

'It's been lovely Eric… thank you so much.'

She leant toward him and kissed his cheek. He turned his head and their lips touched. It was not the kiss of a Hollywood film where the orchestra played a symphony to accompany the moment. This was a gentler affair. Yet Eric heard the violas, the violins, the cellos, and the drama of their harmonies, melody lines, and rhythms. Rhett Butler was embracing Scarlet O'Hara. A few moments later, she was gone, not with the wind, but with a wave and a smile.

The next day after bible class, Eric took the plunge, agreeing with Len to take Margaret and Vera dancing the following weekend. This called for urgent action on his part. His plans to learn a few dance steps, formulated in the thunderstorms and humidity of the ride home from Bridgnorth, had failed to come to fruition. He still had two left feet. The notion of formal lessons at Killen's Dance School was not a welcome one. He just needed a few basic steps. Fortunately, Lady Luck was on his side, the opportunity arising a few hours later when at home for Sunday dinner.

There was no surprise as to the food his mum was cooking for the afternoon meal, the usual rabbit and potatoes, but the source of the game was more surprising.

'Here you are Eric,' said his mum, 'this is from your brother.'

She passed him a letter. He read Billy's neat handwriting.

Dear Mum,

I hope you like the rabbit. I helped the farmer harvest the wheat last week, and when the field was nearly done, all these rabbits jumped out. He told me to catch them by hitting them over the head with a stick, and I caught a slow one. It seemed a bit cruel to me, but there's a lot of cruel things on the farm. Mrs Stoneycroft sometimes goes into the farmyard to get a chicken and kills it by screwing its head. I'm back in school for the new term, and I'm glad Miss McDonnell is still our teacher. I hope that you are all keeping well, and that you enjoy your rabbit feast.

Billy

P.S. I went to the circus last week and was pulled out of the crowd by a clown who made me jump on a trampoline. The audience laughed a lot.

Eric folded the letter and handed it back to his mum.

'He's surprised me, you know,' she said, placing it in a small drawer of the walnut bureau against the wall.

'In what way?'

'Settling so well on the farm... I thought he'd be back in a couple of weeks.'

Eric wondered if this is what she expected or what she wanted.

'I mean,' she continued, 'he's been picking potatoes, helping shoot pheasants or something, and now he's catching rabbits... mind you, I don't think he realised the one he got was pregnant... she would have been slow.'

'I think it's been good for him, though. It's helped him grow up a bit.'

'Yes, yes... I know what you mean,' her distraction a signal she did not want him to be growing up, at least not in her absence.

He felt for his mum, having to deal with the contradiction of wanting her child at home yet wanting him safe and well away from home. It was ultimately an irreconcilable situation.

There was a knock at the door.

'That'll be Hilda,' said his mum.

Eric went to open it.

'Hello Aunty.'

'Eric... my word, you are looking smart,' she said. 'And correct me if I'm wrong, but it looks like there might be a little courting going on.'

He couldn't fail to be impressed with the intuition of his mum's sister.

'Maybe,' he replied coyly.

'I knew it, I knew it,' she said, busying her way through the vestibule and into the hall where she hung up her coat before moving into the back room.

'Eva, Eric's got a girlfriend,' she said, her cheeks flushed a slight shade of pink.

'Have you?' his mum smiled.

Eric reacted to the teasing with a dismissive air.

'Well, we went to the pictures, but...'

His aunt was having nothing of it.

'But nothing! If she let you take her to the cinema, then she must be sweet on you.'

The sisters were enjoying the gentle ribbing.

'What's her name?' asked his mum.

'Vera... I met her at bible class...' Eric hesitated, 'actually... I'm taking her to the Grosvenor on Saturday.'

Hilda emitted a high-pitched coo, followed swiftly by a practical thought.

'How's your dancing?'

'Not too good really...'

'Then let's do something about it.'

'Erm...'

'While your mum's doing the dinner, we'll get Victor Sylvester on the gramophone.'

The front room of Barrington Road was seldom used, preserved for those rare occasions when the vicar popped in for a cup of tea, a biscuit, and a little chat about funds to repair the church spire. The pristine armchairs and settee were protected by lace arm caps and head rest covers, a polished, hexagonal-shaped mirror in dark oak hung from the picture rail above the marble fireplace, and a large Axminster rug sat on the tiled floor, leaving enough room for a sideboard, a gramophone in the corner, and a short lesson in ballroom.

Hilda was small in stature, Eric close to six feet tall, and so it was not exactly a match made in Astaire and Rodgers heaven, but the student was happy to give it a go. With the help of Sylvester's 'Anniversary Waltz' playing on rotation, his aunt refined his rough and ready technique, and though it appeared at times a mild rigor mortis had set in, within a short while, there was a definite improvement.

As the last few bars of the record played for the tenth time, Eric heard the front door open. It was his dad who glanced inside the front room to see his son and sister-in-law in hold.

He uttered a highly predictable, 'Bloody hell.'

His arrival coincided with the call that dinner was ready, the rabbit tasty, much better than the usual fare. Billy had done well. At the end of the meal, Eric cleared the table and was ready to sit down to let his food digest, when Hilda returned from the kitchen.

'Now Eric, I have a little surprise for you.'

'Sorry?'

'A present.'

'But it's not my birthday,' he said, a touch bemused.

She went to the end of the hall and came back with a triangular-shaped cardboard box, which she handed to him.

'I thought, well, you can't take a piano when you join the RAF, but you could take this.'

He opened the container to reveal a black leather case. Inside there was a shining, wooden ukulele.

'Aunty, you shouldn't have...'

'Bloody hell,' his dad grumbled in the background.

'Don't be silly Eric, it's the least I could do,' she said.

His mum was stood at the kitchen door, wiping her hands with a tea towel.

'Are you going to give us a song then, son?'

Although Eric was used to providing the musical accompaniment, he was not normally the singer. But today, with this gift and Hilda's dance tutorial, he was indebted.

'George Formby?'

The sisters agreed enthusiastically with the choice, his dad reacting with a shrug of the shoulder, hiding his face behind the Sunday People. For the next half hour, Eric became the comic singer from Wigan with a thin, nasal twang, 'When I'm Cleaning Windows', 'Chinese Laundry Blues', 'My Little Stick of Blackpool Rock' and 'You Can't Keep a Growing Lad Down' all given an airing. Even his dad was tapping his feet by the end. Eric returned the ukulele to the case and thanked Hilda again. He had enjoyed the sing song. Now he was looking forward to the dance.

Vera sipped her tea and rested the china cup on its saucer. Eric, sitting next to her, had an unobstructed view through the open doorway of couples dancing across the breadth and width of the ballroom floor. The band sounded good, none of them spring chickens, the tuxedo-wearing members all receding hairlines and crowns. Presumably the younger lads were off helping the war effort somewhere, but their sound proved you can't beat a bit of experience in such matters. Vera joined him stretching forward to see what was going on.

'We'll get up there in a minute,' he said, the words lacking conviction.

'That's alright,' she said, 'whenever you're ready.'

'Vera,' he turned towards her, a serious, earnest expression occupying his features, 'I'm not very good you know.'

'I'm sorry?'

'At dancing... I'm not very good.'

'Well I'm sure you're better than him.'

They both caught sight of a tall, young man trying his hand at the foxtrot with all the grace and fluidity of Frankenstein's monster. The sight heartened Eric, and it was good timing. The leader of the band indicated the next number was a waltz. Not only that, it was 'Anniversary Waltz' by Victor Sylvester. Eric almost smashed the crockery in his haste to get to the dance floor, and he had to take care not to pull Vera's arm out of its socket when leading her towards the ballroom. But his alacrity paid off, the pair standing in hold right at the moment the band started to play.

Hilda's tuition came back in an instant, as he counted 'one-two-three, one-two-three, one-two-three,' although there was an early setback.

'Count in your head, not aloud,' she whispered.

Unsurprisingly, Eric lost his timing, and for a few seconds was giving Dr Frankenstein's creation a run for his money, but he quickly and literally found his feet to relax into a pattern. The waltz lacked the passion and fervour of the Latin dances, but the touch of Vera's body against his as they moved with surprising grace was nothing short of thrilling. They crossed the floor, his right hand resting on the small of her back, his other clasped against the soft, delicate skin of her palm. They passed Len and Margaret, his friend winking and smiling in acknowledgement. But just as he was unwinding into this new world of ballroom joy, a familiar, haunting sound destroyed the moment. The wail of air raid sirens permeated the carefree entertainment. The aircrews of the Luftwaffe were on their way.

The music and the dancing came to an abrupt end, everyone hurriedly, yet without panic, gathering their things and setting off for a nearby shelter. The change in mood was instantaneous. Eric, who had been drifting on a tide of friendship and camaraderie, was back in the here and now, a here and now of enemy bombs, death and destruction. The war had come between him and his new girlfriend. He reflected with resignation that it was certainly not going to be the last time either.

CHAPTER 10

The morning's long walk to school brought home the recent change in seasons, summer now a distant memory. There was the crunch of shoes on discarded autumn leaves scattered across the lane, the last of the hedgerow berries calling to be picked, and the fungi peppering tree trunks and the ground below. Billy watched a spider weave an intricate web adorned with droplets of morning dew and heard the trills and warbles of sparrows and blackbirds filling the air. But gradually this autumn vista and soundtrack was overpowered by the customary sight and sound of a sleek Jaguar car, the farmer's daughter sat on the back seat with Dick Tracy at the wheel, and he moved mechanically to the side of the road to let the vehicle past. He had stopped thinking about the inequity of his exclusion from young Patricia's car journey, yet he was still intrigued by the owner of the Jag, the man with the face of a movie star. But by the time he reached school, his deliberations had faded, and he was ready for the first lesson of the day.

Miss McDonnell's Scottish pedigree was glowing this morning. The wisps of red hair escaping from their hold, the ice blue eyes set against her pale, freckled skin, and her blouse the colour of purple thistle accompanied a tartan skirt, a kilt without a sporran.

'I have good news for you today boys,' she announced.

Billy became alert, sweeping the hair back from his forehead and rubbing his eyes with the front of his fingers.

'We're going to form a choir... and we're going to give a concert.'

The news was not exactly greeted with elation, but she had a trump card.

'The choir will be boys and girls...'

Now there was interest. Billy and the other lads may have been, at best, in the early stages of puberty, but adding a few females to such activities invariably added an element of fun.

'What are we going to sing Miss?' said Kenny Kirkbride.

Billy had a good idea of the answer even before she spoke.

'Some of my favourites,' she gushed, 'like 'Caller Herrin'... 'Roamin in the Gloamin'... 'The Bonnie Banks O'Loch Lomond'...'

With the mention of each song, she was transported further and further away, wandering through the glens, traversing the craggy rock inclines of heather-covered hills, navigating the calm waters of the loch in the valley.

'Any others Miss?' Kenny persisted.

'Any others?' said the teacher, awaking from her moment in the Highlands. 'Certainly... perhaps 'Swing Low Sweet Chariot'.'

This was a surprise, an American spiritual with no tinge of Celtic ancestry. Billy raised a hand.

'Where's the concert being held Miss?'

'Ah yes, this is the exciting part. We have been invited to play at the RAF Training Camp.'

Tiny Tom, one of the lads at the back of the class who conveyed an appearance that erred on the emaciated side of things, had a pertinent question.

'Do we get a meal?'

The rumours about the cuisine enjoyed by Air Force recruits suggested the camp was on par with the Ritz in providing limitless supplies of Roast Beef, Lamb and Pork. This apparent banquet fit for a Roman Emperor was, of course, some way from the truth, although food was certainly more plentiful and varied than elsewhere. Tiny Tom was already licking his lips about the prospects, yet Billy was not too bothered. Thanks to Miss McDonnell's generosity, he no longer had to rely on jam butties for dinner at St Mary's, and back at the farm there was always a good-sized square meal.

'I'm sorry Tom, but we'll be there to sing not eat.'

Tiny Tom slumped back into his chair, his vivid dreams of gorging on a side of beef drowned in gravy overtaken by the prospect of phonetically challenging songs performed in Gaelic tongue.

Billy again put up his hand, thinking about his brother and his aspirations.

'Will we meet any pilots?'

'I'm afraid that's unlikely. The camp is now for WAAFs, which stands for the Women's Auxiliary Air Force.'

He felt a trace of disappointment. It was no longer a place where Eric could do his initial training, unless he turned up for his first day wearing one of Auntie Hilda's tweed skirts.

'Right boys, we will practise later but first... trigonometry.'

Maths was far from Billy's favourite subject, but he was heartened by his ability to keep pace with the lads from the grammar schools. Back in Wallasey, separated from the clever ones after his disappointing scholarship results, his academic progress had been slight. But here in Bridgnorth, the equality engendered by evacuation was helping him reach new heights of educational achievement. It was certainly a confidence boost.

'Let's start with a question. How many degrees are there in a right angle?'

Billy's arm shot up.

After lunch, it was time for the inaugural rehearsal of the St Mary's Choir. Billy counted nine girls that had joined the boys from his class to form a twenty strong unit. The main hall of the school had a decent-sized stage on which Miss McDonnell arranged the standing positions of the troupe to create the best sound. Billy was on the back row with his fellow baritone Kenny next to a few of the taller lads including Arbuckle who made up the bass section. The smaller boys including Tiny Tom were trebles on the front row, while the girls, all sopranos, filled the rest of the spaces. The teacher moved from the stage to stand in front of them. She was holding a knitting needle as a baton.

'Welcome to our new singing ensemble,' she said, her excitement barely concealed. 'Let us start by singing 'Caller Herrin'. There's no need for harmonies yet, just sing it as you normally would.'

They all knew the song. Anyone taught by Miss McDonnell was liable to become an expert on Scottish ditties about fishing. She signalled to her fellow teacher and North of the Border enthusiast Miss Baxter on the piano, and with a swish of the knitting needle, the singing began.

Wha'll buy my caller herrin'?
They're bonnie fish and halesome farin';
Wha'll buy my caller herrin',
New drawn frae the Forth?

It was a strange thing, Billy thought as he sang, but the lyric was strangely powerful, his senses channelling the strong odours of trawlers, fish, and fishermen.

When ye were sleepin' on your pillows,
Dream'd ye aught o' our puir fellows,
Darkling as they faced the billows,
A' to fill the woven willows?

The smell was getting stronger, almost catching his throat. It was making singing a little problematic.

Wha'll buy my caller herrin',
They're bonnie fish and halesome farin';
Wha'll buy my caller herrin',
New drawn frae the Forth?

The truth dawned upon him that one of the girls was responsible for the North Sea aroma. Gladys, standing immediately in front of him, lived above the fish shop in Hightown and worked there on a Saturday.

An' when the creel o' herrin' passes,
Ladies clad in silks and laces,
Gather in their braw pelisses,
Cast their heads and screw their faces.

By the end of the song, Billy was surprised at the burgeoning pungency of the young soprano. He knew at times he convected the farmyard smell of Potseething, but this girl was a living, breathing version of the Grimsby Docks. And there was no let up when the choir moved on to the next song. It seemed you did not have to sing about herring to induce its pong.

When dinner time arrived, Billy stuck to the ritual of sitting down to eat his jam sandwich before Miss McDonnell blessed his palm with silver and directed him towards the canteen. Today there was a special treat for the choir... herrings and boiled potatoes. The mystery solved, he apologised in his head to Gladys.

****

It was the day of the choir concert at the RAF base, a Saturday, and those taking part had been told to meet outside St Mary's school at five o'clock. The morning had seen the usual routine for Billy, the radio accumulator, the cashing of the postal order, the vanilla slice, the game of football, the inevitable defeat, although there had been a first. He had been in Bridgnorth for over nine months, but until now had not travelled on the Cliff Railway, a hydro-powered funicular ride that connected Lowtown with Hightown. He had paid his fare and met Gladys from the fish shop in the carriage and was pleased to confirm a complete absence of herring aroma.

Unsurprisingly, the tardy Billy was last to arrive at the school rendezvous, the wagon sent by the RAF on the verge of leaving without him. He boarded to cheers from the others and to Miss McDonnell shaking her head, though in a smiling way. The journey to nearby Stanmore was a short one, travelling up the Stourbridge Road, and it was not long before the choristers were reading a large, rectangular sign that proclaimed, 'No.1 WOMEN'S AUXILLIARY AIR FORCE DEPOT - BRIDGNORTH'. The vehicle turned into the main gate, the setting sun casting long shadows over the sentry box from which a duty guard waved the visitors through. They drove past two aircraft and a tall flagpole, its base sporting a portcullis coat of arms emblazoned *Haec Porta, Moenia Viri*, 'Here are the gates, the men are the walls'. The boys identified the planes as Spitfires, their presence a mystery. This was a training camp without a runway. Perhaps it was some kind of cover to fool the Germans. It might explain the Bridgnorth bombings the year before.

The group from St Mary's were escorted from the wagon and into a dining hall set up as a concert venue, the seats arranged in rows facing a modest-sized stage. Billy and his fellow choir members were asked to climb the few steps on to the boards and told to sit and wait until the audience arrived. To the left of them was a single chair, on which Kenny found a 'Sergeants Mess Dinner' programme for the event. He shared it with Billy

110

and Tiny Tom. The first page was headed 'MENU', Tom salivating as they read the dishes being served.

Tomato Soup
Fillet of Cod
Roast Chicken, Roast Potatoes, Vegetables
Sponge Trifle, Fruit Salad, Custard
Biscuits and Cheese
Black and White Coffee
Wines
Cold Sideboard, Ham

'Do you think we might get some food?' Tom asked.

'Don't know,' said Billy. 'It doesn't look like it.

Tom looked crestfallen.

The next part of the programme was headed 'TOASTS'.

'They're having toast as well!' said Tom, astonishment painted all over his face.

'No yer daft thing,' said Kenny, 'that's when they pour a drink and lift their glasses.'

'Oh.'

Tiny Tom might have been the thinnest in the class, but he was certainly not the brightest. There were planned toasts to 'The King', 'Absent Friends', and 'Victory'.

The final page gave details of the 'Musical Programme' as arranged by Flight Sergeant Grimshaw. The 'stars' listed were:

DANCER - L.A.C.W. Fairhurst
ENTERTAINER - F/Sgt Grimshaw
VIOLINIST - A.C.W. Chapman

The evening was to finish with 'God Save the King!'

They could hear general merriment in an adjacent building, presumably the meal now well underway. Billy had eaten earlier and so was not perturbed by the feasting going on next door. But the same could not be said for Tiny Tom who shuffled uncomfortably, wincing at the clink of every plate and every glass. Eventually, a few cheers were heard that concluded with a cry of 'Victory'. The final toast was done and dusted. Next up was the entertainment.

The makeshift theatre was soon filling with friendly, smiling WAAFs all dressed in RAF skirt uniforms, their long hair backcombed and styled into tightly contained waves and rolls. Billy glimpsed to his left and caught the eye of Gladys. She returned a smile. He tried to reciprocate, but it was more of a grimace. He often noticed the girl from the fish shop staring at him and had endured a little ribbing on the part of his classmates about her. For Billy, it was the wrong one. Gladys' friend Rita was a tall, striking looking girl with green eyes, high cheekbones and a broad smile. She looked foreign but never gave Billy as much as a second glance.

Miss McDonnell approached, clearly having sampled the menu, her cheeks flushed. She explained the choir were first up in a few minutes time and then went off in search of her knitting needle. Billy watched in surprise as Tiny Tom left the stage and exited the hall, presumably in need of a 'Jimmy Riddle'. But five minutes later with the audience packed to capacity, he had still not returned. Furthermore, only Billy had picked up on his disappearance. In fairness, his absence would make no difference to the sound of the choir. In rehearsals, Miss McDonnell had heard an especially out of tune drone amongst the singing and identified young Tom as the culprit. Rather than send him packing, the teacher allowed him to stay on the proviso he didn't sing. His job was to mouth the words as silently as a church mouse.

Flight Sergeant Grimshaw, the 'Arranger' and 'Entertainer', although it was a fair bet the latter tag was a bit exaggerated, was now standing on stage in front of the choir ready to address the audience. As one of the few men in the building, he began by telling a few mild jokes, the laughter correspondingly mild, even tepid. And yet this was a crowd eager to please. Max Miller would have a field day. It was then time to introduce the choir. As he did so, Tiny Tom returned, tiptoeing his way back up the steps to re-join his colleagues. Miss McDonnell, knitting needle baton in hand, looked confused as Tom with his cheeks puffed out like a mumps patient resumed his place on the front row.

Billy, immediately behind him, whispered, 'Where've you been?'

Tiny Tom's answer was inaudible but comprehensible at the same time, his open mouth revealing a strange cocktail of chewed chicken, roast potatoes, and trifle.

The piano played the introductory bars to 'The Bonnie Banks o' Loch Lomond.' Up went Miss McDonnell's needle and the singing began.

By yon bonnie banks an' by yon bonnie braes
Whaur the sun shines bright on Loch Lomond
Whaur me an' my true love will ne'er meet again
On the bonnie, bonnie banks o' Loch Lomond

Billy was relieved to see the crowd of WAAFs enjoying the song, not least because Tom was sticking rigidly to his job of opening his mouth without singing. Furthermore, his pockets were stashed with bits of food purloined from the dining area. He continued to find pieces of cheese and biscuits to eat during the performance.

O ye'll tak' the high road, and Ah'll tak' the low road
And Ah'll be in Scotlan' afore ye

For many of the diners, particularly those on the front few rows, it was an encore of the menu they had just eaten, and a deeply unpleasant encore at that.

Fir me an' my true love will ne'er meet again
On the bonnie, bonnie banks o' Loch Lomond

Yet to the enormous credit of the audience, Tom's gluttony was overlooked, demonstrating both their good nature and good mood. After the opening number, the choir sang 'Caller Herrin', followed by 'Roamin the Gloamin' and 'Swing Low Sweet Chariot', and at the end of their slot, warm applause rang out. Billy felt good, as did all the choir members. He smiled broadly, but instantly saw Gladys smiling dumbly at him. The pretty Rita only had eyes for Flight Seargent Grimshaw.

'Wasn't that great Billy?' said Tom, still stuffing his face.

Billy was forced to squint. A piece of cheese had lodged in his eye.

CHAPTER 11

This was it. Eric stared at the buff-coloured envelope, the blue-black longhand of 'E N Whitfield, 24 Barrington Road, Wallasey, Cheshire' almost childlike in form, although he acknowledged his standards in this regard were as sky high as the aircraft he planned to fly. The letter nonetheless radiated gravitas. Above the shaky handwriting in bold, underlined print were the words 'On His Majesty's Service' next to a Gloucester postmark stamped with Thursday's date and a reminder to re-use in accordance with the requirements of the 'War Economy'. Anxious to read its contents, Eric nevertheless took his time and carefully opened the envelope with a penknife.

The letter inside was abrupt and certainly not couched in terms of 'I am pleased to' or 'I would be grateful' etc. The country was at war, and this was no time for pleasantries. Most of the text was typed, but the date, name and location were written in the same blue-black ink as the name and address. However, this was an educated hand, more in keeping with the seriousness of the content. Eric approved.

You are hereby required to attend RAF Cardington at the address below for a medical on 17th December 1941. Should you not present yourself as ordered you will be liable to be proceeded against'.

This was just over a week away. He read on to discover his selection panel was a full two weeks after the health and fitness assessment. Nonetheless, if all went well, he would not be placed on reserve, and his active service would commence on New Year's Day. It had been over seven months since he volunteered just before his eighteenth birthday but at last the wait was over. He re-read the letter before folding it carefully and sliding it back into the envelope.

He then heard the key in the front door. This would be his mum back from an early morning quest for bread. Her steady step made its way along the hall and into the back room, where her gaze immediately locked on to his left hand.

'Is that... from the RAF?' she asked, cradling the bread like a new born baby.

Countless mothers up and down the land were coming to terms with the impact of war on their families, the younger ones billeted away as evacuees in the countryside, the older ones keen as mustard to do their bit, signing forms and receiving instructions to give up their freedom for King and Country.

'Yes,' he said, '... came this morning.'

'What does it say?'

'I've a medical a week on Wednesday at a base called Cardington.'

'Where's that?'

'Bedfordshire... not far from Northampton.'

'And what happens after that?'

'Well I think I come home and then go back on New Year's Eve for the selection panel.'

His mum visibly relaxed, placing the bread on the dining room table.

'So you'll be home for Christmas?'

'I think so.'

'Oh, I am pleased about that.'

His mum was still missing Billy. His brother had been in Bridgnorth for nearly a year, and although she wrote to him every week, she had not seen him since Easter. The bombing of Liverpool in November had been a reminder that the Blitz was far from over, and she had reluctantly agreed for her younger son to spend Christmas away as an evacuee, little wonder her delight at Eric's likely presence for the inevitably muted festivities. But the joy passed quickly, her face adopting a troubled expression. She began stroking the brown paper that covered the bread, her breath in short starts.

'I do worry about the war Eric,' she said quietly.

It was a rare moment of outwardly expressed concern.

'Of course you do,' he said, hiding the RAF envelope in his jacket pocket. 'I'm sure every mum feels the same… it's perfectly natural.'

'That business with the Japanese doesn't help. It all seems to be getting out of hand.'

She picked up the bread again.

News of the attack on Pearl Harbour had taken everybody by surprise, especially the Americans, and had certainly escalated things. With Japan declaring war on both the US and Britain, the stakes were getting higher by the day, a fact that served only to fuel Eric's desire to join the war effort proper and do something about it. Nonetheless, he still spotted the need to reassure her.

'Don't worry about me though Mum… I'm going to be fine.'

He believed every word. His mother, however, did not appear to share the optimism.

Eric got up to leave for work ten minutes earlier than normal, so he could walk to Seacombe Ferry. Although in good shape, he remained determined to grasp every opportunity to improve his fitness and therefore his chances of getting through the medical with flying colours. Taking a leaf out of Billy's book, he under-estimated the time needed and had to run down the landing stage to board the Royal Iris II just before the ferry hands, two old salts with grey beards, threadbare navy sweaters, and mouthfuls of catarrh, raised the gangway clear of the boat.

It was a bleak December morning, yet as he lifted his trilby, he had to use the palm of his right hand to wipe away a few droplets of sweat from his brow. The other commuters sought refuge in the covered lower deck, but Eric climbed the stairs to the exposed upper section, sitting down next to the tall mainmast where he removed his scarf and undid the top buttons of his winter coat. Alone, it was a moment to reflect upon the significance of the RAF letter still concealed inside his jacket pocket.

From high above the clouds, he heard the sound of propeller engines infiltrating the usual blend of lapping water, wind, foghorns and ships, inviting the young, aspiring aviator to dream about the freedom of the skies. A sudden blast of North Easterly wind caught the ferry, and it lurched to one side and then the other before levelling out to reveal Liverpool Bay, the pathway to the North Atlantic where so many ships and men had succumbed to the undersea warfare of German U-boats. If Eric needed a reminder as to why he had spurned the Royal Navy, this was it. His mind then jumped to Dunkirk in the late spring of 1940 when vessels such as this had sailed the English Channel to rescue thousands of retreating British Expeditionary Forces. Eric's imagination pictured scores of injured and mortally-wounded foot soldiers stretched across the decks, bloodied, desperate, and defeated. Rifle, bayonet, man-to-man combat were not for him. He was happy with his choice as an RAF man, more specifically, Pilot Officer E.N.Whitfield.

When the ferry reached the Pier Head, Eric walked with purpose and haste to the GEC offices in Liverpool, which had somehow survived the Blitz and the bombings, a fortuitous outcome given the company's key role in developing a radar capability for the British and supplying engineering and electrical products for the military. He sauntered past the reception desk and up the stairs to the first floor office. His department manager was already at his desk.

Mr Wells had his head buried in a ledger and scarcely acknowledged the arrival of the purchase order clerk. Wells was a decent man, mild-mannered, though lacking the warmth of his predecessor, the late Mr Leadbetter.

'Mr Wells, may I have a quick word?' said Eric, fingering the envelope in his hand.

'Yes, what is it?'

He carried on writing without looking up.

'I've received this letter.'

'I see,' he muttered, dipping his nib into the inkwell, eyes fixed on the desk.

'It's from the RAF.'

'From the RAF?'

At last he had his attention, the older man placing down his pen with precision. Eric passed him the letter. As the manager concentrated on the contents, his balding head of grey hair plastered to the sides with Vaseline moved from side to side like a tennis umpire. He concluded with a whispered tut. Eric waited for him to say something. The silence seemed to last a while, but finally he spoke.

'This is most inconvenient young man.'

Eric was rather taken aback at the response. If he hadn't volunteered for the RAF, he'd have been conscripted into the Army or the Navy anyway.

'I appreciate that, but…'

'Yes, yes, I understand the imperatives of war, but it doesn't make it any less bothersome.'

'Assuming they let me home after the medical, I can still work for a couple more weeks.'

A weary, but resigned air overtook Wells. He handed the letter back.

'You see Eric, you're a fine employee, and people like you are not two a penny… though I'm sure you're doing the right thing.'

And with that final pronouncement, Mr Ernest Wells returned to writing up the entries in his ledger, Eric slowly turning around and heading back to the solitude of his own desk. He gathered a number of purchase orders, straightened them out, and used a clip to secure them in a bundle, depositing them in the desk tray headed 'Pending'. His boss knew. His mum knew. That just left Vera.

****

The knock on the front door of Barrington Road was ferocious. Len was always in a hurry and had a tendency to announce his arrival as if a dire emergency.

Ted Whitfield looked up from his newspaper, grumbling under his breath, 'Bloody hell.'

'That'll be Len,' said Eric, picking up his coat and hat. 'I'll see you later.'

'Alright son,' said his mum, knitting what appeared to be the start of a shawl.

It was a few days since the RAF call up, his mum seemingly reconciled to the situation. His dad was always harder to read. His exterior, gruff and crotchety, belied a sentimentality that ran deep, hidden from view, but discernible nonetheless. Eric opened the front door to be greeted by the beaming smile of his best friend.

'Eric!' said Len. 'Are you ready for a quick one?'

'I trust you meant pint?'

'Hang on a minute, that's one of my lines.'

With Eric unexpectedly setting the pace, the friends walked briskly up Liscard Road on the way to the Boot Inn, their favourite public house. Len did most of the talking. He was full of his plans for settling down with Margaret, and how one day they would have a brood of kids.

'Five girls and five boys would do me, enough lads to play football, and enough girls to look after me in my old age.'

Eric shook his head and smiled. It was not until they were propped up against the bar, pints of mild in their grasp, that a natural break appeared for him to give Len the news.

'I've had my call up papers from the RAF.'

Len's pint glass, already on its way to his lips, froze. His smile, diminishing for a few seconds, returned as he composed himself and slapped his friend on the arm, slopping some of Eric's beer on to the woodblock floor beneath their feet.

'Ruddy hell Eric... good man,' he said, in mock, well-spoken officer tones before turning to face the others in the bar and shouting, 'gentlemen, this brave young chap has been called up by the RAF! Let's give him three cheers... Hip Hip!'

'*Hooray!*'

'Hip Hip!'

'*Hooray!*'

'Hip Hip!'

'*Hooray!*'

Much of the clientele were aged, and so the proclamation had not been the most boisterous, Eric experiencing self-consciousness and pride in equal measure.

In between sips of his pint and further banter with Len, he noticed a slight disconnection from time to time on the part of his friend. The news was a big thing for him, his drinking partner going away. Moreover, it might have tapped into an element of guilt with Len working at Lairds in a reserved occupation. However, by the time the final dregs of their second pints were drained, the irrepressible Len had recovered his poise.

'Come on Eric, let's go and get the girls.'

Twenty minutes later, Eric was sat next to Vera, drinking tea on the settee just outside the ballroom at the Grosvenor. He was awaiting his call sign of Victor Sylvester and the 'Anniversary Waltz', Len and Margaret already up doing a foxtrot of sorts. He fidgeted nervously, knowing this was the moment.

'Vera?'

'I know.'

'Sorry?'

'I know.'

'You know what?'

'That you've been called up.'

'Erm… who told you?'

'No-one.'

'Then how do you…'

She put her finger on his lips to stop him talking.

'A woman's intuition… I could tell by your face.'

It was an exchange that informed Eric there could never be secrets between the two of them.

'I go for my medical…'

Again she put her finger to his mouth.

'Don't talk about it now,' she said, softly squeezing his hand. 'Let's just enjoy tonight, hey?'

On cue, the strains of Victor Sylvester could be heard.

'May I?' he said, offering his hand.

'You may.'

He led her to the floor where the dancing proved effortless. No ballroom aficionado would have looked on and thought 'My God, here's the new partner for Ginger Rogers,' but in Eric's mind, his feet had been taken over by Astaire himself. As they waltzed, breezing past the other couples, Vera's dark hair brushed against his face and a waft of her delicate scent almost made him sneeze, the one moment he nearly lost his rhythm. But he maintained his composure, glad that the air raid sirens remained silent on this occasion. They danced for tune after tune, until Vera pulled him away to leave the floor.

122

'Get your hat and coat,' she said.

'Sorry?'

'Get your hat and coat.'

'Where are we going?' he said, confused at the sudden departure.

'To the swings.'

'The swings?'

The evening was mild, a good night for a walk. Outside the blackout was in full force, the only lights visible the feeble, dimmed headlamps of an occasional bus or warden's vehicle, but their eyes quickly adjusted to the darkness. They strolled along Grosvenor Street arm in arm talking quietly about the dancing, Len and Margaret, Alfred Hitchcock's *Suspicion*, in short, anything but the war and Eric's call up. After turning into Martin's Lane and crossing Liscard Road, they approached the park entrance.

'The gates are locked Vera.'

'That doesn't matter, follow me.'

He faithfully trailed behind her, until she found a section of railings where the iron bars had been wrenched apart.

'It's where the dogs get in,' she said.

They squeezed through before trampling across the long grass to the playground.

'Let's see-saw,' Vera suggested.

'I'm heavier than you... I could leave you stranded up there.'

'I'll take the chance.'

Eric was good as his word. After depositing his hat on the park bench, he sat on the see-saw and leant back, extending his legs in front to leave Vera dangling high above.

'I could stay here all night you know,' he said.

'You just dare!'

He teased her for a little, eventually jumping up and forcing her to drop, Eric careful, nonetheless, to cushion the blow just before her seat hit the ground.

'Eric!' she shrieked.

He laughed.

They crossed to sit on two of the larger swings, propelling back and forth, synchronising their movement. It was a peaceful evening, no lights, no people, and precious little noise. The next ride was the roundabout, Eric pushing, and Vera squealing in a mostly understated, hushed way.

'I'm feeling a little dizzy now,' she said. 'Can we have a sit down?'

'Alright.'

They returned to the bench.

'Watch your hat!'

He stopped himself at the last moment from crushing his trilby, placing it on his knee. Sat next to one another, Vera rested her head on his shoulder, and they both stared into the distance, saying nothing.

She eventually broke the silence, whispering, 'It just seemed the right thing to do... play on the swings... be children again.'

Eric's right arm was around her shoulder, his left, stroking her hair.

'Yes, I know what you mean.'

'Tonight feels, you know... like we're saying farewell to something... maybe our innocence.'

Eric stiffened, 'Eh, you don't...'

She slapped the air in admonishment, 'Not that you naughty thing... I'm talking about you going off to war. Who knows what the future holds?'

'I'll be fine, don't you worry.'

The ensuing silence confirmed that his confidence was not shared. It was like the exchange with his mum all over again. As Eric drifted into thoughts of what may lay ahead, he heard Vera speak.

'Kiss me Eric.'

'Erm...'

'Kiss me… properly.'

'Properly?' he hesitated.

'Properly.'

He leant across and kissed her.

The distant engine noise and meagre illumination of the number 16 Wallasey Corporation bus reminded the couple they were not alone. They agreed it was time to go home, leaving the park through the same gap in the railings like a poodle and a retriever. When they reached Liscard Roundabout, Eric watched Len emerge from the Monkey House toilets. He was fixing his flies.

'Eric!' he shouted. 'Where did you get to?'

'The swings,' Vera answered.

Len was temporarily flummoxed, before saying, 'Well, why not?'

Margaret appeared from a doorway to join her boyfriend, and Eric felt her hand on his arm, 'Good luck in the RAF,' she said.

'Yes… thanks Margaret… thank you.'

Luck? Would he need luck? He hoped that God's care was not a matter of luck, more a matter of faith. Bible study may have started as something to do on a Sunday and enabled him to meet the lovely Vera, but it had awakened a belief previously brittle, fragile, and slight. He hoped, indeed prayed, that this conviction would be a guiding light and comfort for the challenges in store.

The foursome wished each other a Merry Christmas and Happy New Year, this likely to be their last night out as a group for some while. Eric and Vera sauntered up Seaview Road, walking slowly, sub-consciously delaying their own goodbyes. Outside her house, they stood there for a few moments. There was no talk about the war, the RAF, medicals, assessments. In fact there was no talk at all, other than 'Goodnight,' although not before they had kissed… properly.

CHAPTER 12

Billy was sat at the large wooden table in Potseething's kitchen, the room dominated by an enticing aroma from a cauldron of stock simmering away on the wood burning stove. He gathered the script for *A Christmas Carol* and skimmed the pages for words spoken by Bob Cratchit. At the far end of the room, Patricia played with two rag dolls in an armchair, while her mum toiled with some washing in the sink.

Billy had been delighted to get the part of Bob, not least because it reflected his growing up. When he first arrived in Bridgnorth almost a year ago, he would no doubt have been cast as one of the Cratchit children, the role of the father an unrealistic prospect. Miss McDonnell, however, had been impressed with his performance as Talbot Edwards, Keeper of the Jewels in *Captain Blood* and had readily offered him the part of Cratchit Senior in the St Mary's Christmas Play.

He recalled with mixed feelings the bittersweet curtain call of a few weeks before, when enthusiastic applause rang out from the appreciative audience comprising mainly mothers, fathers, brothers and sisters of the Captain Blood cast. Whilst fellow evacuees on stage waved to their adopted parents, Billy could only acknowledge an imaginary figure, the Stoneycrofts having failed to attend. It was a lonely moment, yet he excused them in his head. Potseething Farm was some distance from the school, a fact he knew only too well from his daily trek. Regardless of their absence, he had since come to view the Talbot Edwards experience as one of the highlights of his year, and so when Miss McDonnell mentioned a Christmas production of the Charles Dickens classic, he had been one of the first to volunteer.

Billy returned to his script and thumbed the pages, speaking softly to himself as he read.

'Yes, my dear, I wish you could have gone. It would have done you good to see how green a place it is. But you'll see it often. I promised him that I would walk there on a Sunday. My little, little child. My little child.'

In one of the most obvious pieces of casting in the annals of thespianism, the role of Tiny Tim had gone to Tiny Tom. He was as delighted as Billy to get one of the key parts, but his food obsession remained an issue, harbouring ludicrous thoughts of eating during the performance like the Cratchits did in the book. Billy read on.

'Very well observed, my boy, I hope they do. Heartily sorry for your good wife. If I can be of service to you in any way, that's where I live. Pray come to me.'

'What are you reading there Billy?' enquired Rose.

The question took him slightly by surprise

'It's... erm... *A Christmas Carol.*'

'Is that the one with Scrooge?'

'That's right... I'm playing Bob Cratchit.'

'Well that's nice.'

And that was that. No more questions, no more enquiries.

The Farmer walked in and slowly lowered his backside on to his favourite armchair, choosing not to remove his coat. December was the least demanding month for farming, but old George still had to toil, this morning a case in point, out ploughing the fields in the winter cold.

'Did you want a cup of tea?' said Rose, now feeding her washing through the large wooden rollers of the mangle.

George took in a lungful of air, pursed his thin, chapped lips, and exhaled a jet of bad breath.

'Aye... nice an' milky mind.'

He looked weary, as if the years of hard graft were catching up with him, a perpetual grimace etched into his craggy features. The contrast with the busy energy of his wife was marked, and the age gap between the two appeared to be widening on a daily basis. More than ever, they seemed father and daughter.

Billy continued to read his lines, whispering so as not to be heard.

'But however and whenever we part from one another, I am sure we shall none of us forget poor Tiny Tim'.

Old George glanced up at Billy, as if noting his presence for the first time.

'Ye al'roight boy?

'Yes thanks.'

'What ye doin'?'

He explained about the Dickens play and his part. The farmer shrugged his shoulders and resumed a jaded persona, slumped in his chair. There was no further interest from George. The morning had confirmed one thing for sure. The Stoneycrofts would not be coming to his next performance treading the boards.

****

The last day of term at St Mary's had been and gone, and it was now just two days before December 25th. The school performance of *A Christmas Carol* was underway, Billy standing at the side of the stage adjusting his breeches, uncomfortably a few sizes too big for him. He discarded thoughts of them dropping to the floor at an inopportune moment and concentrated on his upcoming scene.

Kenny Kirkbride was doing a sterling job as Ebenezer Scrooge, another example of perfect casting. His classmate's reputation for stinginess had been earned with distinction over a long period of time. He had recently made a gobstopper last three days, despite its covering of fluff. Pulling his pants up again, Billy fervently wished they were as tight as Kenny.

It was nearly time for one of Bob Cratchit's main scenes, the one in which Tiny Tim's family make the best of their festive meal watched over by Scrooge and the Ghost of Christmas Present. Alongside Billy was the pretty Rita playing the part of Mrs Cratchit, Gladys as their daughter Martha, Arbuckle playing Peter, and Tiny Tom as Tiny Tim. Miss McDonnell drew near, her face beaming, evidently delighted with how the production was faring despite the play's lack of Scottish dialect, although Billy did recall the day she referred to the author as Charles McDickens.

'Now I have some lovely news for you,' she said, her smile somehow broadening further.

'What's that Miss?' said Gladys, as intrigued as the rest.

'When you sit down for your meal, you are going to be eating real food.'

'Real food?'

It was Tom. His ridiculous dream was coming true.

'Yes... you all deserve it.'

They all celebrated, noiselessly. The curtain closed in readiness for the scene with the feast, and a few minutes later the dialogue was underway.

MRS CRATCHIT: *I've made the gravy hissing hot.*
PETER: *I've mashed the potatoes.*
MARTHA: *I've the dusted the hot plates*
BOB CRATCHIT: *Come Tim; let me take you to the table.*

Billy picked up Tom and draped him over his shoulder. Thankfully, this Tiny Tim was slight and easy to carry, although Bob Cratchit's main concern was that his breeches remained intact. In fact he was so anxious to deposit his lame son that he almost threw him on to the chair. Trouser shame averted, he sat down to eat with the others. The dishes and bowls laid out on the table contained cooked goose, mashed potatoes, apple sauce, stuffing, and gravy, the steam from each dish rising to form a collective haze over the banquet. The cast all banged the table as the food was served.

ALL: Hurray!
BOB CRATCHIT: Never was such a goose cooked.
PETER: Such tenderness.
MARTHA: Such flavour.
TINY TIM: Such a size
MRS CRATCHIT: Such cheapness
BOB CRATCHIT: Indeed, all themes of universal admiration

The idea of treating the cast to a real feast started to backfire spectacularly. First of all, the audience could hardly understand a word spoken, clear intonation impossible with a mouthful of roast dinner. Secondly, Tiny Tim was acting totally out of character. The cripple in Dickens' text was weak, fragile and largely helpless. The version in the St Mary's Christmas play was ravenous, competitive, and on a couple of occasions, able to walk with ease to the other end of the table to get more goose. And thirdly, the cast ran out of lines. Imaginary food could be eaten precisely in line with the script. Genuine food took time to chew, swallow and digest, the difficulty first becoming obvious when the family were supposed to be eating the Christmas pudding.

MRS CRATCHIT: Here is the pudding.
PETER: It's like a cannonball
MARTHA: So hard and firm
BOB CRATCHIT: And blazing in a smidgeon ignited brandy.

Unfortunately, they were all still munching on their roast dinners, the figgy delight a figment of the imagination. By the scheduled end of the main meal, things were almost desperate.

BOB CRATCHIT: *It seems all have had enough.*
MARTHA: *Indeed, I am steeped in sage and onion to the eyes.*

Not so Tiny Tim. He had only just started and was ready to tuck into a second plate of food. The pudding was still to be served. There was only one answer… improvisation.

MRS CRATCHIT: *How much do you like goose Martha?*
MARTHA: *Not as much as turkey.*
MRS CRATCHIT: *Why not Martha?*
MARTHA: *It can be at bit greasy.*
MRS CRATCHIT: *But don't you think turkey is a little dry?*
MARTHA: *Sometimes.*

Rita and Gladys were performing wonders, keeping the dialogue flowing with the type of conversation you might overhear in the fish shop, Gladys no doubt familiar with such inanities from her Saturday job. Billy didn't get a look in but was glad. Making impromptu conversation in this context was not something he could manage.

MRS CRATCHIT: *What about fish?*
MARTHA: *Now you're talking*
MRS CRATCHIT: *Why's that?*
MARTHA: *The great thing about fish is that it's not rationed.*
MRS CRATCHIT: *Oh, of course.*

Hang on, thought Billy, surely they didn't have food rationing in

Dickensian times? But such details did not concern the two budding actresses. Gladys as Martha was forced into a brief monologue about the different types of fish products available, while Rita as Mrs Cratchit left the stage to fetch the pudding. She was back shortly to throw the steaming bowl on to the table. The dialogue long spoken, Mother and Daughter resumed their chatter.

MARTHA: And it doesn't matter if you live in the country.
MRS CRATCHIT: Why's that?
MARTHA: They transport the fish by lorry.

The twentieth century fish shop chatter between the two girls was severely undermining the evocation of Victorian England. Meanwhile, a scramble was going on between Peter and Tiny Tim to get a spoonful or two of the dessert. In the struggle, the bowl fell to the floor and the pudding spilled on top of the stage. Tiny Tim leapt from the table like a salmon to claim a giant's portion for himself. The next few minutes were perhaps the longest in Billy's relatively short life, as he waited for his lame son to stop sprinting around the table for food scraps. As Martha and Mrs Cratchit discussed cockles, Tiny Tim finally emitted an enormous belch to signify he was full up. The play could at last continue as Charles Dickens intended.

The remainder of the production passed by without incident, and Billy, still holding up his trews, was soon enjoying another curtain call, this one especially agreeable, drinking in the applause while standing hand in hand with his wife, the delightful Rita. Unfortunately, once they left the stage, Rita charged off and was nowhere to be seen, their temporary marriage over.

Billy changed from his breeches, scarf and top hat into everyday clothes. He wished all the best to his school friends gathered in their family groups and left to begin the long walk home to Potseething Farm to prepare for Christmas.

****

Due to the limitations of war, the Midnight Carol Service at St Nicholas' was taking place at 1.00pm on Christmas Day, Billy in situ pumping away on the organ bellows behind the irascible Mr Ogden. The evacuee was now a dab hand at this task, and his early blunders when losing concentration had faded into the past, as had the embarrassing squeak thanks to a few drops of engine oil. The organist was still prone to agitation over the slightest thing, but Billy was now immune to the facial contortions. In fact, he had developed a healthy disregard for the grouch by pulling tongues at him when hidden from view at the rear of the pipes, an action that invariably made him feel better. The main problem now was boredom. Today's idea was to pass the time reading letters from home.

Despite carrying very little by way of possessions, he had somehow conspired to lose much of the weekly correspondence from his mum, but he had retained a few that he stuffed earlier into his pocket before he left the farm. He pulled out the most recent letter, received only yesterday accompanied by a Christmas present. The gift was a jigsaw with a generic countryside scene, the kind of puzzle he used to enjoy but was less keen on these days. Furthermore, living now on a daily basis with green pastures, trees, and stone walls, a picture of industrial England may have been more appropriate. Nonetheless, he was grateful for the thought and the effort taken by his mum. And in this regard, he was philosophical about the scenes earlier at breakfast when Patricia had unwrapped her gifts at the kitchen table. Old George and Rose may not have bought him a present, but that didn't mean they were unkind people. He still enjoyed living on Potseething Farm.

133

The organist played the introduction to 'Good King Wenceslas' prompting the congregation, overflowing from the pews into the aisles, to join in with the singing. Meanwhile, Billy read his mum's letter, as he effortlessly pumped the bellows.

Dear Billy,

Merry Christmas! It seems strange for us to be celebrating here, while you are so far away in Bridgnorth, but hopefully things will be back to normal next year. I hope you like the present. It isn't easy finding something to get you, but I know you like a jigsaw. The choice wasn't great, but there are a lot of pieces, and so it shouldn't be too easy. Your dad is still working at the Co-op Laundry and is off for a couple of days this week, so that will be nice.

As for Eric, he passed his RAF Medical last week in A1 condition. He goes for a panel interview next week and will join up proper after that. He seems to be looking forward to it. We are going to your nan's for Christmas Dinner with Auntie Hilda and Auntie Ada. Obviously, with food rationing, it's a little difficult to prepare a meal the way we normally would, but we'll do our best. It's probably the last time for a while we'll have Eric to play the piano at a get together, so I'm sure we'll make the most of the occasion for that reason as well.

I hope your Christmas goes well at the farm and that there is enough food to go around for you to enjoy the festivities. I will write again soon. Take care as always,

Your loving Mum.

With the carol coming to its end, Billy returned the letter to his jacket pocket. The Reverend Kirke, mercifully better after serious illness, thanked the churchgoers before reading Matthew 2:15.

'And it came to pass, as the angels were gone away from them into heaven, the

shepherds said to one another, Let us now go even unto Bethlehem, and see this thing which is come to pass, which the Lord hath made known unto us…'

Billy was not listening, his mind wandering towards more earthly and mundane matters. He thought of Trampy. Would he be spending today in the caves or maybe the Potseething barn? It probably didn't matter either way. In Trampy's world, there was no Christmas, no war, and no worries. He supposed in a funny kind of way, he and the vagrant had that in common. This didn't feel like December 25th, he was removed from the war, and even those day-to-day anxieties he had at home, such as going to school, had disappeared. Yes, he was just like Trampy; apart from the clothes and the stench… at least he hoped so, that young boy's comment at the circus still resonating for all the wrong reasons.

After the reading, the churchgoers sang 'We Three Kings of Orient Are', 'Away in a Manger', and 'It Came Upon the Midnight Clear', the carols interspersed with further nativity readings from Luke and Matthew. Before the final hymn 'God Rest Ye Merry Gentlemen', the vicar read his sermon, its theme promoting the Bible as a refuge and comfort during these difficult times. Yet for Billy, these were not especially difficult times. He may have been many miles from home, missing his family, and staying in Spartan surroundings with country people who singularly failed to lavish attention upon him, but in a strange kind of way, he had never been happier, relishing his new found independence and feeling very much at home in this rural backwater. This unusual Christmas would soon be over, but he was truly looking forward to the prospects of the New Year… a Happy New Year.

CHAPTER 13

From the stationary train, Eric acknowledged his mum and nan standing with the crowds on the platform at Liverpool's Lime Street Station, the people dwarfed by the enormity of the curved iron and glass roof fashioned in bygone Victorian times. He was in a third class compartment closest to the tender and sitting by the window, his small suitcase and civilian respirator resting on the luggage rack above his head. The joining instructions had made it clear, despite Aunt Hilda's good intentions; the ukulele would have to remain at home. In many ways, Eric felt liberated. The war was a long way from won, and there was growing evidence that the battle for the skies held the key to victory. From today he could make his mark as a pilot and help his country overcome the enemy.

A loud hiss preceded a shudder, and the train began to move forward, launching a jet of smoke towards the criss-cross of the girders above. Eric gave one last, understated wave before the train and its long trail of coaches exchanged the covered shed of Lime Street for the daylight of Liverpool's neighbourhoods. He had made this same trip for his medical two weeks before and was therefore prepared for the slow, laborious journey of trains and connections that would terminate at the modest Cardington Station. Tired, he closed his eyes to reflect upon the last week.

His final day in the office had been an unassuming affair, a handshake of 'good luck' from Mr Wells and a few 'take care' wishes from the females in the office and canteen. To make more of a fuss would have seemed inappropriate. These were extraordinary times that demanded ordinary behaviours. And Saturday's visit to the cinema with Vera to see *Suspicion* had been a strangely muted affair, the couple seemingly united in preparing for their time apart by playing down the significance of the moment, avoiding a tearful and upsetting departure. Even with his family, there had been no great fuss, the fortnight's gap between his medical and selection panel providing a useful, graduated acceptance of the forthcoming changes. However, it was clear to everyone involved that whatever happened, nothing would be the same again.

He slept for much of the journey, almost missing his connection at Crewe, but in the early afternoon, a yawning and stretching Eric awoke to the sound of the locomotive slowing down and stopping at Cardington Station. He and his fellow RAF passengers disembarked from the stuffy and warm train to face the biting cold of a winter's day in central England. He knew the drill and headed straight towards a line of small RAF vans waiting outside ready to escort the arrivals to the base, each vehicle with an upright, unsmiling Corporal standing alongside. Eric and three other lads were allocated and ushered to one by a stern official.

The short drive to RAF Cardington was made in silence, the only noise the revving engine and screech of tyres on tarmac and concrete. Turning into the base by the main gate and guard room, they took an immediate right past the gymnasium to park up outside the Squadron HQ, an otherwise modest building but for the impressive stone columns by its front entrance. Within a couple of minutes, a group of about forty men had assembled in the car park, unaware that walking was about to be superseded by something more regimented.

A short, thick-set man approached and climbed on to an orange box to give him height. His uniform was immaculately pressed, his side cap tilted at the perfect angle, his shoes glistening from a sterling effort with boot polish, spit, and brush. Here was somebody who could suppress a smile with aplomb and bellow for England.

'Right you lot! I'm Sergeant Rawbottom.'

Nobody attempted a snigger.

'First things first, you're going to deposit your belongings, so form two straight lines and then stand straight... at the double!'

On his last word, the pitch of his voice moved up an octave, the men hurrying to achieve the required formation.

'Right you 'orrible lot! When I say march... you march!'

They readied themselves.

'Quick... march!!! Left, right, left, right, left, right, left, right...'

The motley crew did their best but were a sorry sight, impeded by the carrying of suitcases and gas masks. It had been a similar fiasco when he arrived for his medical, Eric still unsure as to why he struggled with the timing of such a simple step. At the entrance to the clothing store Sergeant Rawbottom bawled at them to halt. Once divested of their luggage, it was time to march again.

'Left, right, left, right, left, right, left, right...'

This was a big camp, more town than village. When they reached the NAAFI waiting room, the NCO once again brought the procession to a stop. An officer, oozing authority, emerged from the building.

'This way chaps.'

His friendly tone was at the opposite end of the audible spectrum to the Sergeant's yell, and it helped relax the more anxious amongst the intake. Inside the NAAFI conditions were cramped, but they all managed to find some standing space. The officer was about six feet four, in sharp contrast to the short-legged NCO. No orange box platform was required here.

'OK men, you are all volunteers who will serve in whatever position we determine, although you are here today to undertake tests and a selection panel interview to assess your suitability for aircrew. However, before we start, you will need to be sworn in.'

Eric joined the others in willingly raising a hand and repeating the oath.

'I swear by Almighty God that I will be faithful and bear true allegiance to His Majesty King George the Sixth, His Heirs and Successors, and that I will, as in duty bound, honestly and faithfully defend His Majesty, His Heirs and Successors, in Person, Crown and Dignity against all enemies, and will observe and obey all orders of His Majesty, His Heirs and Successors, and of the Air Officers and Officers set over me. So help me God.'

The officer continued.

'Congratulations, you are now officially in the Royal Air Force.'

Eric did not listen to the extraneous words that followed the statement. It was official. He was in the RAF.

Next up was the panel interview. Five interrogating officers seemed excessive, but their questioning was relatively gentle and armed with a good secondary education, decent examination grades, and an unblemished employment record, he breezed through its demands. The tests that followed were more taxing. Essays, mathematics, words, numbers, shapes, coordination, fitness, some challenges more difficult than others, but all-in-all he was happy with his performance. He certainly hadn't experienced that feeling of panic, common in such situations, and he had left the final exam room confident of earning a place in aircrew, hopefully to train as a pilot.

After the assessments, the group were marched to the canteen to eat, marched around the base on a tour that took in the two giant hangars that once housed the R101 Airships, and marched to Hut 333 on the edge of the camp where they stayed the night. The billet was freezing cold, Eric's bed furthest away from a boiler contraption giving off minimal heat. But it had been a long, tiring day, and he soon drifted off to dream about the Grand Old Duke of York... marching up to the top of the hill then marching down again.

At 6.00am on the dot, Eric awoke to the din of two cymbals crashing together, courtesy of the not-so-venerated Sergeant Rawbottom.

'Rise and shine you 'orrible lot! Time for a little run.'

He had enjoyed better starts to the day, forced to jog three laps around the perimeter of the base and then made to wash and shave with ice cold water in the sub-zero temperatures outside. Only then was he marched to the NAAFI for a delightful breakfast of bacon and eggs. But no sooner had hot tea joined forces with the fried food churning in his stomach than the NCO whisked off his charges for another aimless run around the base, followed by another bout of uncoordinated marching and yet another run. The recruits, close to despair, were more than relieved when told to return to their billet to await an instruction to collect their test results.

Eric fidgeted on an uncomfortable chair in a waiting room within the main administrative building of the camp. He was witnessing Sergeant Rawbottom delivering the verdicts of the selection panel interviews and assessments with typical insensitivity. The dreams of more than a handful of the RAF's newest servicemen were being dashed, Eric increasingly concerned he was about to join them. He glanced around. Some men were grinning, others despondent, demeanours signifying with clarity their individual results. The process was dealt with alphabetically, and so Eric was the last to discover his fate. He almost jumped when he heard his name called.

'Whitfield!'

It was Sergeant Rawbottom, shouting as if a mile away.

'Yes sir?'

Eric stood up and stared straight ahead at some indistinct point in the distance.

'You've been recommended for aircrew as wireless operator / air gunner.'

Eric struggled to comprehend. Plenty of lads had not made it to aircrew, assigned to ground station duties instead, so he was lucky in that sense. But wireless operator and air gunner? What about pilot?

'Sir?' said Eric, averting his gaze to avoid eye contact.

'Whitfield?' replied the NCO with deep suspicion.

'Is that right... wireless operator?'

The sergeant gawped at him, as if face to face with the killer of his pet spaniel.

'Is that right, SIR?' he said, grounding out a sturdy emphasis on the missing word.

'Is that right, sir?' corrected Eric.

The not-so-tall Sergeant had to stretch to bring his nose to within a few inches of the new recruit, his face contorting, his crumpled features dripping with contempt.

'Are you calling me a liar?' he spoke softly, but with unconcealed threat.

'No sir.'

'Good... 'cos I don't like liars.'

He leant back a little and looked Eric up and down.

'I suppose you were hoping to be a pilot, like most of the deluded sods that come here.'

'Yes sir.'

He suddenly thrust himself forward to within a fraction of Eric's face.

'Let me tell you something Whitfield. To serve in the RAF is the ultimate honour, whatever rank or position you're given, and to be selected for aircrew is a privilege for which you should get down on your hands and knees and thank the Lord.'

Eric continued to stare into a cinematic haze ahead, the heavy breathing of the sergeant his soundtrack.

'Pilots?' Rawbottom continued. 'Pilots are the cream of the RAF, but I'm afraid your cream has just curdled... understand Whitfield?'

'Yes sir.'

'Good.'

The attitude of the sergeant was hard to take. Eric needed an arm around the shoulder, not an embittered, angry bully twisting the knife. Fortunately, there was little opportunity to mope. The marching was about to recommence.

'Left, right, left, right, left, right, left, right...'

The NCO led the group to the clothing store to get their uniforms, the experience starting badly for Eric.

In the queue for shirts, a po-faced serviceman behind the counter grunted, 'Size?'

'Erm...'

He felt a ball of disquiet gathering mass in his stomach. He hadn't a clue as to his shirt size? His mum bought his shirts.

'Size?' the man repeated.

In desperation, Eric turned to the next recruit, a dour, slow talking Yorkshire man called Dick.

'What's my shirt size?' said Eric.

'Yer what?'

'What's my shirt size?'

'How the bloody 'ell w'ud I know yer' shirt size.'

It was a perfectly reasonable answer to a perfectly unreasonable question. It had not even been rhetorical.

'Look in the one yer' wearin',' shouted Dick's pal, also held up in the line.

It was a good idea, so Eric suffered the indignity of removing his shirt and scrutinising the garment for a label.

'16!' he roared, as though appealing to a cricket umpire for LBW.

He moved on to the next section, easing the queue behind him.

'Size?' demanded another downbeat character in charge.

'16.'

'What?'

Eric immediately recognised his mistake. This was for shoes and boots. 'No... that's my shirt.'

'Shoe size?' the store man persisted.

His mum bought his shoes. History was rapidly repeating itself; although this time he avoided asking Dick. No matter, the man from Doncaster was ready to offer an answer regardless.

'Size 8 I'd say. What d'yer think Sid?'

'That's a 10 if ever I saw one.'

Eric quickly slipped off his brogue and frantically looked inside. He couldn't find anything and was about to make a guess, when Dick tapped him on the shoulder.

'On sole pal... it's on sole.'

A circled number 9 was imprinted on the leather of the instep.

'9!' he cried in another appeal for leg before.

This had turned into an unexpected trial, and as Eric gingerly made his way towards the main uniforms section, foreboding seeped from every pore. Fortune, however, was on his side. The department was some distance - and not just geographically - from Savile Row where tailors crafted garments to the precise measurements of clients. RAF Cardington had something less exact, a bloke who looked you up and down and then wrote a few numbers on a chitty before giving you the slither of paper. These were your sizes, at least according to the judgment of this one man, yet Eric was delighted with the arrangement. His mum also bought his jackets and his trousers.

'Left, right, left, right, left, right, left, right...'

They were marching again, carrying the newly issued supplies in a kitbag to another hut, this one with beds and lockers. An orderly arrived to check the men had all requisite things, and when satisfied, made it clear it was time to march again. However, just as Eric was about to leave with the group, he was pulled to one side by Sergeant Rawbottom. He watched the others, under the tutelage of another sergeant, disappear as they marched off to yet another part of the base.

'Left, right, left, right, left, right, left, right...'

The NCO was smiling a broad grin. It was a disturbing sight, the Cheshire Cat with the cream, the cheese, and everything else in the pantry.

'Whitfield, Whitfield...' he purred.

'Yes sir?'

'At ease Whitfield, at ease.'

It was a command easier said than done.

'Thank you sir.'

'Now Whitfield, what was your job before you joined up?'

The sergeant was walking back and forth in front of him.

'Purchase Order Clerk, sir.'

Eric may have been at ease, but his eyes concentrated on anything in the room other than the sergeant.

'Ah, Purchase Order Clerk,' he said, stopping and glancing up to the rafters. 'Not exactly essential for the war effort I suppose.'

'No sir.'

The NCO resumed his walk.

'And who was your employer?'

'General Electrical Company, sir...GEC.'

'GEC, that's right, they make Osram light bulbs don't they?'

'Yes sir.'

'Not much use in blackout conditions though.'

'No sir.'

'Mind you, those aircraft you're never going to pilot, I suppose those dials need illuminating.'

He continued to stalk the ground in front of him, a big cat waiting to make the kill.

'And the buildings in the camps and bases of places like this, they need lights as well.'

'Yes sir.'

'Which must explain why anyone working for GEC is treated as being in a reserved occupation.'

Eric blinked and swallowed, 'I don't understand, sir.'

The sergeant stopped again and took one step towards him.

'Let me put it this way,' he said, leaning forward to speak directly into his ear. 'You're going home Whitfield, you're going home.'

Before he had time to come to terms with the bombshell, Rawbottom was marching the solitary recruit back to the Clothing Store to return his main uniform, size unknown, shirts size 16, shoes and boots size 9. He then marched him to another waiting room, its interior a characterless combination of wood, chairs and a table. Here he was left alone, the Sergeant departing, the highlight of his working day over.

Eric's mind was in turmoil, his dreams crushed. He was destined to spend the rest of the war travelling across the River Mersey on the Royal Iris to raise purchase orders and make blue-back ink entries in leather-bound ledgers. He cursed GEC, Sergeant Rawbottom, the war, in fact, everything and grimaced at the thought of returning home, all those recent goodbyes and farewells devalued by his sudden return. He would be a laughing stock.

He heard the door open. It was the officer who had sworn in the men yesterday. Eric stood bolt upright.

'Sir.'

'At ease Whitfield.'

He sat next to Eric, informality his trademark.

'You must be disappointed.'

'Yes sir.'

'Well I'm here to explain one or two few things.'

This officer was the antidote to the harrying and intimidating style of Sergeant Rawbottom.

'Thank you sir.'

'What you need to do old chap is get permission from your employer to allow you to join up. I see from your files that you are involved in clerical work, and so I would be surprised if this was too much of a stumbling block. You are still treated as enlisted, but you will be placed on reserve. Once released by your employer, this frees us to recall you from your reserve position. My only cautionary point is that you're normally sent to the back of the queue in these circumstances, and so it may be some months before you're called back again. But let me reassure you. You will be back. I'm sure of it.'

'Yes sir, thank you sir.'

The officer slapped him gently on the back and said, 'Good man.'

Eric dithered while sourcing the courage needed.

'Sir?'

'Yes Whitfield?'

'About my tests sir…'

The officer was well briefed.

'Wireless operator and air gunner?'

'Yes sir.'

'No doubt you were hoping to be a pilot.'

'Erm… yes sir.'

'Let's go outside.'

A line of servicemen marched past as the two men stepped out into the cold. The Officer looked up at the grey blanket of cloud.

'You see those skies Whitfield?'

'Yes sir.'

'It is in those skies that we will win the war. Not at sea, not in the trenches, but in the air. I can't give you details today, but our chaps are producing some tremendous aircraft that will help achieve these aims. The new machines will be immense, requiring a team of highly skilled specialists to fly them. The pilot is just one of the team, a very important member, but still only a part of the team. The pilots alone will not win the war for us, it will be the crews, yes the pilots, but also the flight engineers, the navigators, the bomb aimers, and of course, the wireless operators and gunners. I say this without any hesitation. History will judge men like you in the highest regard, as those who did more than anyone to maintain the freedom and liberty of this royal throne of kings, this sceptred isle, this other Eden, this precious stone set in the silver sea…'

Both men fleetingly lost in this moment of poetic inspiration were brought back to earth by yet another line of squaddies marching past from A to B. Eric felt tremendous gratitude towards this officer. He had been the arm around the shoulder he needed and more.

'Now, I have a vehicle to take you to the station,' he said, returning to more practical and mundane matters. 'Oh, and incidentally, your uniform and supplies will be packaged and given to you on your return, so there'll be no need to go through the stores rigmarole again.'

Eric thought of the ordeal from earlier, grateful for the small mercy.

'Thank you sir.'

'Good man... and good luck Whitfield.'

An hour later, he was on the train home, the same third class carriage, the same stations, the same journey, but not the same hopes and aspirations. He thought of Mr Wells at GEC, seemingly unaware that the job of purchase order clerk was reserved. In fairness, he couldn't think of anybody in the GEC office affected by such a situation before. Eric was clearly an anomaly. Yet despite the false start to 1942, he was determined to remain resolute. He may have been returning home, but he was still Aircraftsman, AC2 Eric Norman Whitfield. With a little bit of goodwill on the part of his GEC employer, his time would come. One day, he would help save this sceptred isle, this other Eden, this precious stone set in the silver sea.

CHAPTER 14

January and February 1942 had brought severe winter conditions to the country, the first month of the year dominated by snowfall, the second by the coldest temperatures of the century. Billy shuddered at the memory of the nightly walk up the freezing stone staircase in the farmhouse to his austere and sparse bedroom, icicles clinging as doggedly to the inside of the window as the outside. Going to bed, the heated, covered brick had permitted only meagre protection from the savagery of the cold, and the daily trial of leaving the warmth of his blankets to dress for school or church had made him feel like Scott of the Antarctic. But now it was the middle of March and the weather gods were smiling again, mild temperatures paving the way for a repeat of Potseething's annual farming cycle with the preparation for lambing, the blowfly treatment, the arrival of a new calf, and the top dressing of cereals.

Today's walk to school was certainly easier. It was only a matter of days since trudging through snowdrifts big enough to cover most of his torso. Nature appeared to agree, the first buds of spring and tuneful warbling of distant birds making their presence known. Billy heard the hum of the Jaguar taking Patricia to school and moved to the side of the road without even thinking. He had long stopped taking notice of the farmer's daughter and the mysterious driver, apart from that day recently when the vehicle became trapped in snow, an exception he had enjoyed perhaps too much.

On reaching school, Billy experienced the novelty of not having to remove five layers of clothing, a simple hat, scarf, and coat combination the only items requiring a hook on the wall. He walked into the familiar classroom of desks, chairs, and blackboard, ready for one of the best things about St Mary's. It was the day they were to produce the monthly newsletter.

The number of pupils in his class had started to fall, a few boys having returned home. Indeed, the school's future was coming under threat. A feature of his mother's letters over the last fifteen months had been the absence of any talk about the war. Yet the one received last weekend had stressed the absence of bombing raids and the apparent return to normality. Although she didn't say as much, the underlying message appeared to be a plea for him to come home. The same thing was happening to his classmates. Billy didn't like the thought, but he was beginning to think his Bridgnorth adventure might be coming to an end.

The day started with a geography lesson studying an Ordnance Survey Map of Northumberland, close enough to the border to satisfy Miss McDonnell's exacting, patriotic requirements. The second half of the morning was given up to producing the newsletter.

The Bridgnorth Evacuee News had been going for a number of months and had proved a great success, both among the would-be journalists in the class and the readership. The magazine session began with a production meeting of sorts chaired by the teacher with nominated pupils contributing ideas for the issue. Billy, as usual, was tasked with producing the crossword, and he immediately embarked upon its creation. Meanwhile, Miss McDonnell asked the others for stories from home to include. He knew what was coming next.

'The funniest thing happened to my Uncle Bert last week in Wallasey,' said Arbuckle, chuckling away to himself.

Everyone knew that whatever happened to Uncle Bert last week in Wallasey, it was not going to be funny. It never was. Miss McDonnell would always politely discard his supposed rib-tickling anecdote before the final version went to press.

'Oh yes?'

The teacher's voice quivered a little in apprehension.

'You see, he grows fruit and vegetables on his allotment, and last week he picked a strawberry that looked just like me.'

Arbuckle was very pleased with himself.

'It must have been a big strawberry,' Kenny joked.

'It was,' said Arbuckle, impervious to any sensitivity about his size.

Billy's recently acquired farming knowledge, however, had spotted a flaw in the story, and so had Miss McDonnell.

'But strawberries are not picked in March,' she said. 'They tend to be ready in the summer, around about July.'

Arbuckle was crestfallen, his attempts at getting a published article crushed yet again. It was a pity in some ways. The tale definitely had amusing connotations, a change from the normal lame account of said uncle losing a favourite sock. It was just a shame that it was a pack of lies.

Discussions continued and quiz questions bandied about, while Billy concentrated on devising his word challenge. He soon had a first draft and informed Miss McDonnell accordingly.

'Well done Billy,' she said, glancing around the room. 'Tom?'

'Yes Miss?'

'Can you have a go at Billy's crossword?'

'Alright miss.'

This was bad news. Tiny Tom struggled with anything that veered towards the academic. Asking him to verify the puzzle was akin to asking George Formby sing a requiem at a funeral. Billy reluctantly handed over his creation. Tom launched into the challenge with gusto, and there were initial frantic scribbles as he completed a few of the clues. But he was soon left scratching his head, producing a shower of dandruff that coated the shoulders of his jacket like a snow scene from a winter grotto.

'Hey Billy, you've got a few clues wrong,' he said with unwavering certainty.

'Which ones?'

'Well, five across for a start.'

Billy read the clue out loud.

'Where you live, four letters. What's wrong with that?'

'Come off it,' said Tom, displaying unusual smugness, 'Wallasey has, 1-2-3-4-5-6-7-8 letters... eight letters, not four.'

'The answer's 'Home' not 'Wallasey', yer' daft monkey.'

Tom was slightly crestfallen by the revelation, but he fought on.

'Then what about one down?'

Bill read out the clue.

'Decayed matter found in bog, four letters... and?'

'Well, one across is easy, Son of a King, six letters... that's 'Prince' isn't it?'

'Yes.'

'Well if that's correct, there's a problem with one down.'

'What do you mean?'

'Decayed matter found in bog, four letters... beginning with P?'

'That's right... 'Peat', Peat begins with P.'

'Oh,' said Tom dejectedly.

The wind had well and truly been taken out of his sails. In fact, his ship was about to sink.

'What did you have?'

'Dung.'

'Dung?'

'Yes,' he rallied with spirit. 'Decayed matter found in bog, four letters, 'Dung'.

Billy shook his head. He needed another reviewer.

The following Sunday, Billy was in the Potseething kitchen reading the newly published edition of the Bridgnorth Evacuee News, surprised to see an article on the back page about Arbuckle's Uncle Bert losing a favourite sock. Miss McDonnell had finally been broken. He studied the first general knowledge quiz question, 'What is the Capital of Argentina?' and chuckled to himself at the memory of Tiny Tom's suggested answer of 'A'. He still didn't know if it was a joke. He suspected not.

There was a knock at the door that Rose answered, returning shortly to pass Billy an envelope.

'Here's your mum's letter... the postman delivered it to the wrong farm yesterday.'

Inside the envelope was another one addressed to Mr and Mrs Stoneycroft.

'This is for you,' he said, handing the small brown letter to the farmer's wife.

Billy took out his postal order, rueing again the deviation from yesterday's normal routine, missing out on the cream slice. He glanced up to see the farmer's wife staring at him in a way he had not seen before, slightly lost in her thoughts, in truth more through him than at him. The moment, however, was fleeting, and she quickly returned to normal

'Has your mum written to you?' she asked.

He checked the inside of the envelope.

'Yes.'

'Well I think you'd better read it.'

He did. It was momentous news. He was going back to Wallasey... at Easter... for good.

The revelation induced mixed feelings. Although he'd look forward to seeing his family again, he wasn't ready to go home. He had settled into the simplicity and pace of this rural life, relishing the independence that the arrangement afforded him, and such was his contentment, he routinely gave little consideration as to the hardship and rigour of living in a home without running water or electricity. He stopped listening to Rose as she discussed the practicalities; his mind preoccupied with what came next, the prospect of returning to the iron discipline and sterility of Gorsedale School especially filling him with dread. He worked out he would leave Bridgnorth a week on Thursday. That gave him eleven days including today, and he vowed to make the most of it. He folded the letter and picked up the Bridgnorth Evacuee News again, ready to get lost in the drama of Uncle Bert's lost sock.

A few hours later, Billy was walking through Bridgnorth Castle Gardens on his way to the Church of St Mary Magdalene. This particular Sabbath was a change from the normal ritual of bellowing duties and Sunday school at St Nicholas' in Oldbury. A month or so back, the Reverend Kirke had spoken to him in private, suggesting he give serious thought to the act of confirmation. The evacuee promised to consider the matter in the coming week, but seven days on when the vicar asked if he'd made a decision, he requested further time for deliberation. Pressed again the following Sunday, Billy was forced to air the slightly embarrassing question.

'What's confirmation?'

'Oh I see,' said the Reverend Kirke, patience incarnate. 'Confirmation signifies the time in your Christian life when you vow to uphold the faith into which you have been baptised, when you make the commitment to be a disciple of Jesus Christ Our Lord for the remainder of your life.'

This was as clear as mud to Billy, but he gave the vicar, a man brimming with caring and kindness, the benefit of the doubt and agreed to attend the next confirmation ceremony, a ceremony happening today.

The ludicrous image of Bridgnorth Castle came into his sights. Thanks to the effective demolition skills of Cromwell's Roundheads in 1646, its derelict remains had been left to slope at an angle even more severe than the famous Leaning Tower of Pisa. Billy strolled past the ruins, fighting

154

off the usual compulsion to scale its heights, the protruding brickwork and edges an open invitation to climb. Despite the recent removal of the bandstand to use as scrap metal for the war effort, the contrasting serenity and order of the surrounding gardens remained. Facing the old Norman Castle, St Mary Magdalene Church was a commanding edifice, its green dome and tower designed by Thomas Telford an especially distinctive feature. While St Nicholas' was homely and quaint, this was indisputably a more fitting place for the Bishop of Hereford to perform today's duties, full of grandeur with impressive columns and clear glass arched windows.

Once inside, Billy surveyed the interior and was struck by its size and its brightness. Although uncharacteristically punctual, he was still the last to arrive, and a slightly impatient ecclesiastical man in a flowing black gown instructed him to join a line of mostly young people. Addressing the group, he welcomed everyone to St Mary Magdalene and explained that this was a rehearsal for the service proper.

'I should warn you that today's service is taken from the 1662 Common Book of Prayer,' he announced in sombre tones, 'and is in 17th Century English. It may, therefore, be a little difficult to follow. However, I'm sure this walk-through will help you all in this regard.'

Standing at one end of the line, Billy spotted the organ right next to him, an impressive instrument, far more imposing than Mr Ogden's. He stretched his head and upper body to examine it from a distance, wondering what kind of bellows powered the beast, but he failed to spot anything. However, hidden from the eye line of the church man giving the instructions, his curiosity got the better of him, and he sidled away to get a better look. Despite a thorough inspection, he saw nothing of interest other than a few spiders and silently returned to the line unnoticed. The man in the gown continued to mumble instructions, Billy's mind drifting to take in the rest of the church. He noticed an unusual wooden font and an apse overseen by three colourful leaded windows. Churches could be such impressive buildings.

'… and I trust that you are all now fully versed in what you need to do this afternoon.'

Billy gulped. The tutorial was done and dusted, and he hadn't listened to a single word.

The group waited to one side of the nave while the pews filled with regular churchgoers. When no spaces remained, two senior clergy figures appeared from nowhere, both draped in ornate robes and gowns, the Bishop of Hereford standing out with his gleaming crozier and gold embroidered mitre that made him seem about seven feet tall.

What followed was all very serious, lacking the affability and friendliness of an occasion under the tutelage of the Reverend Kirke, and Billy was soon regretting the failure to give full attention earlier. At the start of the confirmation section, the Bishop spurted some nonsense in a foreign language, and the group responded in unison, Billy mumbling some improvised words half a second later. He remained off the pace throughout the whole ceremony, especially when his name was called out and he instinctively raised an arm as if in school. To the observers in church, it was like watching a Busby Berkeley routine where all participants were in perfect synchronicity, with one exception. Billy was that exception.

His biggest mistake occurred during Holy Communion. The group had been told in rehearsals to take a small sip of wine during the symbolic re-enactment of the Last Supper, but when Billy was handed the goblet, he glugged a mouthful like his dad with a first pint of stout. It made him cough violently and regurgitate a piece of consecrated bread, the food missile bouncing off the Bishop's robe and on to the floor. The only consolation for Billy was the religious professionalism of the Bishop who scarcely acknowledged the incident, although his eye did twitch slightly when the evacuee bent down and picked up the bread to put it back in his mouth.

156

Billy departed from St Mary Magdalene a short while later, officially a disciple of Christ. He was off to another service at St Nicholas' to pump the bellows and give news of his confirmation to a delighted Reverend Kirke. However, as stumbled his way into the Oldbury church, unsteady on his feet and reeking of alcohol, he had to conclude that at the age of thirteen, he really ought to have just had a sip.

****

Billy may have been leaving the town for good, but his last day at St Mary's School was not an especially melancholic affair. Classes finished at noon for Easter, many of the evacuees going home for the holidays, and so when he said goodbye to the likes of Kenny, Tiny Tom and Arbuckle, it felt more like the end of term. At the conclusion of the final lesson, he retrieved his coat and was about to exit the building, when he halted, thought for a moment, and returned to the classroom. Miss McDonnell was tidying around and initially failed to realise he was standing there.

'Oh... it's you Billy.'

'Yes Miss.'

She furrowed her brow.

'Did you want something?'

He looked down at his shoes, wiggling his toes inside the leather caps.

'Yes Miss.'

'What is it?'

The teacher had been the single most important person during his fifteen month stay in Bridgnorth. The family at Potseething had been good to him, but he had never been accepted as part of their clan, arriving as an outsider and leaving as an outsider. The Reverend Kirke was another kind soul, but the vicar's remit was spiritual well-being, and Billy was not very spiritual. Miss McDonnell, however, had taken a genuine interest in his

157

welfare and his development. From an educational perspective, she had enabled him to thrive alongside grammar school contemporaries, always encouraging, always supportive. She had let him paint, sing, act, compile crosswords and, of course, eat in the canteen.

He struggled to find the right words but eventually said in a matter of fact way, 'Thanks for the dinners Miss.'

'That's alright Billy...'

Before she could add anything else, he was on his way. He passed Gladys and Rita as he left. Both ignored him. It seemed the affections of the girl from the fish shop had transferred to someone new, whilst her friend remained completely disinterested and elusive. He knew he would see a fair number of these peers back home, as they were all from the Wallasey area, but there was a fair to middling chance he would not come across Miss McDonnell again. Regardless, he vowed never to forget this teacher and her little piece of Scotland within St Mary's School for Evacuees in Bridgnorth.

It was a fresh afternoon when he stepped outside, a gust of wind whipping up and catching his breath, though the breeze remained mild. About to head home, he went on a detour. He had the whole afternoon before dusk settled, permitting one last chance to take in the town and surrounding area. Tomorrow morning he would be on the early morning train to Birkenhead.

He chose the long walk up the Kidderminster Road, eventually reaching an aged 'Cemetery' signpost. Here he turned right and followed a footpath that climbed its way past gravestones and into woodland before ascending the undulating 'Jacob's Ladder' to the top of High Rock. He sat down there to rest, his ears buffeted by the sound of the wind. The view from here was impressive. Through the bare branches of trees, the River Severn dominated the scene, meandering its way to dissect the contrasting geographies of Lowtown and Hightown, its banks a winter-muddied brown, its water, a silver-grey reflection of the clouds above. The green fields added colour and held back the spread of the conurbations that clustered in the periphery of the town's sandstone hill. Billy swallowed the air with avarice as he had done when alighting from the train back in January 1941. It was fresh, healthy, untainted by industry, and it would not be his for long.

He then had a thought, a big thought, and it made him feel so much better. His upcoming birthday would be his fourteenth, old enough to leave school. He would be fourteen! He could leave school! He had no need to return to Gorsedale after all. Prior to Bridgnorth, the world of paid employment had been a distant prospect, but after his work on the farms, with the shooting parties, and in the church, he had the confidence and experience to face the challenge with relish. He had no idea about the job he would do, but it had to be a better than Gorsedale, that stale old institution with its iron discipline and nineteenth century text books. The thought unshackled him, and he almost skipped from his spot on top of the hill.

The return journey was always going to be easier. Electing to go back to the farm via Hightown, he took the funicular railway and ambled to the Castle Gardens for a final look at the graceful St Mary Magdalene Church and the landscape pointing south with Oldbury in the distance. Tomorrow, he would exchange all this for terraced streets, brick shelters and barrage balloons. It was not a great swap.

Billy picked up the bulging pillowcase and tucked it under an arm. Packing his scant possessions, he had found the small piece of shrapnel he brought from home for good luck. On balance, it had worked. So much had changed since arriving in the same garb with the same possessions, not least of all Billy Whitfield himself. He had grown for a start, probably three or four inches, and was not as slight in frame. It was a good job his clothes had been too big for him back then.

'They'll ride up with wear.'

How often had he heard that from his dad as he stood there looking like something from the circus?

But the biggest transformation was from within. He was now confident, independent, and more young man than boy. He took one last glance at the bare bedroom, the damp patches on the wall, the two army beds pulled together, the makeshift blanket mattress, and then walked downstairs to the kitchen. There was nothing unusual about what greeted him, the wireless playing in the background, Old George outside working hard, Rose cleaning, and Patricia in the armchair playing with her dolls. It was just another morning at Potseething Farm, another day of the usual routine, except for the fact that Billy was going home. Nonetheless, the Stoneycrofts appeared to be going out of their way to keep things normal. There was to be no special fuss or send off.

'Have you got everything?' enquired Rose.

He held the pillowcase with its pathetic contents aloft.

'Yes thanks,' he replied nonchalantly.

'Good.'

'Right, I'll be off then.'

'What time's your train?'

'Nine o'clock.'

'Nine o'clock?' she said with a tinge of alarm. 'Well, if you hurry, you should just about make it.'

'Thanks for everything Mrs Stoneycroft.'

'That's quite alright. Now hurry along. You don't want to miss your train.'

'Bye,' he shouted to Patricia.

She played on, the merest of acknowledgements uttered from her lips.

He walked out of the farmhouse, closed the front door behind him, and without looking back left Potseething Farm for the final time.

Fifty yards down the Oldbury Road, he heard the rattle of a cart and the clip-clop of a carthorse. It was Farmer George coming towards him, looking tired and dispirited. On spotting Billy, he slowed down and stopped.

'Ow Bist,' he said.

'Mr Stoneycroft?'

'Yes son?'

'What does 'Ow Bist' mean?'

'Buggered if I know.'

His response indicated a complete lack of intrigue on his part. He didn't know and didn't care to find out.

'I'm off to get my train,' said Billy.

'Aye, that's roight.'

The farmer removed his hat and tilted his head forward, using his left hand to rub his forehead and his eyes. When he had replaced his headgear, he stared ahead, lost in deliberation.

'I'll have to go...' said Billy, 'I don't want to be late for my train.'

'Aye lad, ye be off... ye be off.'

Disconsolately, the old farmer shook the reins and resumed his journey, Billy left staring at the pitiable image of man, horse and cart making their way slowly down the lane back to the farm.

He then heard a familiar voice

'Billy Boy!'

It was Trampy walking along the lane in the same direction of the farm. The vagrant was wearing his summer sack, the morning breeze doing Billy no favours, wafting the pungent odour from this man of the outdoors directly up his nostrils. Even so, he was pleased to see him.

'Hello Trampy.'

'Ye goin 'ome lad?'

'Yes.'

'For good?'

'Yes.'

He extended his right arm to invite a handshake, his palm, sandpaper rough, dirt engrained in every crease. The two shook, Billy's teeth grinding at the vice-like grip of his shabby friend.

'Ye look after 'yeself now.'

He nodded before saying, 'Sorry Trampy, I have to go or I'll be late for my train.'

'Ye go lad.'

'Thanks again.'

Billy turned for the brisk journey to Bridgnorth Train Station but had only walked a few steps, when he heard his name again.

'Billy Boy!'

'Yes?'

'Ye keep up paintin' lad. There's talent there.'

'Thanks.'

Trampy held up a thumb and then began to amble down the lane, Billy setting off for the station again.

And there was to be one final moment that compounded the greatest mystery of his fifteen month stay at Potseething Farm. As he passed St Nicholas' Church and said a silent adieu to the Reverend Kirke, the familiar rumble of the sleek, Jaguar SS21 invaded the quiet. He turned his head to see the usual occupants, Dick Tracy and Princess Margaret, but today there was somebody else in the vehicle. Sitting in the front seat and leaning towards the driver was Rose Stoneycroft. They looked a proper family. Perhaps that's why the old Farmer had appeared so forlorn.

Giving no thought as to why they hadn't offered him a lift to catch his train, the departing evacuee quickened his pace. Not for the first time, Billy Whitfield was cutting it fine.

162

PART TWO

NUREMBERG

CHAPTER 15

'For God so loved the world that he gave his only begotten son that whosoever believeth in him should not perish but have everlasting life.'

'This is the gospel,' said Miss Finch, 'in all its fullness, preached in just twenty five words from the lips of our saviour himself.'

Eric was impressed. 'The End' appeared in his bible on page 921, yet John 3:16 had summed up the essence of Christianity in one sentence. He tended to keep his faith to himself, and certainly had no plans to become evangelical in his ways, but if he ever needed to call upon a quote from the Holy Book to explain his convictions, this would be the one. Miss Finch taught the class a useful acronym, G.O.S.P.E.L. so as to remember the verse. He copied the words with care and precision on to the lined paper, red ink for the capital letters, black for the rest, vowing to later place these pages inside the relevant section of his bible.

A break for tea soon followed, Eric ambling across towards the trestle table where Vera today was on teapot duties. The previous habit of making a dash to the cups and saucers had long gone, principally as there was no Len in tow, his friend having lost enthusiasm for bible study around the same time he started courting Margaret. Eric, last to be served, joined Vera in a corner away from the other attendees.

The pretty brunette took a sip from her cup and grimaced. It was not a good brew. Eric agreed, and they both placed their cups on to the floor beneath their chairs.

'How's Billy settling back into Wallasey?' she asked.

'Not too bad really.'

'Well, that's good to hear.'

'Mind you, the School Board man paid a visit the other day.'

'Your Billy's been playing truant?'

'Not exactly... when he came back from Bridgnorth, he thought he was old enough to leave school, but you can only do that if you've had your fourteenth birthday by Easter. Now he's got to go back and stay there until the summer.'

'Poor Billy...'

'I know... he wanted to return to Bridgnorth.'

'Did he?'

'Yes... but that was a non-starter, not least of all with Mum.'

'Does he know what he wants to do when he leaves?'

'No... he's no idea... he said farmer the other day.'

They both laughed.

'And what about you, Aircraftsman Whitfield? How are you coping with things at the moment?'

'Alright I suppose.'

It had not been an easy few months since returning so unexpectedly from the Selection Board at Cardington. He had found it an uncomfortable, dispiriting experience, rapidly tiring of having to explain why he had been placed on reserve by the RAF. Work at GEC had been equally tiresome, the drudgery of the daily routine in razor-sharp contrast to the hopes and dreams of helping the country win the war, unsurprisingly finding no consolation from the importance of Osram light bulbs to the military machine. At least in this regard, Mr Wells had granted him permission to leave, and his recall for Aircrew training was now simply a matter of time. As for home, his mum had been pleased to see him back so quickly, and in no time at all you'd have thought the false start had never taken place. But he sometimes found Barrington Road too quiet, giving too much time for reflection, though in fairness since Billy's return things had changed. It was certainly more lively, his dad's language taking a turn for the worse.

'Bloody hell son… you're not on the bloody farm now.'

Yet above all, it was his relationship with Vera that had suffered the most. The pair had paced themselves for his departure at the end of December, not anticipating such an abrupt reappearance. They had since done the usual things, the cinema, a little dancing, bible classes, but they were not progressing particularly as a couple, and he wasn't sure why. Eric freshly appraised the woman next to him. She was attractive, warm-hearted, kind and attentive, in many ways, his ideal woman. He ought to be climbing to the top of Blackpool Tower to proclaim his good fortune. Instead, he had retracted within himself and continued to give little back in return. Maybe it was the uncertainty of the future. Maybe it was the war.

'If everyone has finished this lovely tea,' said Miss Finch, 'could we now return to our seats and continue the class?'

Lovely tea? This was not the adjective Eric, Vera, or even the highest being of all would have used. God might love the world, but he definitely didn't love this tea.

****

The entries behind the terraced houses of Barrington Road and surrounding streets were paved in cobblestones, grey, rutted and irregular beneath the feet. Either side of the narrow passageways, walls seemed to close in, the uniformity of red brickwork checked by the backyard doors with dark, peeling paint and rusting latches. The everyday scene was a product of the industrial revolution, in which the only sign of Mother Nature was the group of flies swarming around the recently deposited mound of dog muck. Billy closed his eyes, a wistful edge to his recall of abundant hedgerows, green pastures and wild flowers from his walk to school in Shropshire. Today, in place of birdsong and the bleating of sheep, the dominant sound was that of bluebottles feasting in the alleyway. And with dismay, he noticed that his right shoe had just trod in the brown sludge left with nonchalance by Fido at number 12. Billy was on his way to Gorsedale for a delayed first day back, his time as a school leaver cut short by the officious, little man with bald head and ill-fitting suit who had preached about the dire consequences of truancy.

He emerged from the cobbles and into the street, attempting to wipe the dog mess from his sole by scraping it against the edge of the kerb, a task only partially successful. The school was now almost in sight, a reminder that this journey was quick, if not scenic, the polar opposite of his Potseething to St Mary's daily marathon. And for a brief second or two, the memory induced an urge to turn the clock back a few weeks, but he swiftly regained his composure and walked through the school gates to join the other lads in the yard.

'Hey it's Whitty!' shouted one of them. 'What you doin' back 'ere?'

He explained about his fourteenth birthday mix up, his plight greeted with a little ribbing but mostly sympathy. The bell rang. Billy steeled himself for a resumption of the old routine with its daily walk through the main entrance to come face to face with the deputy headmaster, cane in hand, standing in the middle of the corridor, suspicious, mistrustful, his narrow eyes darting from side to side before prodding his rattan stick and barking. 'Walk straight Whitfield, shoulders back.' Yet he was not there. He had gone to war, as had seemingly all the younger men. The remaining teachers were largely veterans, too tired to get angry. His spirits lifted. Perhaps his final term was not going to be so bad after all.

After register and a dreary morning assembly, the first class was a mind-numbingly dull history lesson about the Tudors, and so it was a big relief when break arrived, the lads decamping to the school yard for twenty minutes, an unwavering routine regardless of weather. Fortunately, this was early May and uncommonly warm. To Billy's surprise, the plan was to play football, a surprise because ball games had been outlawed back in the day. Things were changing, he thought.

The word 'ball' proved to be a loose definition. One of the boys pulled from his pocket a piece of wood that he had crafted in his last woodwork lesson. This doorstop was to be the makeshift ball in their game, one goal chalked against the wall, the other a gap in the bike sheds. The first captain chose Billy as goalkeeper, a dubious honour given that a chunk of South American hardwood was about to be hurtled in his direction.

The game was end to end stuff, with goals at a premium, in the sense that nobody had yet scored. But that was surely about to change with the opposition's best player through with only Billy to beat. The goalkeeper had prevented a few certain goals with a judicious, outstretched boot, but the save he made from this strike was top drawer, expertly stopping the 'ball' with his forehead. The minor trickle of blood that ensued was a small price to pay for keeping his team in the game. He picked up the doorstop, but his timing was bad.

'Whitfield!'

The cry came from old Mr Kingston, the maths teacher, positioned by the door, resting on his walking stick.

'Yes sir?'

Expecting a dressing down, the answer was surprising. 'Fine save young man... fine save.'

When he had left the house earlier in the morning, he had expected to exchange the warmth, camaraderie, and togetherness of St Mary's School for the harshness, spite, and maltreatment of Gorsedale with its parade of bullying masters. Yet the new regime was benign... dull, lacklustre, but benign.

The next lesson was maths with the same Mr Kingston, and today's topic was the wonderful world of fractions, taught with frightening monotony by the old man. And with all the boys struggling to stay awake, stifling yawns and holding their eyes open with index fingers and thumbs, their plight appeared desperate. Fortunately, there was to be an escape. The teacher had served during the Great War as a pilot in the Royal Flying Corps, the predecessor to the RAF, and he was a man always ready to reminisce about his old days in the air. Today was no different.

'Put down your weapons men,' he shouted.

Across the room, the students placed pencils and pens on to their desks.

'Today, I want to tell you about the bombing raids I undertook as a pilot for the Royal Flying Corps.'

The announcement was not greeted with universal enthusiasm. Some of the boys had heard this yarn a hundred times before. Billy, however, was intrigued, wondering if one day an aged Eric might regale people with tales from his time in the RAF.

'It was July 1915,' he started, 'and I was flying over France in one of the first aircraft, a Bristol Scout C, which was a rotary engine biplane. I was one of the chosen ones. Most of the other pilots were on reconnaissance or photographic missions, but not me.'

He was now at the controls of the single seater over Amiens, flying helmet, goggles, and leather jacket providing rudimentary protection from the elements.

'No you see... I was a bomber... one of the pioneers, my assignment to unleash the fiercest weaponry known to mankind upon the charging Germans spread across the fields of battle below so as to blast them to Kingdom Come.'

He snapped back to the present, glancing from pupil to pupil.

'What weapons you may ask?'

He paused. No-one asked, but he carried on.

'Well, I'll tell you. I didn't have 500lb bombs. I didn't have machine guns. I didn't have incendiaries. No... I had a cocoa tin, gunpowder, wick, and a box of matches.'

From those new to the story, there was a little snigger.

'When I was flying over the target, I had to get my Bournville container, empty out the remaining cocoa, fill it with gun powder, feed the fuse through a hole in the tin, light the thing, and then wait for the right moment to throw it out of the cockpit to the ground.'

He adopted a faraway look again. He was back in 1915.

'I can remember as if yesterday, leaning over the side of the aircraft and watching my home-made bomb tumble to earth. One of the Hun spotted the device and called for his fellow soldiers to hit the ground. The cocoa tin struck the soil and exploded. I was ready to steer my Bristol away, mission accomplished, when I saw the Germans, each and every one of them, get to their feet. The damage caused by the bomb had been restricted to an area not much bigger than a postage stamp. I might have caused more harm with a pea shooter.'

At this point, Mr Kingston started laughing, his chuckles interspersed with the occasional 'Pea Shooter!' A few of the lads, including Billy joined in with the mirth, which lasted longer than it really warranted.

Eventually, it was time to resume the maths lesson. Billy reckoned about half of the class were happy to leave behind the tales of the Royal Flying Corps, while the other half wanted to hear more. Unknowingly, he was working on his fractions.

The afternoon brought further relief with the last lesson of the day, which took place outdoors. In pursuance of the 'Dig for Victory' goals, the school had taken the aesthetic beauty of the spotted orchids, freesias, and tulips in its quadrant and replaced the flowers with potatoes, cabbages and peas. The practical tutorial offered the opportunity for Billy to impress the others. When the teacher expressed disappointment that the King Edwards were not growing as hoped, the ex-evacuee called upon his Potseething experience to point out that the spuds should be planted to a depth of about four inches, the rows thirty inches apart, and the planting gap in each row about eighteen inches. The rest of the class looked on in awe at this display of agricultural expertise, compounded when he held court on the issues of the carrots, broad beans and cauliflowers. The teacher's eyebrows arched in surprise

'Excuse me sir?' said Billy.

'Yes… Whitfield isn't it?'

'Yes sir... what happens when the vegetables are harvested? Who gets them?'

The teacher's face turned a mild shade of beetroot, coincidentally another of the veg in the school garden. Billy knew the answer to his question straightaway. The Gorsedale masters were clearly looking forward to the summer of 1942 supplying vegetables by the bucket load for their own parlours and kitchens.

In this part of the empire, 'Dig for Victory' was, in truth, 'Dig for Teacher'.

****

Eric was standing next to his mum as she stirred a pan of stew on the stove, its contents a murky brown dominated by potatoes. He savoured the wonderful aroma of the broth, bubbling at its edges, steam rising to the kitchen ceiling. It was time for dinner.

A few months ago, Eva would have sat at the dining room table, younger son in Bridgnorth, elder son in the RAF, experiencing a few pangs of longing and worry, Ted's understanding and responsiveness as absent as her two boys. But today the cheery edge to her personality was in full flow.

171

She even sang as dished out the food. Her husband, however, did not share her good mood.

'Bloody Germans,' he snarled, putting down his newspaper and taking his plate from Eva.

'What now Ted?'

His wife's question was tinged with reluctance.

'Exeter… they've bombed bloody Exeter.'

'At least they've stopped bombing here,' she replied, passing generous plated portions to Eric and Billy. 'We have to be thankful for that.'

'That's the bloody point…'

'Less of the bloodies Ted.'

'It makes sense to bomb here', he ranted. 'Liverpool's a major shipping port. But what's Exeter's got? A bloody cathedral and a population of village idiots.'

'They're not village idiots Dad,' said Eric. 'They're just like you and me.'

He recalled an RAF recruit he had met at Cardington called Leslie. He was from Devon, his father a surgeon, some way from the village idiot.

'That bloody Adolf Hitler is nothing but a vindictive swine,' said Ted, destroying a large slice of potato with corresponding malice.

The others were busy eating, but Ted was in full flow.

'They reckon it's revenge for us bombing one of his cities. He's just a bloody madman…'

He tutted and shook his head.

'Few would argue with that,' said Eric. 'Could you pass the cabbage please Mum?'

'You see,' his dad continued, 'the British believe in fair play and so our lads only bomb military targets.'

'With cocoa tins,' piped up Billy.

They all looked at him, confused.

'What are you on about son?' said Ted.

With a mouthful of stew, Billy recounted Mr Kingston's anecdote about the Royal Flying Corps bombing raids of the Great War.

Ted turned to Eric. 'Let's hope they give you better weapons son when you're up there.'

'Of course they will…' interjected Eva, her carefree spirit ebbing away.

Eric placed his knife and fork on the plate, and took a short rest from eating. He looked out of the window and above the netting to stare at the sky.

'The RAF have these Avro Lancaster heavy bombers,' he said, 'powered by four Rolls Royce Merlin engines… top speed nearly 300 mph… wingspan the length of two cricket wickets… and rather than cocoa tins Bill, a bay large enough to carry 8,000 lb bombs.'

'That's a lot a money for a bomb,' said Billy.

'It's pounds in weight not cash,' chuckled Eric.

'Oh.'

'You've done your studies haven't you son,' said Ted.

Eric brushed aside the remark. Always the quickest eater in the house, Billy had finished his tea first.

'Will you fly a Lancaster, Eric?' he said.

'I won't be the pilot, but I'll be on the plane as part of the crew and so, yes, I hope it is a Lancaster.'

'Shall we put the wireless on?' said his mum, always uncomfortable within the vicinity of this subject.

In many ways, the interminable delay to the start of her elder son's active service - it was almost a year to the day he first volunteered - was prolonging the agony, giving her too much time to think about things. Eric hoped his call up letter arrived soon. She turned the dial of the radio, housed in its robust, walnut cabinet. After a few whistles and screeches, they heard the familiar sound of Lord Haw-Haw, the alter-ego of William Joyce, the Irish-American who had defected at the outbreak of war to become a major cog in the Nazi war propaganda machine.

'*This is Germany calling, this is Germany calling…*'

She went to move the dial on, but Ted lifted up his hand. She waited. The Nazi propagandist with his perfectly clipped upper-class accent began reading out the names of newly captured British prisoners of war, RAF victims from the downed aircrafts of bombing raids gone wrong. Eva had gone from the chip pan into the fire. Eric did the decent thing. Ignoring his dad's protestations, he got up from the table and tuned the radio to another station, one in which the high-pitched and shrill treble of Gracie Fields threatened to smash the glass of the vase on the sideboard.

'Hey, it's Sally of our Alley,' said Eric, his forced zeal and interest transparently insincere.

'The only thing in our alley is dog muck.'

'Billy!' said his mum.

'Well it is.'

He held up the sole of his shoe for all to see the remnants of Fido's offering.

'Look!'

'Bloody hell.'

CHAPTER 16

The long wait was over, Eric now officially on active service. The letter had instructed him to report to RAF Padgate in Warrington on 28th July 1942, where he was experiencing a second dose of the Cardington induction from last New Year. The promise about his uniform had held firm, the cellophane wrapped garments handed to him intact on his arrival, and he was pleased to see the clothes remained a good fit. Padgate was the RAF's No.2 Recruitment Training Camp, designed to give raw recruits their first experience of military discipline. In common with Cardington, it was vast with rows and rows of wooden huts for accommodation, interiors polished like a drill sergeant's boots, toilet blocks, NAAFI dining halls, cook houses, parade squares, and the ubiquitous lines of marching men. Eric's brief stay featured an array of lectures about the RAF; numerous injections; his scalp checked for head lice; the severest of haircuts; an even more severe visit to the dentist; and marching... plenty of marching. Aside from sleep, the only break of sorts came during meal time.

On his third day at breakfast, Eric was sat at an empty table in the NAAFI with his bacon and eggs. He had learnt during his short time in the RAF that the limitations of rationing did not apply in the service. The food was excellent, the early morning 'wake up and get out yer' beds for a five mile run', less so. A fellow recruit approached, his auburn shaved-head somehow an even harsher version of Eric's own cropped look.

'Alright to sit here pal?'

'Sure.'

He placed himself opposite and held out a welcoming hand.

175

'Reg Wilson, pleased to meet you.'

They shook.

'Eric Whitfield, likewise.'

Reg may have looked like a convict about to be deported to Australia, but his blue eyes were bright, the window to a lively and energetic mind.

'Can I ask where you're from Eric?'

'Wallasey...' adding the inevitable, '... near Liverpool.'

'A Scouser?'

'Sort of... what about you?'

'I'm from Ludlow.'

The syllables in the word were savoured and drawn out, a minor countryside tinge to his accent.

'Isn't that near Bridgnorth?'

'Pretty close.'

'My younger brother's not long back from there... he was an evacuee.'

'The town on the hill.'

'Yes... I cycled there last year.'

'From Liverpool?'

Eric didn't correct the Mersey reference.

'Yes.'

'Cripes, that's a bit of trek isn't it?

'Six hours each way.'

'Bloomin' 'eck,'

'On the hottest day of the year.'

'Well all this should be a breeze for you.'

'If only!'

Another recruit, one who appeared to be sucking a large boiled sweet, joined them.

'Sit down Sid,' said Reg. 'This is Eric from Liverpool.'

He nodded and winced.

'Sid's had a bad time at the butcher's. Three extractions and seven fillings wasn't it?'

Sid resorted to hand and body gestures to confirm. He then took a mouthful of egg, swallowing half, the remainder expertly dribbled down the front of his RAF shirt and tie.

'Sid's been selected to train as a navigator. What about you Eric?'

'Wireless operator and gunner.'

'Same as me!'

Sid pushed his dish of bacon and eggs to one side, the effort too much for his dental swellings, Reg quickly taking advantage and emptying the contents on to his own plate.

'Any idea where you're going for your Initial Training?' said Eric, swabbing his mouth with a napkin.

'Not yet, but here's the thing,' said Reg, glancing around as if revealing government secrets to a spy ring. 'I've heard on the grapevine, we might be going to Butlin's.'

'Butlin's? The holiday camp people?'

The lowering of Eric's brow turned his face serious. Reg reciprocated the look.

'That's right... a place called Filey on the East coast in Yorkshire.'

Sid muttered something completely indecipherable... indecipherable to normal ears, but Reg understood every word.

'Did you?'

'Eh? What?' said Eric.

'Sid went to Butlin's in Skegness just before the war... says it was great,' explained Reg.

Eric liked the sound of this. It was the last day of July, the holiday month of August about to begin, and there was the prospect of his first wave of proper training taking place in a holiday camp. He pictured rowing boats on lakes, fairground rides, toffee apples, swimming pools, and dancing. His decision to join the RAF was becoming more and more vindicated by the second.

After swilling down his breakfast with a mug of tea, Eric was conscripted with Reg, Sid and the other men in the dining hall to march at the double to one of the parade squares. The NCO was a dead ringer for Sergeant Rawbottom at Cardington, dispensing the same line of cruelty and malevolence.

'At ease!' he bawled. 'If I call out your name, I want you to gather on the right of the square. If I don't call out your name, you stay where you are!'

He began to scream names.

'Anson, Bennett, Carruthers, Forrester...'

Eric listened patiently until...

'...Thompson, Whitfield, Wilson, and Young.'

About fifteen of the recruits responded to the call including Reg. The sergeant addressed the group.

'Right you lot, you've been allocated for Initial Training to RAF Hunmanby Moor in Filey on the Yorkshire coast. It's just a shame you're going in August and not February when the weather might freeze your balls off!'

He turned to another senior.

'Sergeant, take this lot to get their things.'

It was time to march again, Eric noticing a wink from Reg as they started. He winked back. The grapevine had proved reliable. They were going on holiday to Butlin's.

'Bring on the candy floss,' he thought.

Eric and Reg were enjoying the coach ride from York Railway Station on the way to their new home for the next five or six weeks in Filey. As they approached the camp, Eric glanced at the sky, its low, thundery cloud shrouding the area in a grey cloak of darkness. If these were the holiday camps in Yorkshire, Eric didn't want to see the prisons. The base was a network of concrete paths, barren soil, and utilitarian accommodation, and as the vehicle came to a halt, the alighting trainee airmen had their first encounter with the raw wind gusting in from the North Sea.

'Bloomin' 'eck Eric, this is bleaker than Birmingham on a wet Wednesday in February,' said Reg, attempting to run fingers through his hair, a reflex action that suggested he had a red mane prior to the savagery of the barber at Padgate.

'You can replace Birmingham with Birkenhead,' said Eric, reflecting on the absurdity of his earlier holiday resort preconceptions.

'Right you shower,' roared yet another Sergeant Rawbottom carbon copy coming in at about five foot two. 'My name is Sergeant Poole, and my job is to make your life as miserable as possible during your stay here. So, why don't we get off to a good start by going for a run?'

The recruits looked at one another. They were all kitted out in their uniforms, shirts and ties. Surely they would change into their PE gear. The sergeant made one miserly concession, allowing them to remove their side caps, and before they could say 'You must be joking sarge', they were off, running around the perimeter of the camp, not once, not twice, but three times... in fact, he threw in one more for good measure. Wheezing and gasping after the extreme exertions, the young runners had no breath left to help them think. It was a good job. Rational thought might have seen them attack and disembowel the sadistic sergeant.

They gathered up their belongings and were soon marching with forced enthusiasm to their billet, a concrete shell christened *Chez Nous* for the weeks ahead. Its exterior was austere, bleak and desolate, its interior, not as welcoming as the exterior. The sole concession to comfort was a heater in the centre of the floor, not especially useful during an English summer, even one impacted by the cooling breezes that had journeyed from the far reaches of Norway and Finland. Each man had a camp bed and a locker, in which they carefully placed their kit possessions.

Eric turned the key in his and whispered to Reg, 'It's not exactly the French Riviera is it?'

'I must have done something terrible in a previous life,' said Reg, pulling the face of a man who has downed a pint of curdled milk.

'It's got to be time for food now, don't you think?'

'Right you shower, get your PE kits on, at the double.'

It was Sergeant Poole back to ensure there was neither rest nor food for the wicked. Eric tried to keep up with the others by changing in rapid time but couldn't stop himself falling back on to the bed as he tried to pull up his shorts. He was grateful that the Sergeant had missed the incident. Eric didn't want to stand out in any way, although in truth it was far from a homogeneous unit. He had seen Pathé news reels of RAF training camps with flawless physical specimens exercising in textbook symmetry, nothing like this lot of short, tall, skinny, and broad recruits woefully unprepared for the next session of purgatory. The ragged, hungry and tired specimens were marched along a myriad of pathways, some with gradients difficult to navigate, eventually coming to a halt next to an assault course. Further exertions beckoned.

'Ten seconds gap between each starter,' Poole shouted. 'Go on my whistle!'

The group was organised roughly in alphabetical order, Eric last to go, and the problems ahead soon became obvious. Ten seconds was not a long time, and it only took two or three struggling on a component to create traffic chaos behind. The six feet wall was straightforward for lads of average height, but some of the trainees were - to use the technical term applied by Sergeant Poole with matchless irony given his lack of stature - short arses, and their attempt to scale the brick built challenge was akin to a show pony jumping Beecher's Brook. Teamwork prevailed to shove those in difficulty over, but then it was the turn of the big men to hold things up. The underground tunnel fashioned in the earth was snug for the regular frame, but one chap had the barrel chest of a mountain gorilla, and it was no surprise to see him quickly entombed by his effort to squeeze through the burrow. He was somehow pulled out by his new colleagues, though in doing so brought down some of the soil and scrub, rendering the challenge even more hazardous for those behind, especially Eric bringing up the rear.

The scramble net was an easier task, except in the case of one poor chap who fell through a hole and ended up dangling for a few, precarious seconds like a Victorian murderer on the gallows, before he fell to the ground with a bump. Yet it was the final leg that introduced the new boys to the bona fide world of torture, the group having to wade through muddy streams and hazardous ditches at the pace of Jesse Owens. By the end of the course, the rib cages of the trainees heaved with industrial intensity, their lung capacities had been shrivelled by the preposterous labours, and their erstwhile PE kits were now caked in drying mud and foliage. And there was to be one ultimate, cruel moment.

'Right,' said Poole. 'Let's go and do it all one more time, shall we?'

A sea of faces coated in incredulity stared back at the NCO. Inside, Eric was screaming for it all to stop, imagining a nearby cliff top he could leap from to bring the misery to an end. But the destructive thoughts were fleeting, ended abruptly by the sound of laughing, an evil, theatrical cackle of a pantomime villain. It was Sergeant Poole. He had been joking. The sadist had a sense of humour, albeit one about as funny as an abscess on the posterior.

Marched back to their concrete chalet-cum-bunker to change into their uniforms, a palpable relief greeted the news they were off to the NAAFI, Eric gratified to discover food standards as high as Cardington and Padgate. It provided much needed respite. But all too soon, it was back to the physical grindstone of marching, drilling, and a first stab - almost literally when his thumb was lucky to survive a stray blade - at combat and rifle techniques. And when it came to the last physical toil of the day for the recruits, Eric was astonished to discover it made the assault course seem like a stroll in the park.

Uniforms were exchanged for PE kits again, the young men thankful for more than one set of singlet and shorts after the muddied daubing from the obstacle course. Sergeant Poole, who had the strength of a lion, the stamina of an Arabian horse, and the sadistic tendencies of the Marquis de Sade, trotted at the head of the group.

'Right gentlemen… we're going to the beach for a bit of fun… so follow me.'

Setting a brisk pace, he led them to the edge of the camp, through a wooden stile, and down a rough track that opened out on to Hunmanby Sands and the North Sea. The Sergeant ensured the men ran close to the lapping water of the incoming tide where the sand was the consistency of porridge, their feet sinking a few inches with every step. The slog of pulling limbs up and forward immediately took its toll. After five miles of gruelling effort, the sands gave way to a rocky terrain, the uneven stones beneath their plimsolls a welcome exchange for the marsh conditions left behind. The relief, however, was short-lived.

'About turn!' ordered a completely unruffled Sergeant Poole.

The five mile return journey beckoned, scurrying along the same wet sand strip as before, but this time, the wind would be in their faces. Eric had arrived at Padgate believing he was fit. He now knew different, the aches and pains in every bone, muscle and sinew of his body a constant reminder to the fact. The rest of the group were in the same boat, although some worse than others. Poor Reg had a face so red; it bore a passing resemblance to a stick of Blackpool rock. Off they went again, commanded at the front by the human dynamo that was Sergeant Poole.

About an hour later, the bedraggled and exhausted athletes left the sands to re-join the dirt track back up to the base. The beach was never going to be the same again for Eric, all memories of Egremont or New Brighton with picnics, ice creams, sandcastles and paddling lost forever, replaced by the agony, torment, and persecution of the trek along Hunmanby Sands. Thanks were duly given to the Good Lord that the day was over.

CHAPTER 17

On his last day of work at GEC before rejoining the RAF, Billy's brother had engineered the chance of an office job for his younger sibling who had left school a few days earlier - this time with legitimacy - at the end of the summer term. The interview had not been the most testing of challenges for the fourteen year old, managing to answer a few elementary questions without making a fool of himself. The competition was evidently not too testing either because he was appointed unopposed to the job of filing clerk and told to report for work the following Monday morning at 9.00am.

Billy looked at his watch. It was 9.05am, and he was still on the tram to Bold Street, once again corroborating the truth that timekeeping and Billy had a tendency to clash. He surveyed the passing buildings and streets, noting the pockets of devastation inflicted by the bombs of the Luftwaffe thankfully absent now from the area for many months. He entered the GEC building ten minutes late, not the best start, but entirely predictable. The receptionist told him to sit down and wait. He twiddled his thumbs and studied the decor, observing the grandeur of the polished wood, the opulence of the ornate chandeliers, and the refinement of the painted portraits on the wall. An older man passed, stopped and then stared at him for a few seconds. He reversed a few feet, continuing to gaze, his actions unnerving.

'Is your name Whitfield?' the man said.

He had recognised him, hence the stare. Billy stood up.

'Yes.'

'I thought so… you've a look of your brother.'

'Eric?'

'That's right, I'm Mr Wells,' he said, looking up at an imaginary sky. 'He worked for me and never made a mistake... exemplary... and he was a good man too…'

Billy thought of the past tense. Surely it should be 'is a good man'.

'Obviously you don't have his good looks, style or deportment,' he continued, 'but I can tell you are siblings.'

He had only been employed by GEC for a matter of minutes, but already his elder brother was proving a hard act to follow.

The lift opened, and the man who had interviewed him walked out towards reception.

'Good morning Mr Wells,' he said, speaking over his spectacles.

'Good morning Mr Butler.'

The new starter had never heard people talk to one another in such a stilted, formal way, other than in films, and he found it mildly disturbing. Wells departed, leaving Butler to guide Billy towards the lift, the manager wordlessly pressing the 5th floor button to usher a few creaks and groans from its mechanical parts as the elevator made its way to the top of the building.

'This way,' said Butler, opening the lift door, his grey hair greased like a chip fished out of a pan of congealed lard.

Billy dutifully followed to enter a large, noisy room full of secretaries hovering above good-sized typewriters, their fingers rapidly depressing the keys to recreate the sound of a fast train travelling over tracks. He was amazed at their pace, but even they were surpassed by the women on the comptometers, their hands a blur as they aggregated the bundles of documents in front of them with mesmerising speed.

'Ellis!' shouted Butler.

A young man, not much older than Billy, stood up. He had the body of a man, the face of a boy, tight red curls, a turned up nose, and a mouth set in a permanently fierce expression.

'Yes Mr Butler?'

'Will you show young Whitfield around this morning?'

'Yes Mr Butler.'

'He can sit in the desk next to young Roberts.'

'Yes Mr Butler.'

Billy almost expected to hear, 'Three Bags Full Mr Butler', followed by heels clicking and a salute, such was the deference shown by Ellis to the man in charge. It was a small reminder that while Billy was respectful of authority, it was not something of which he was in awe. Butler retired to his office, leaving the two young men to introduce themselves to one another.

'Terry…'

'I'm Billy.'

It was not the friendliest greeting, but he was here to earn money not make friends.

'First things first,' said Terry. 'You need to go to the chandler's to get a dozen sky hooks.'

'Sky hooks?'

'They'll know in the shop.'

'Where's the shop?'

'Out of the front entrance, turn right, then first right, follow the road around, turn right, and it's on your right.'

Billy remembered the four rights. It should be an easy find.

'Do I need any money?'

'No, we have an account.'

There was a sneer to Terry's face that he found difficult to appraise, but he concentrated on the job in hand and took the lift down to the ground floor and left the building in search of the shop. He took the four right turns to discover a familiar sign… 'General Electric Company'. He was back where he started, returning in shame to the office to explain he had lost his way. Terry reiterated the directions.

'Right, left, left, right.'

Billy decided not to challenge him on the change of information.

'By the way, what's the name of the shop?'

'Sayers.'

'Thanks.'

Down the lift and out again into the August sunshine, Billy's quest this time was successful, finding Sayers without a problem. He waited patiently in the small queue, a little disconcerted when looking beyond the glass counter to the display of cakes, pastries and bread. It was his turn to be served. The sales assistant had the lined face of a Peruvian Inca, her grey hair clipped back and tucked behind a white band.

'Yes love?' she said, her voice husky, a lifetime of cigarette smoking evident within its wheeze.

'A dozen sky hooks please?'

'A dozen what love?'

'Sky hooks.'

'We don't sell them love, have you tried the chandler's next door?'

The new boy had been tricked.

Billy sidled out in embarrassment but quickly recovered his confidence when stepping into the adjacent shop, encouraged by the tools, nails, screws, and every other conceivable hardware item on display. This was definitely the place to buy a sky hook.

'A sky hook?' said the puzzled shop assistant, the 'hook' pronounced like a barn owl hooting.

'Yes.'

'Never 'eard of dem lad.'

'Oh.'

'Ave yer tried de cake shop?'

The assistant was laughing, Billy evidently not the first new recruit at GEC to follow the well-trodden path of asking for a sky hook in Sayers. Returning to the fifth floor, the pugnacious expression of his tormentor had slipped. Terry Ellis was delighted.

All things considered, Billy's first week at GEC went reasonably well. He managed to get there on time the other four days, even if arriving with one minute to spare and gasping for breath. Aside from filing and general fetching and carrying duties, his main diet of work involved reconciling large batches of invoices to a control total using a calculating machine with a mechanical handle and tally roll. It was, in truth, repetitive work. The managers were in the main austere and stern, but the typists and comptometer operators universally friendly. Billy paired up with another affable sort, Joe Roberts, the clerk adjacent to his own desk. Joe was a seventeen-year-old Scouser with black, wavy hair, a quick wit, and he took Billy under his wing, protecting him from the less than welcoming Terry. They spent their lunch times together at Woolworth's Café in Church Street for a regular treat of Sausage, Chips and Peas, or the occasional variation of Sausage, Mash and Peas.

Billy glanced up at the clock on the wall. It was nearly time to go home, his inaugural week's work done and dusted, though not before the regular task of carrying the typewriters to the basement via the lift. These were heavy-duty and valuable pieces of office machinery that those in charge wanted in a bunker protected from a possible Nazi bombing raid. Many in the office took this as proof that management considered the equipment more precious than the staff.

Brute strength had never been one of Billy's natural attributes with arms more suited to flower arrangement than lifting hefty machines, the labours of potato picking in Bridgnorth memorably authenticating the fact.

True to form, with a Remington metal brute in his arms, he staggered his way towards the lift. He was sharing the duties with Terry whose cheeks were pinched crimson with the effort, but given his biceps were as broad as his neck, he was able to hold his typewriter aloft as if a balloon. Billy was attempting to open the lift's metal grill door, when he felt a sudden push in his back. He fell to the floor, the typewriter landing a second later on his wrist. The noise reverberated around the hard floors and walls of the office, alerting people to rush out and discover the cause of the commotion. Prone for a few brief moments, Billy tried to come to terms with firstly the pain, and secondly what had just occurred. Terry had pushed him... for no reason, he had pushed him. Sensing a trickle of sweat on his forehead, he wiped it dry with his hand but only succeeded in spreading blood now seeping from a cut across his wrist.

'Is everything alright?' said Edna, one of the secretaries, dark haired, attractive, about to make somebody a wonderful wife no doubt.

'Yes,' said Terry, 'the return carriage is a little damaged but it looks repairable.'

'I meant him,' she said sardonically.

'I'm alright' said Billy.

Edna fetched the first aid box and applied a bandage as a tourniquet.

'What 'appened Bill lad?' asked Joe

The patient exchanged a quick glance with Terry and knew immediately he could not tell the truth.

'I slipped,' he replied.

The others accepted this at face value, but Billy noted Joe was suspicious. He knew Terry too well. The time was 4.55pm, and Mr Butler allowed Billy to leave five minutes early, the injured office junior depositing a *Hansel and Gretel* trail of dripping blood on the tram, landing stages, ferry, and bus, all the way home to Barrington Road.

One look at the soaked bandage and his mum marched him

immediately to the Doctor's on Poulton Road. In common with many of his age, Dr Hopkins had been forced out of retirement to cover for a younger man on medical active service. Now in his seventies, his faculties were in decline, bafflement a constant companion. His clothes, two sizes too big for him, hung from a slight frame, and he had the general appearance of a mad professor, bald head with unkempt grey hair dangling either side, tiny spectacles resting on the bridge of his nose over which faraway eyes took in the patient.

'Come in young man and take a seat,' he said. 'Now let me guess, sore throat? There's a lot of it about you know.'

'It's this,' said Billy, holding up his war wound.

'Your left ear? Infected is it?'

He curled his fingers to stop pointing at the side of his head.

'No, my wrist, I've cut it, and it's still bleeding.'

'Oh I see… indeed.'

This was some way from a textbook medical diagnosis. The patient was asked to place his upturned arm on a table top, enabling the doctor to remove with care the bandage and clean the wound. It revealed a nasty gash.

'You'll need stitches in that young man.'

'Stitches?'

'Yes, but you don't need to go to hospital. I can do it here… now where did I put my needles and suture?'

The doctor rose from his chair and went to a cupboard with three shelves housing a myriad of brown bottled medicines and potions. After a minute or so of confused and haphazard searching, he returned carrying a small glass container.

'Now this is the best thing for an ear infection.'

'But it's my wrist,' complained Billy.

'Of course it is… of course it is.'

The old medic returned to his panoply of trusted remedies and opened a small drawer.

'Ah, here it is...'

He had unearthed his needle and thread. It was time for a bit of sewing. Despite the strong chloroform-type smell in the room, there was to be no anaesthetic applied before the doctor got down to business, Billy wincing as the clinician bound the wound with all the skill of a man darning his socks. Nevertheless, the end result was satisfactory, and he left the surgery with a newly applied bandage that was staying nice and dry.

It had been a strange finish to his first full week of paid work, particularly the way in which Terry had pushed him, but he banished those thoughts to the periphery. On the positive side, he had earned ten shillings. Unlike Bridgnorth, however, he would not blow the lot on cream slices from the cake shop. In the aftermath of the sky hook incident, staying away from the bakers was not going to be too difficult.

The following Monday morning Billy arrived at GEC five minutes late to be greeted by a none-too-pleased Mr. Butler. He kept his head down and immediately took refuge in the tallying of a large batch of invoices. As the morning went on, it became apparent that Terry was showing no remorse for last Friday's incident. He was not sorry. Or was he? When Terry was asked to deliver the internal mail, Edna noticed something.

'Hey Terry, is that a black eye you've got?'

Terry mumbled something to affirm.

'What happened?' she said.

Joe piped up and winked at Billy, 'Yer' fell over didn't yer Terry?'

Terry hesitated before confirming in a subdued way, 'That's right, I fell over.'

The words lacked conviction. It was a sweet ending courtesy of Joe's own brand of justice. Suffice to say, Billy was never pushed again.

CHAPTER 18

Initial Training at the RAF was unquestionably the most challenging experience of Eric's nineteen years to date. The daily ritual included many recurring trials; the ten mile slog along the beach of Hunmanby Sands to sap the energy of an Olympian; the constant marching from place to place with the breath of the drill sergeant forever blasting the ears; and the severity and rigours of the inconceivably mud-soaked assault course in an otherwise dry and parched place. Even the *Chez Nous* concrete chalet bestowed its own tiresome and repetitive routines with the cleaning of floors, polishing of buttons, shining of shoes, folding of blankets, and the laying out of kit for inspection, the results of which were a consistent failure to meet the impossibly stringent standards of the NCO. Yet it could have been much worse for Eric and his cohorts, their stint taking place in the months of August and September. He recoiled at the thought of the poor beggars subjected to this regime during the barbarity of a North Sea winter, the image of a freezing cold wash and shave in the outdoors especially painful.

There was little breathing space for the recruits, and although meals at the NAAFI provided welcome respite, there was only one part of the week when Eric was able to find genuine peace and solace from the everyday demands of training, 'Chaplain's Hour' on a Wednesday. Surprisingly few in the camp took advantage of the comfortable surroundings in which to enjoy tea and chat with a man of the cloth, a man as gentle and undemanding as the NCOs were tough and exacting. A talk by the Reverend usually lasted about fifteen minutes, followed by questions from the recruits. Reg usually accompanied Eric to these occasions, and he revealed himself more cerebral in religious matters than Len at bible classes back in Wallasey. He had a tendency to ask the difficult but pertinent question, and today was no exception.

'Excuse me Chaplain,' said the young man from Ludlow, 'can I ask about the Ten Commandments?'

His china cup looked incongruous next to the roughness of his hands.

'By all means,' said the Reverend, his little finger protruding at a ninety degree angle from the grip on his own tea cup.

'It's the sixth one I have trouble with, *Thou Shalt Not Kill*. Let's say that one day I'm flying over enemy territory on a mission, and we drop our bombs, destroying the target but killing people on the ground, innocent people. My point is how can the Church condone these actions when it breaks one of the most fundamental of the Ten Commandments?'

'Good question... erm?'

'Wilson.'

'Good question Wilson.'

Eric watched on, the Chaplain seemingly buying time to answer Reg's tricky challenge. The man of God brought his fingers together to form an apex and smiled benevolently.

'The Bible does not necessarily give us all the answers that we seek in such matters, although there is certainly the viewpoint that when attacked by an aggressor, a nation has the moral right to defend itself.'

'An eye for an eye, a tooth for a tooth?' offered one recruit from the back.

'Perhaps... but tackling *Thou Shalt Not Kill*, many believe the word 'kill' is akin to 'murder' or 'an unlawful killing'. In biblical terms, the word 'slay' tends to be used to label a death caused through war or conflict.'

Another attendee interjected, marginally veering into Len territory.

'Surely Adolf Hitler is the devil with a toothbrush moustache and fighting Satan is what the bible's all about.'

'That's a fair point as well... may I read Ephesians Chapter 6 Verse 12? I believe it will provide some insight into answering these difficult questions.'

The Reverend's manner changed from fireside chat to the pulpit, and he projected his voice to fill every cubic inch of the room.

'For we wrestle not against flesh and blood, but against principalities, against powers, against the rulers of the darkness of this world, against spiritual wickedness in high places. Wherefore take unto you the whole armour of God, that ye may be able to withstand in the evil day and, having done all, to stand.'

Eric made a note of the reference.

'Yet above all,' concluded the Chaplain, 'as devout Christians, it is our duty to pray to God that this time of war and conflict is supplanted by a time of freedom, reconciliation, and above all peace.'

There was close to a small round of applause, but the men kept their appreciation to themselves, the meeting breaking up shortly after.

On returning to the billet, Eric took out his Holy Bible and opened it from the back, turning to the blank page that preceded the map of Armenia, Syria and Mesopotamia. Utilising brown gummed tape to adhere lined paper inside the book, he used a red pen to write 'WARFARE' and 'THE ENEMY' in capitals, and a black one to write 'Satan and his hosts', underlining the words carefully. He then turned to Ephesians 6:12 as read by the Chaplain and copied the text, his handwriting as immaculate as ever. Closing the book, he considered it one of the most important lessons learnt from the bible. He went to sleep that night a settled man, a warrior ready and primed to do battle.

****

It was now early September 1942, and as AC2 Whitfield lay in his bed awaiting the Sergeant's clarion call of 'hands off cocks on with socks', he reflected upon the timing of his call up to the RAF. After the setbacks of the War's early years, optimism was high that the tide was turning in favour of the Allies. Within the Air Force, the message from Commander-in-Chief Arthur Harris was crystal clear. Bomber Command would win the war for Britain. And key to that victory was the Avro Lancaster, the aircraft in which Eric hoped to take to the skies as a wireless operator or gunner. The endless round of lectures attended in the last few weeks had taught him aircraft recognition, armaments, engines, hygiene, sanitation, law, discipline, administration, organisation, mathematics, meteorology, navigation, the basics of Morse code, principles of flight, anti-gas procedures, and signals. He was soon to finish in Filey and start his technical training at a destination unknown. There was no doubt in his mind that he was now ready for the challenge of winning the war for his country.

'Hands off c…'

It was the familiar bawl of Sergeant Poole at 6.00am, time for an early morning run along the beach. His opinion of the NCO had changed since that horrendous first day, Eric gradually appreciating him as cut from a different cloth to that of Cardington's Sergeant Rawbottom. There was nothing vindictive about this man. Given the short time he had to transform the physical condition of his latest batch of raw recruits into lean, fit specimens, a cruel to be kind approach was essential. Five weeks ago, the same group of trainee airmen had wheezed, coughed and spluttered their way along the sands, each step a nightmare, an affront to the perceptions of their fitness levels. In contrast, today's effort was an archetypal display of stamina and endurance, taking place only minutes after the first waking moment of the day. The troupe, as fit as racehorses, would now be ideal material for the Pathé news film makers, demonstrating the adaptability of the human body and mind.

After breakfast, ground combat tuition with the aiming and firing of rifles was followed by the filling of ammunition clips at the shooting range and then some real heavy work carrying concrete beams across the site. Butlin's Filey was only half-built, but the owners had been granted permission to carry on with its construction so it could open at the end of the war, hence the conscription of Eric and his colleagues as temporary unpaid 'navvies'.

The afternoon featured weapons training that included the stripping and reassembling of a Bren Light Machine Gun, a lecture on different types of poisonous gases, and a film about the dangers of venereal disease. To a large extent, the carnal warnings were an irrelevance. At the end of each day, when the head of the exhausted trainee hit the pillow, thoughts of girls and temptations of the flesh were a galaxy away from the mind. And with no leave passes granted, the opportunities for any 'How's Your Father' were effectively non-existent anyway. Nonetheless, a movie short with graphic shots of diseased genitalia was aired to ensure any residual desires were crushed, trampled and discarded. Hammering home the message, a Wing Commander gave a homily on the dangers of the 'good time girl', 'pick-up' and 'prostitute'.

'She may look clean, but she will spread syphilis and gonorrhoea,' he warned with severity. 'And remember this... you can't beat the Axis if you get VD.'

Eric left the room happy to remain virginal. In fact, celibacy appeared a highly attractive choice for the future.

Walking alongside, unconsciously cupping his groin for protection, Reg whispered, 'Bloomin' 'eck Eric, I think I'll stick to me' regular partner.'

'Eh? What regular partner?'

'This.'

He held up his right hand. Eric shook his head and smirked.

Further pointless drilling and marching ensued, after which the group were told to report to the Administration block for the allocation of further kit and to discover details of their next posting. Eric joined a queue and collected a second kitbag, helmet, goggles, flying suit, leather gauntlets, gloves, life jacket, and emergency whistle. Laden with his new supplies, he joined Reg at the end of another queue, the curse of a surname beginning with 'W' striking again.

'I wonder if we're transferring to the same place,' said Reg.

'Logically, you'd think we might... both of us on wireless training and that, but this is the RAF and....'

'AC2 Whitfield?'

The voice was loud and unfriendly.

'Yes sir.'

He stood up and walked towards the unsmiling officer behind the desk. He was handed an envelope.

'Your next posting is Number 3 School of Technical Training, leaving tomorrow,' said the official.

'Thank you sir.'

Eric returned to his seat and read the letter

'AC2 Wilson?'

'Yes sir.'

Reg went through the same routine, returning shortly to sit down.

'Where are you going Eric?' he said.

'Blackpool.'

'Oh bugger.'

'What do you mean?'

'I'm going to Number 3 School of Technical Training.'

'That's Blackpool you ninny!'

'Is it?'

'Yes.'

'Spiffing!'

The word was enunciated with his countryside dialect and sounded undeniably comical; Eric doubting his friend would have said 'spiffing' before joining the RAF. Funnily enough, he had expected all recruits to be sourced from the 'educated classes' as per the films and newsreels, yet the reality was very different, at least if you ignored the officers where the silver spoon was still shining brightly. His group was a fair representation of the country, with lads from Scotland, Newcastle, Leeds, London, Cornwall, Birmingham, Cardiff, and, of course Wallasey and Ludlow. Their backgrounds varied from sons of shipwrights, butchers, coalmen and miners, to sons of doctors, architects, and solicitors. In any normal situation they would not be mixing, but the common experience bonding these young men together as a force was stronger than anything he had encountered before, a bond that could only strengthen the nearer they came to actual operations.

So Blackpool it was, and after the gullibility about the holiday camp that never was at Filey, thoughts of the Tower, the Tower Ballroom, the promenade, the beach, and the fairground rides of the great seaside town meant nothing. They were definitely not going on holiday. The war had put the lights out on such pleasures, and in the case of Blackpool's Illuminations, literally so.

CHAPTER 19

Eva Whitfield sat down to read the letter from Eric, Billy in the background enjoying his breakfast.

29th November 1942

Dear Mum and Dad,

I hope you are all keeping well and bearing up to everything. Thank you for your letters. I always enjoy reading them. I'm sorry I've not written more often, but this doesn't mean you're absent from my thoughts and prayers. Training here in Blackpool is hard but rewarding, and although impatient to do my bit for the country, I'm getting closer by the day to be in a position to help.

There's no camp here like at Padgate or Filey, and so I'm staying in digs at the far end of the promenade with a chap called Reg, a fellow Aircraftsman from Ludlow. Our landlady's called Mrs Kay. She's a real character who smokes cigars and is abrupt with everyone other than me and Reg. And before you ask, she feeds us well. We never go hungry. I'm learning Morse code in a factory that makes the Wellington Bomber, but it's not easy. I've been here three months and I'm only up to 9 words per minute. Reg is a genius. He can already do 14. But I'll keep persevering.

We're still not allowed to leave the town. One recruit is in trouble for trying to visit his family in Manchester last weekend. He was caught by a couple of guards who seem to be everywhere on the outskirts of town. We do, however, have a fair amount of leisure time, certainly more than we had at Filey. We go swimming at the public baths once a week, to the Tower on a Sunday evening to sing along to the Wurlitzer organ, and I play football every Saturday afternoon. (You can tell Billy I went to Bloomfield Road to watch Blackpool FC, and Stanley Matthews played for the RAF).

It seems unlikely I'll be home for Christmas. I've exams early in the New Year, after which I'll finally get some leave. Please send my best wishes to everyone. I promise to write to you again soon.

Your loving son,

Eric

'How's he getting on Mum?' said Billy, wiping the grease away from his mouth with a shirt cuff.

'Billy!' she said, admonishing her son. 'Use a hankie, for goodness sake.'

'What does it say?'

Eva shook her head in resignation.

'He's staying in digs at the far end of the town... his landlady smokes cigars and is rude to everyone other Eric and his friend.'

Billy slurped his tea, remembering a few evacuees in Bridgnorth who went through a similar thing.

'Does he talk about his training?'

'Only briefly... he says he's learning Morse code. Oh, and he saw Stanley Matthews play for the RAF.'

Billy was impressed.

'Matthews?'

'It's just a shame he won't be home for Christmas,' she said, looking out of the window distractedly, speaking more to herself than Billy. 'It'll be lovely to see him again. It seems such a long time since he was here.'

She was brought back to the present by her younger son's request.

'Any more tea Mum?'

'Billy, I think you better go or you'll be late for work.'

She could have added 'again' or even 'yet again', his timekeeping a constant menace. On the plus side of things, his time of arrival at the office was consistent, getting there at about ten past nine. If the world stopped for about ten minutes, the problems of his tardiness would be over. He picked up his coat, left the house, and dashed down the road to catch the bus to the ferry, turning the corner just as it pulled away from the stop, his frantic wave ignored by the driver. Today, he was going to be half an hour late. He now had to think of an excuse.

'Hello Billy, I was so sorry to hear about your cat,' said Edna. 'Do you think it'll live?'

'I hope so.'

The cat story had managed to save his bacon, but he hadn't banked on the probing concern shown by the women in the office, particularly Edna.

'I've a ginger tom called Tiger,' she said. 'What's your cat's name?'

'Erm...' he glanced around the room, hesitating long enough to raise her suspicions, 'Ledger.'

'Ledger?' she said disbelievingly.

'Erm... yes.'

She took him to one side, her brown eyes penetrating his.

'Listen Billy,' she whispered, 'you need to get out of bed earlier. If you keep being late, you'll get the sack. You don't want that do you?'

Billy wasn't totally sure of the answer. He didn't like the work. It was monotonous, and he lacked an aptitude for it, a failure of concentration perhaps his greatest weakness, not a great thing when reconciling large batches of invoices. His real wish was to be a draughtsman, utilising his artistic skills to prepare technical drawings, but nobody around him shared these aspirations. He thought of Miss McDonnell in Bridgnorth. She'd have encouraged him. Ultimately, however, he recalled Eric's efforts to get him the job at GEC and knew he owed it to his brother.

'No, I don't,' he replied.

'Good...' said Edna, ruffling his hair affectionately, '...now get back to work... and pray for that cat!'

She smiled knowingly. Billy smiled back and returned to his desk.

The morning dragged, but somehow the clock on the wall ticked its way to one o'clock. Eric teamed up with Joe Roberts to venture out into the November cold and walk at a brisk pace towards Wimpey's for today's treat of a hamburger. But as they crossed Ranelagh Street, the friends were stopped in their tracks by a man who jumped out in front of them.

'Photo gentlemen?'

He was carrying a professional folding camera and flashbulb.

'No ta pal,' said Joe, 'I've a face for de wireless.'

They tried to walk past the photographer, but the man persisted.

'Listen gents, how about two shillings each.'

'Yer' joking aren't yer pal? D'yer know how much we earn?'

'No, you don't understand, I'll pay you.'

'Yer what?'

'I need a shot of young office workers for a trade magazine, and you two fit the bill.'

Billy had to admit they looked smart. Underneath his fawn-belted Mackintosh and Joe's woollen overcoat, there were well-groomed suits, shirts, ties, and highly polished shoes, their image nicely finished off with stylish leather gloves.

'Dat's a deal, don't yer think so Bill?' said Joe, already combing his dark, wavy hair in preparation.

Billy agreed. This was going to be easy money.

Thirty minutes later, he was not so sure.

'Just one more shot gents...' said the photographer, unable to disguise a mounting irritability in his voice. 'And this time Billy, can you walk normally and not like a seventy year old with arthritis?'

'Come 'ed Bill lad,' said Joe. 'Yer can do it.'

All he had to do was walk, something surely he had mastered from the age of one. With a few further snaps, the man with the camera was just about satisfied, handing over the four shilling fee, undeniably begrudging at least half of it. He promised to send a copy of the photograph to the GEC office.

The two clerks raced to Wimpey's and ate their food in record time, Billy's indigestion the price paid for his first and almost certainly his last modelling assignment.

When the small envelope arrived at GEC, it was addressed to Joe Roberts Esquire. Billy's Scouse pal had never sounded so grand.

'It's 'ere Billy lad,' murmured Joe, as he walked past waving the letter.

'Great.'

Billy picked up an invoice and headed to Joe's desk.

'It can't be very big,' said Billy, decidedly unimpressed with the likely size of the image. He was not expecting something to display in Piccadilly Square but had hoped for something larger than a postage stamp. Joe removed the small, black and white photograph. It was about 3" x 2".

'We might need a magnifyin' glass,' he said, bringing it closer for a better view.

In fairness, it was a decent picture, the young men strolling elegantly and with purpose through the busy metropolis of city centre Liverpool, but they were being upstaged. Dominating the photo on the right hand side was an older man in a flat cap, chewing on a pipe and appearing out of his depth in such a busy, built-up area. He clearly belonged to a rural setting, resting on a hay bale and radiating the odours of farm muck. Maybe the photographer deliberately wanted to capture the old world against the new. Either that or he was not the best at his craft. Taking a closer glance, Billy was slightly surprised at his own image. The face was young. He certainly didn't look older than his fourteen years of age. But the clothes could have been hanging from a grandfather. Billy was fourteen going on sixty four. He returned to his desk, feeling more grown up than ever, Bridgnorth and his time as an evacuee already more than a world away.

He may have adopted the persona of an old age pensioner, but today youth was calling, Billy ready to become a member of the Liverpool Boy's Lunch Hour Club, a facility set up to keep younger employees gainfully occupied during the middle of the working day. The single chime at one o'clock saw the young office worker jump from his desk and hurry towards a large department store in Williamson Square. Running up the stairs, two at a time, he reached the top floor and entered a large room above the shop, immediately joining a big lad called Buster in the queue for a bowl of home-made lentil soup and generous helping of freshly baked bread. Buster devoured his food in less than a minute and spent the rest of the time at the table scrounging spare crusts and soup leftovers from the others.

After the feast came the sports, starting with a game of shove halfpenny, Billy quickly demonstrating a natural, delicate technique to beat with ease the heavy-handed Buster whose every coin overshot the board with a velocity liable to endanger anyone within the vicinity. Tiddlywinks football was next, and it was another straightforward task for Billy to win. Buster's hands were like plates of meat, and his inclination to press too hard on the disc saw five counters destroyed. It was no surprise when the big man was banished from playing.

Disappointingly, the pleasures of the Boy's Hour had to end, although Billy returned to the office buoyed by the new routine, one that could only help the day pass a little quicker. Today, however, the sight of tally rolls and invoices induced new lows of tedium, the clock seeming to tick ever slower as the afternoon progressed. There were even occasions when he wished perversely for the return of the Luftwaffe - absent from the city for many months - to shake things up. After an eternity, the sound of five chimes indicated it was time to go home. He had earned another shilling.

Thirty minutes later Billy was at Seacombe Ferry about to climb the stairs of the number 14 bus home, when he heard somebody call out his name.

'Billy? It is Billy isn't it?'

An attractive looking woman, black hair, violet eyes was getting on behind him. It was Vera, Eric's friend. He had met her on a couple of occasions last summer before his brother had left for the RAF.

'Yes... hello,' he replied.

'Shall we sit downstairs?'

'Alright.'

Without protest, he followed and sat down on the seat next to her, the pair exchanging a few pleasantries about the weather and work. The conductor then pressed the bell, and the bus responded by jerking forward into life, Billy staring out of the window to watch a first drop of rain fall on to the glass, his eyes tracking the droplet's journey down the pane.

'How's Eric?' she suddenly asked.

'He's in Blackpool at the moment.'

'So I've heard.'

Vera spoke a little absent-mindedly, pulling a stray thread of cotton from her coat, rolling it, and placing it in her pocket.

'Does he write often?'

'Not really.'

They were interrupted by 'Fares please', Billy's ear almost sliced off by the conductor's ticket machine slung at hip height like a cowboy's holster.

Coins exchanged for tickets, Vera continued to press.

'Do you know when he might be coming back to Wallasey?'

'I'm not sure, but he doesn't think he'll be home for Christmas.'

It was her turn to stare out of the window, the rain now heavier by the second.

'I suppose it must be difficult for him to find time to write. I've heard the RAF push them very hard in training.'

His brother had attended football matches at Bloomfield Road to watch Stanley Matthews. He ought to have the time. But the younger Whitfield showed some sensitivity and maturity by agreeing.

'Yes, I think that's right.'

The conversation dried up, Billy glad a few stops later to say goodbye and depart the bus. He scurried down Hampstead Road, thankful for the protection of his raincoat. He thought of Vera. She was friendly, pretty, and seemed really nice, yet Eric had chosen not to write to her. Recalling his dad's moan of 'bloody women… I'll never understand them,' it seemed to Billy that when it came to Eric and Vera, it was the man proving difficult to comprehend.

CHAPTER 20

'Christmas in Blackpool... who'd have thought it?' said Reg.

He was slumped in an armchair, wearing a party hat on the back of his head with a glass of beer in one hand and a cigar in the other. Eric was sat opposite with the same props but appeared less dishevelled. He didn't do dishevelment.

'I know...' said Eric, raising his glass and proclaiming, 'Merry Christmas pal.'

'Up yours!'

Both RAF trainee airmen were recovering from the gastronomic treat that had been Christmas dinner. For an hour or two, rationing restrictions had not existed, the lads gorging on soup, roast turkey dinner, and plum pudding, a feast for the eyes, taste buds, and stomach. Mrs Kay had served up food portions as oversized as her cigars, and both Eric and Reg were now ready to burst, the beer hardly helping with their digestion.

The landlady with the sharp tongue for anyone other than her 'paying guests' strolled into the lounge smoking a German U Boat. She was a big woman, wearing an overall that clung to her broad torso and gathered below her bust, a bust that reminded Eric of the barrage balloons still festooning the skies of many British cities and towns.

'By 'eck, I'm glad them buggers 'ave gone,' she said, 'miserable as sin they are... the pair o' them.'

Her rasping voice, pitched like a baritone sliding towards the bass register, bore the signs of a lifetime's devotion to the art of smoking. Two dear old ladies, fussing around like mother hens, had just popped in to leave a Christmas present in the form of a bottle of homespun scent. Mrs Kay had ushered them away with the kind of haste normally reserved for unsolicited door-to-door salesmen.

'Smells like a pig to me,' she said, holding the bottle tip to her nose.

There was a ring at the doorbell.

'Bugger me… they're back.'

She marched purposefully to the front door, where Eric heard her tone change to one that was unusually welcoming.

'Come in Gladys… and bring those lovely ladies in with you.'

'Thank you Fanny.'

Clearly, it was not the ladies with the pig perfume.

Her friend entered the room and was as jolly and gentle as Mrs Kay was curt and unrefined. She was small in height, a little overweight, and a person who seemed to find everything hilarious. But the attentions of Eric and Reg soon changed course, when a couple of WAAFs in uniform followed her into the room. Both had long hair backcombed on top, pinned to the sides, and worn long at the back. Attractive and affable, the redhead was called Gwen, her fresh complexion portraying a level of vitality rarely seen, especially during such troubled times. Her friend, a bespectacled brunette by the name of Kitty, was less confident, but pleasant nonetheless. Mrs Kay and her friend disappeared to the kitchen leaving the four young RAF trainees in the room.

'Where are you staying?' said Reg, straightening out his Christmas hat.

'In digs with Mrs Bloom… in the road parallel to this one,' said Gwen.

Fanny's friend was another landlady.

'Just the two of you?'

'Yes… we started off in a guest house with about ten other WAAFs, but the food was terrible, so when the chance of going to Mrs Bloom's came up, we jumped at it.'

'She's lovely and a great cook,' said Kitty.

'What's it like here?' said Gwen, addressing the question to Eric.

'Fine...' he said, looking around before speaking quietly. 'Our landlady's quite a character... smokes big cigars.'

'And tells most people to bugger off,' said Reg.

The girls giggled.

When it transpired they were also training to be wireless operators, Eric veered the conversation away from any talk about words per minute. These were two young, bright women, and he knew without asking they would be as good as Reg at Morse code.

Mrs Kay returned to the room with Mrs Bloom trailing in her path.

'How about a sing song?' she growled. 'I bet you girls like a song.'

They nodded.

'It's such a shame your Alfie's not here,' said Mrs Bloom. 'He's such a good piano player isn't he Fanny?'

'I know Gladys... he is... but never mind. There's a war on you know.'

'I play a bit of piano.'

It was Eric, modestly owning up to his talent.

Reg was perhaps the most surprised.

'You play the piano?'

'I know a few tunes.'

'What are we waiting for then?' roared Mrs Kay. 'Into the front room we go.'

Eric had not visited this part of the house before but was unsurprised to discover spotless wooden and glass surfaces, lace-covered chairs, grandiose curtains, a grandfather clock, an oil painting of a tarn, porcelain dogs, and a photograph of a young man in Royal Navy uniform on the sideboard. But Eric's eye was ultimately drawn to the piano, a pristine upright in mahogany. This was no old Joanna in desperate need of an expert with a tuning fork. He lowered himself on to the leather stool and began to play. It sounded beautiful.

Reg was positioned between the WAAFs on the main settee, the two landladies standing either side of the piano, primed to give a recital. They reminded Eric of an old Music Hall act. In his head he christened them 'Fanny and Gladys'.

'What's in your repertoire son?' asked Mrs Kay.

'Most things... George Formby?'

'That'll do... how about a 'Little Stick of Blackpool Rock'?'

'I'm not hungry after that dinner,' said Reg.

The landladies exploded with laughter at the witticism before calming down to begin their performance. The song settled into the first few bars, Eric surprised to hear the lower register of Reg dominating the vocals. However, looking up from his keys, he saw his friend on the settee, mouth firmly closed. Turning his head to the right, he identified the source as Mrs Kay, Eric now imagining a Music Hall poster proclaiming her as 'Fanny Kay - the voice of a thousand cigars.'

The song ended to enthusiastic applause, mainly from Mrs Kay to be fair, and after some more Formby numbers in which everyone participated, they sang a few Christmas songs. The impromptu sing-a-long concluded with a solo from Mrs Kay performing Paul Robeson's 'Ole Man River' about an octave lower than the original, the porcelain terrier on the mantelpiece threatening to jump off into the fireplace in protest during the loudest parts of the interpretation. It was, in more ways than one, a low key end to proceedings, somewhat lacking the rousing impact of 'Land of Hope and Glory' at the Proms.

'Eh bugger, I need a cigar.'

****

Reg was particularly taken with Gwen and keen for them to meet up again. Eric was less eager but agreed to a New Year's Eve rendezvous with the girls at Woolworth's on the promenade for a meal in the café.

The day itself was a cold one, and standing outside the elegant building with its clock tower and bright façade, Eric cupped his hands and blew hot air against both palms before lighting up a cigarette. Exhaling deeply, the smoke from his Woodbine drifted up towards the brooding and magnificent sight of the adjacent Blackpool Tower with its five hundred feet of iron and cast steel extending to the heavens, the construction rightly considered much more than the poor man's Eiffel. Everywhere he looked, people were dressed in air force blue and so spotting the two WAAFs was not the easiest task, but following an anxious ten minute wait, Gwen and Kitty arrived, both smiling and relaxed.

The four young diners duly made their way up the stairs of Woolworth's and into the café to join hundreds of diners sat at tables stretched out across the vast floor. They were in time for 'Luncheon' and able to enjoy the delights of Thick Vegetable Soup, Fried Salmon Cutlet, Parsley Sauce and Chips, followed by Steamed Fruit Roll and Custard Sauce, all for a bargain shilling a piece. A cup of tea to finish, and it felt like a reprise of the Christmas over indulgence, but it was an enjoyable occasion, both girls great company with many RAF anecdotes of their own.

'How about going for a walk to work off this food?' said Reg.

'Where to?' replied Eric, patting his stomach. 'Ludlow?'

They all laughed. Eric was not normally the joker, but he could occasionally deliver a telling quip.

The group left the warmth of the café for the outside cold, strolling along the snow-covered pavements of the promenade, past the Tower with its ballroom base, and towards the small arcades and countless shops selling sticks of rock. When they reached the 'The House of Mirrors', they went inside for a laugh, and Reg was soon having fun.

'Here you are, look at this.'

He positioned himself in front of a reflection that distorted his figure to that of a small, rotund person.

'I give you Mrs Bloom,' he cried.

The others chuckled. Moving to the next mirror, he was suddenly transformed into a giant.

'Eh bugger, I need a cigar,' he exclaimed in a subterranean bellow.

They all laughed again.

'You are funny,' said Gwen.

It was very obvious that the natural exuberance and *joie de vivre* of Reg had found a like-minded soul in the red-headed WAAF, and after giggling their way around the distorting mirrors, the pair disappeared into the mysterious world of 'Madame Zelda's Fortune-Telling' caravan on the prom. The demure Kitty and reserved Eric sat on a dry bench outside to wait.

'I'm not a believer in that crystal ball stuff,' said Eric, his ears crimson with the cold. 'What about you?'

Kitty exercised her habit of wrapping a strand of hair around a forefinger to thread behind an ear before adjusting her glasses.

'Not sure to be honest,' she said. 'I'm naturally open-minded, but it's hard to believe the old lady inside there can predict the future.'

'Maybe she'll say when the country's going to win the war.'

'I suspect not.'

Kitty was small, probably not quite five feet, and her legs swung a little on the bench.

'I think the snow might be starting again,' said Eric, a solitary snowflake melting on his cuff.

'Does Reg have a girlfriend?'

Kitty's question jarred a little against the predictability of their previous exchanges.

'Not that I'm aware of… he's certainly never spoken of one.'

212

'Gwen doesn't have a boyfriend… well she did have, but he was killed at Dunkirk.'

'Oh, I'm sorry to hear that.'

'Yes, it was very sad… but she says it already seems a lifetime ago.'

'I can imagine.'

Looking out on to the beach, it was a change not to see RAF recruits running along the sands. The regime at Blackpool may have lacked the everyday strict discipline of Cardington, Padgate and Filey, but it was still far from an easy ride, and the beach marathons, although never as bad as those early efforts on Hunmanby Sands, were always a test. Fortunately, this was a rare day off from such exertions.

'Do you have a girlfriend Eric?'

He gulped, again not expecting the question.

'Erm… I think so.'

'You don't seem too sure.'

'Well, erm…'

He was almost stuttering. It was a simple question. There should be a simple answer. He had been away from home for over five months now and had not seen Vera in all that time. He had received a couple of letters from her and written back once but winced at the recall of its contents, a couple of pages of meaningless drivel about RAF training. He envied those lads able to maintain strong and cordial relations with girlfriends and wives from afar. In Eric's instance, such ideals were seemingly incompatible with serving his country. Yet they had not broken up, hence the hesitation and uncertainty in answering Kitty's question. A change of direction was needed.

'What about you Kitty? Is there a man in your life?'

She held up her left hand to reveal a wedding ring.

'His name's Ralph, my true love,' she said before looking out to sea. 'He volunteered to join the RAF, and I foolishly did the same, thinking I'd see more of him…. ridiculous I know… he's now a pilot in Bomber Command.'

Eric felt a twinge of envy. That could have been his destiny but for the vagaries of the selection board at Cardington.

'Without the war,' she continued, 'we'd be at home now making plans to start a family. Instead, I'm here, worrying about him every day, unsure how I'd manage if anything happened to him. It's seems silly to say, but sometimes I wish I'd never met him.'

They both stared out to the distant horizon, a cold breeze brushing their faces, until their introspections were interrupted by the opening of the caravan door, Reg and Gwen stepping out. Eric's pal was jubilant.

'We're getting married,' he yelled, 'and we're going to have five children!'

Eric thought this was far too sudden. He had only met the girl on Christmas Day. Fortunately, Gwen noted his disquiet.

'We're not really getting married,' she said. 'It's just what Madam Zelda told us.'

Eric was immediately reassured. Those fortune-tellers did talk a load of rubbish.

CHAPTER 21

The New Year was three weeks old and ready to deliver Eric's exam results. The wireless operations test had taken place above Burton's on the High Street, and although by no means a catastrophe, he was not overly confident of attaining the necessary pass mark. No such worries for Reg. Unusually, the alphabetical sequence had been transposed, and his friend already knew he had achieved a high mark of 76%, ready to move on to the next phase of his training. Eric was sitting outside an office in the Wellington Bomb factory on the edge of town, increasingly nervous that something had gone wrong. Reg had not been asked to report here. But he was not kept waiting long, a familiar face opening the door to the room and beckoning him inside.

'Come in dear chap and take a seat.'

Eric was startled to come face to face with the same tall officer who had sworn him in at Cardington.

'Thank you sir.'

He sat down in the chair that faced a modest-sized walnut desk. The RAF senior had cultivated a clipped moustache to accompany the clipped accent.

'Right Whitfield, I'm Wing Commander Thompson...' he hesitated, stroking his new whiskers, 'Whitfield?'

'Yes sir?'

'Have we met before?'

'Yes sir, Cardington, January 1942.'

'I remember... you wanted to be a pilot.'

'Yes sir.'

'Well that is interesting,' he said, sorting through a few papers positioned on his blotting paper pad. 'Let's start with your exam results Whitfield,' he said.

'Yes sir.'

Eric's stomach lurched a bit.

'Not bad, but not great... a mark of 57%... but this has given us the idea for you to change course in your training, steering you away from wireless operations. You understand?'

'I think so sir.'

For the briefest of moments, Eric envisaged his dream of piloting an aircraft was finally coming true, yet the only flight involved here was a flight of fancy.

'Your assessors believe you have the aptitude and attributes to make a successful flight engineer. Bomber Command operations are gathering momentum, and this means we need more aircraft and more crew. Unfortunately, there is every prospect we will end up short of good flight engineers, which is where people like you come in. You can help bridge this gap by switching from your current discipline. Do you have any thoughts on this?'

'How long is the training, sir?'

'That's the only down side. It will probably take another ten or eleven months before you are ready for flying operations. But, as you know, the flight engineer essentially flies the aircraft with the pilot, something I'm sure you would find extremely rewarding.'

He was right. The wireless operator and gunner positions were not roles that held any excitement for Eric. Yes, he would still prefer to pilot a Lancaster, Stirling or Halifax, but flight engineer sitting next to the skipper in the cockpit of a four engine bomber would be a very good second best.

'Yes sir... I'd be delighted to make the switch.'

'Good man... you won't regret it. Now, I understand you have seven day's leave, after which you'll report to RAF Innsworth in Gloucester to start your technical training. Here are all the details.'

The Wing Commander had made the change in direction seem optional, but looking at the paperwork, it was obviously a *fait accompli*. He thanked the officer and departed to catch the bus back to his digs.

He was about to put the key in the front door, when it was opened from the inside by Reg who immediately put his forefinger to his lips in a keep quiet gesture. He shook his head sternly, his brow furrowed.

'It's Mrs Kay,' he said in a whisper, 'she's had bad news.'

'What's up?'

As he asked the question, the landlady appeared at the other end of the hall.

'Come in boys,' she said, disconsolately.

Eric and Reg made their way tentatively through to the back room, Mrs Kay dropping into her usual chair, her normal confident and brash demeanour absent. She opened a gold embossed tin and pulled out a cigar, ready to go through the usual smoking ritual but then halted, returning the missile wrapped in tobacco leaves to its container.

'He walked at nine months you know.'

The young men in RAF uniforms didn't know what to say, which was just as well. Fanny Kay only wanted to talk. She continued to reminisce, staring into space as she spoke.

'And he was top of the class at school... such a bright boy... who grew into this strapping, thoughtful young man. When Jack died suddenly, he was so strong. I'd lost a husband, but he'd lost a dad, and he spent all his time making sure I was alright... then when he joined the Navy, he looked so smart in his bell bottoms, his jersey, and his cap, and I was bursting with pride... Seaman Cyril Kay... my boy... my pride and joy...'

She pulled a handkerchief from a pocket and dabbed her eyes, the slightly comic figure with the booming bass voice, giant cigars and strident persona a million miles away from this broken woman.

'It happened in the Atlantic near Greenland,' she said, marginally recovering. 'It was a U Boat of course... they'd lost the convoy and didn't stand a chance.'

She stopped talking, and there was silence for a short while, until the cuckoo clock on the wall struck three o'clock, the woodcutter's hourly appearance from the top opening of the timepiece never so absurd.

'We're very sorry for your loss Mrs Kay,' said Reg.

Eric knew many people who had lost their lives during the war, but he had never been this close to grief before. He recalled the day during the Liverpool Blitz when he went into work at GEC to discover the mild mannered Mr Leadbetter had been killed in air raid shelter overnight. That had been a shock, but this was different. The raw emotion of a mother dealing with the loss of her son was a mere scratch below the surface. The moment demonstrated for him, better than anything else to date, the human cost of war.

The landlady lifted her head and looked at Eric.

'Can you play 'The Lord's My Shepherd' on the piano?'

'Well... I've never played it before... but it has a straightforward melody, so I could give it a go.'

'Shall we move to the front then?' she said, slowly rising from her chair.

There was something funereal about the pace they swapped rooms, adding to the discomfort. When settled in the chair by the window, Mrs Kay signalled for the hymn to begin, her voice, pitched higher than normal, cracked and emotional, the scene poignant and moving.

The Lord's my shepherd, I'll not want
He leads me down to die

The singing stopped, exchanged for quiet weeping, Eric and Reg grateful when Mrs Bloom arrived. Here was someone capable of dealing with a grieving mother. The RAF lads were out of their depth and gladly took refuge in the bedroom upstairs.

Eric told his friend the news about the change to become a flight engineer. Although Reg was surprised at the revelation, it made little difference. They had fully expected to move to different training schools for the next stage of their learning and were already prepared to go their separate ways.

This penultimate day in Blackpool had turned out to be a sombre one, and later in the evening when Eric was drifting off to sleep for the final time in the front bedroom with a view out towards Morecambe Bay, he reflected with sadness that his lasting memory of his time here would now be dominated by the events of today, a reminder as to the fragility of everybody's situation. Little wonder that his last waking moment before sleep was a brief prayer to God to protect his own mother from such sorrow.

The next morning, he and Reg said goodbye to a subdued Mrs Kay and departed for the railway station. As they queued at the ticket office, there was a tap on Reg's shoulder. It was Gwen, his friend immediately embracing her as though a long last family member. Eric spotted Kitty a few yards back, looking on with a somewhat faraway expression.

'Now don't forget to write to me Reg Wilson,' said Gwen, kissing him on the lips.

Released from the embrace, Reg wiped the lipstick from his mouth with the back of a palm.

'Every week,' he promised with the enthusiasm of a playful puppy.

Eric thought of the infrequency of his letters to Vera, guilt imposing itself until a gentle voice interrupted his introspection.

'Goodbye Eric... and have a safe journey'

'Thank you Kitty... and I hope everything works out for you.'

'So do I.'

The manner of her reply was a little dispirited.

He picked up his belongings and made his way with Reg to a compartment within the nearest carriage. Through smudged and grimy glass, Eric looked out to see Gwen and Kitty standing on the platform, the former's exuberance undiminished. She waved eagerly at Reg who responded by jumping up and pulling down the sash window just as the train moved forward.

'Remember Madame Zelda!' he shouted.

Gwen cupped her ear.

'MADAME ZELDA!' he yelled above the clatter and crunch of the locomotive, holding up an outstretched hand. 'FIVE CHILDREN!'

She blew him a kiss that Reg inhaled like Mrs Kay with a cigar. Frantic waving continued until the station disappeared from view and he closed the window, an overdue action on this windy January morning. Eric was pleased for his friend. He had only known Gwen for about three weeks, but they were obviously well suited and happy to be courting. The war was already tearing them apart, yet he felt confident this was a friendship that could endure and outlive such difficulties.

The love-struck wireless operator was now gazing out of the window with a smile on his face, his cheeks reddening to match the colour of his hair. Eric was going to miss Reg Wilson with his funny countryside accent and irrepressible personality. He was reminiscent of Len back in Wallasey, though with a touch more sensitivity and intelligence. His Ludlow drawl made him sound a bit slow, but he was in truth razor-sharp, his Morse code prowess a clear demonstration of the fact.

It was not a long journey and the train soon reached Lime Street, the two friends alighting from the carriage to shake hands and wish each other good luck. They promised to meet up again as soon as circumstances permitted.

Watching Reg walk away to catch his connecting train was a lonely moment for Eric. He had just said *au revoir* to his constant companion of the last six months, a period spent within the confines of the RAF, where freedom was an absentee and everything was done for you. The rediscovered solitude and independence was combining to unsettle Eric. It seemed he had become institutionalised. He turned to leave the station for the tram stop but within seconds heard a shout.

'ERIC!'

It was Reg running towards him.

'What's up?'

'Have you got any coins?'

Reg was as fit as a butcher's terrier, but he was now out of breath, the gasping presumably brought on by excitement rather than exertion.

'Coins?'

'Yes… I want to make a phone call.'

'Where to?'

'Blackpool.'

'Blackpool? Who do you want to call in Blackpool?'

'Gwen… she's above Burton's this afternoon, and I've got the number.'

'That'll be a trunk call.'

'That's why I need the coins.'

Farthings and halfpennies would not be enough, Eric fishing out of his pockets a few sixpences, a florin, and half a crown. He handed over the stash.

'What's the urgency?'

221

'I'm going to ask her to marry me.'

'Eh? That's a bit sudden isn't it?'

'I don't care. Sitting on the train as we left, I just knew she was the girl for me. Life's too short to wait for these things to happen.'

'But what about the war? It won't…'

'Bugger the war!'

There was no answer to that.

Hoping to get some of his money back, Eric followed his pal to the public phone boxes on the far wall by the ticket office, where they joined a queue, the would-be-groom impatiently tapping his feet and agitating the coins in cupped hands, as he waited for a booth to become free. His impatience was rewarded when an older man finished his call, Reg almost catapulting the poor bloke out of the way. With a small piece of paper in his hand, he dialled the number, inserted the sixpences, and waited.

'Ah, hello', he said, relief palpable. 'I need to speak to Gwen Jones. She is upstairs in the RAF training class.'

Reg listened a bit, his face irritated with the response. He cut in.

'Listen my good man, I appreciate this is inconvenient, but my name is Wing Commander McNeish, and I'm a personal friend of your manager. I'm sure he…'

The bluff had done the trick, the shop assistant retiring to fetch Gwen. Reg's agitation during the wait increased, though it had nothing to do with the florin needed in the coin slot. There was a click.

'Gwen!' he shouted, but then went quiet, his words spaced between the bad news from the other end of the line. 'Oh I see… that's terrible… I understand… please send mine and Eric's sympathies… indeed… what did I want? Nothing important… it can wait.'

The money ran out, bringing the call to an end. All the energy and vigour of Reg had gone.

'What's happened?' said Eric.

'It's Kitty.'

'And?'

'Her husband's been killed on a training flight. He was only twenty.'

'Oh no…'

'That must be hard to take… a bloody training flight.'

In the space of twenty four hours, Eric had encountered two deaths, one a son, one a husband, both wreaking havoc on the lives of the people affected.

'I'll write to Gwen,' said Reg, 'and ask her in a letter.' He was down but not out.

They said goodbye for the second time, leaving Eric to wonder at the unfairness of it all. He thought about Kitty, remembering their conversations and identifying in retrospect her melancholia, as though she knew what was going to happen. Jumping on the tram for the Pier Head, he concluded that, despite her youth, she was probably wiser than the rest. In fairness though, as the war became more real by the day, he was probably catching her up.

CHAPTER 22

Eric was welcomed home as the prodigal son with a homecoming meal at his grandmother's, his mum, dad, brother and aunties all present. The occasion culminated with Eric at the piano for a sing-song just like old times, and for a few short hours, there had been no war, no troubles, and no concerns about the future. Over the next couple of days, his dad showed some interest in his training, particularly the switch to flight engineering, and his mum wanted to know about the people he had met along the way. But otherwise, home was no different than before, as though he had never been away. He had again been surprised by Billy, now quite the young man, gaining in stature, his voice breaking. He seemed to be getting on well enough at GEC despite a timekeeping problem, the latter no great surprise to Eric. He remembered those old schooldays leaving for Central School to the sound of his younger brother snoring in bed, destined for another dash through the streets to beat the morning assembly bell at Riverside Primary.

One day towards the end of the week's leave, Eric stepped out into the chill of the early afternoon to meet up with Len for a drink at the Boot Inn. They had exchanged letters during his time away, but there was still much to discuss. Although off-duty, Eric was in full uniform, and unlike Blackpool where RAF attire was as common as pink rock, heads turned in acknowledgement as he passed by, a gratifying experience for the young aircraftsman. He turned from Parkside into Liscard Road towards St John's Church, his meeting point with Len, and was surprised at what faced him. Even from this distance, the usual fresh face was absent, superseded by a drawn look, and as he drew closer, he could see dark rings under the eyes. His old pal looked a worried man.

'Eric...' shouted Len, his greeting lacking its usual vibrancy, enough to confirm that Len McCabe was not the man he had left behind.

'Len... how's it going?'

They shook hands and slapped one another's backs, but the handshake lacked the expected ferocity. Something was not right.

The pair chose to walk through Central Park, the conversation more a trickle than a flow, enabling Eric to take note of his surroundings, the trees with bare branches, the fields hardened by the winter climate, the skies a smudged grey. He had been surprised to find a claustrophobic edge to his home town and so welcomed these open spaces. When they reached the water fountain, unsurprisingly free from anybody stopping for a mouthful this cold January day, Eric turned around to see his brother walking towards them at a brisk pace.

'Eric! Eric!' he called.

'What's up Bill?'

'Where are you going?'

'The Boot... for a pint.'

'Can I come?'

He felt for his younger brother. He was on the way to manhood, getting taller by the day and earning a living from full time work, but he was still only fourteen. He would have a few more years yet before the smooth silk of pale ale, mild or stout passed his lips.

'I'm sorry Bill... they won't let you in.'

'They might.'

'They won't... they'll get in trouble if they did.'

'Oh... alright then.'

Billy turned dejectedly to head home, Eric experiencing sadness out of kilter with the substance of their exchanges. The pair had spent plenty of time together when young, but the passing years had seen them drift apart, the war in the guise of Bridgnorth and the RAF cementing the division. The request to join him for a drink seemed an attempt to bridge this gap, but the licensing laws had intervened to scupper Billy's efforts.

The bar at the Boot was quiet with just a few old drinkers supping pints in a corner. Nonetheless, Eric's uniformed presence still generated an enthusiastic reaction, the barman even offering a drink on the house. The RAF man insisted on paying his way and sensed Len's disappointment at this principled response. The friends took their pints to sit at a small table close to the bar.

'How's Margaret?' said Eric, expertly leaving a rim of froth on his upper lip from the first sip.

'Fine thanks.'

That was it. The old Len would have launched into a catch up of everything going on, but not today. As Eric contemplated the right words to ask, Len talked.

'I've got some news Eric.'

The tone was sombre. He had evidently not found a five pound note on the pavement.

'What news?'

'I'm finishing at Lairds next week… I've been called up by the Navy.'

'I thought you were in a reserved occupation.'

'Only if the employer says so… the Navy asked if I was essential and they said no. So I'm on my way.'

'I see.'

'The trouble is…'

Adopting a confessional stance was not the norm, Len clearly struggling to keep a lid on the demons in his head. Yet Eric was overcome by a compulsion to help. It was the Christian thing to do.

'What's the trouble Len?'

'I can't believe I'm saying this... what with poor bastards killed every day of the week out there fighting....'

'Go on...'

'I shouldn't... you know, but... I don't want to...'

His words trailed off. He didn't need to say anymore. This was it, the cause of his subdued manner.

Eric tried to reason, 'That's quite normal...'

'I've read the papers,' he interrupted, 'those convoys in the Atlantic and Mediterranean, they're bloody death traps.'

Eric recalled Mrs Kay's son lost at sea, Len's anxieties earning immediate resonance, but he discarded the thought immediately.

'Listen Len, they're not going to throw you straightaway on board a ship that's part of an Atlantic convoy. I know from the RAF you'll start with months of training, when you'll be marching and running in your sleep. Then they'll cram your head with theories, practical stuff, all manner of things. And only when you're fully equipped to operate on active service will they post you to a ship's crew, by which time we might have won the war. Did you read about the German defeat to the Russians in Stalingrad? A few of the papers think it a very significant moment.'

'I suppose you've got a point there.'

His reasoning was getting through.

'Of course I have. You need to be trained to deal with what comes your way. And they'll train you.'

After a few more exchanges, Len's old spirit began to shine through, and they were soon reminiscing about the past like a couple of old codgers. They were both incredulous at their Bridgnorth exploits back in 1941, cycling nearly two hundred miles in the type of weather Noel Coward reserved for Englishmen and mad dogs. As he listened to an anecdote from his friend he had heard many times before but always enjoyed, Eric deliberated on the fear expressed by Len. He had outwardly said what most other men thought but were too frightened to say out loud for fear of being branded a coward or traitor. He himself was always likely to keep his anxieties under lock and key, but he admired Len for his honesty. And the outpouring had done the trick, colour now flooding his cheeks, his eyes shining again as he talked of his engagement to Margaret whom he planned to marry when time permitted.

'Congratulations pal, she's a lovely girl.'

'You're not wrong there Eric lad. Cheers!'

'Cheers.'

Len downed the rest of his pint in affirmation of this conclusion before wiping his mouth, leaning back in his chair, and asking the question that Eric part-dreaded.

'What about you and Vera? What's happened?'

'Well,' said Eric, finishing his own drink to buy a little time, 'we're having afternoon tea tomorrow.'

'Look pal,' he glanced around the pub as if a German spy might be listening, 'I don't want to tread on your toes, but she's too good to lose you know.'

'Oh I know... I know.'

The trouble was he didn't know.

There were butterflies in Eric's stomach, as he stood outside the tea shop on Seaview Road waiting for Vera. Peeping through the glass with its 'Afternoon Tea' sign hanging at a slightly skewed angle, he observed most tables full, though an empty one by the window offering most privacy. Despite the rumble of cars and buses, he heard the click of high heels on the pavement and swivelled round to see Vera, her clothes more makeshift than before, but her walk still conveying the elegance of a Parisian model. His nerves were understandable. He had not seen her for over six months and was unsure as to how their meeting would go. Part of him was ready for an earful.

'Away for six months Eric Whitfield and only one letter! And what a letter that was, all about marching and running, running and marching! Call yourself a boyfriend. You're a disgrace, with no consideration for anyone else in this world other than yourself.'

As it was, and as he had suspected deep down, she was warm and cordial.

'Hello there,' she said, 'and how are you?'

'Fine thank you… and you?'

'Not too bad.'

'Shall we go inside?'

He opened the door, holding out his arm for Vera to enter ahead of him, a subdued bell ringing to announce their arrival. Without consulting, she chose the table that Eric had picked out, where the couple sat down to read the menu. There was not a great choice, but they did have the luxury of damson jam, and so they both ordered tea and scones.

'You look very well,' she said, straightening out her clothes. 'And you've lost a bit of weight.'

'They work you hard in the RAF.'

'I can see that.'

He launched into a dry account of the cross country exertions, the beach runs, and the assault courses, repeating the mistakes of his letter, yet he was powerless to stop. The subject matter was safe ground, a refuge from the more difficult themes and questions. The waitress, her grey hair escaping from what resembled a cut-down papal mitre, arrived to end the dull prose. Struggling with a full tray, Eric had to be quick to lend a hand and stop the tea and scones dropping to the floor.

Eric acted as 'mother'.

'So how are things going for you?' he said, at long last demonstrating some interest in his fellow diner.

It was Vera's turn to talk, portraying an account of mundanity, of making do, of people getting on with their lives. Although the air raid sirens continued to howl on a regular basis in response to the Luftwaffe setting their navigation aids for the coast of Blighty, it had been over eighteen months since the last shell dropped on local soil. Yet Vera's disquiet was evident, talking about a desire to do more when she reached her twentieth birthday, the age of conscription for single women. Her mother's ill-health was a stumbling block, but she still harboured hopes of joining the WAAF or the WRNS.

Eric looked down at his plate, empty except for a few crumbs, and at his cup with its usual residue of tea at the bottom. Vera, on the other hand, had barely started. The conversation switched to Margaret and Len, their compatibility, and the news about their engagement. Eric was finally relaxing into their exchanges, when Vera surprised him with a direct question.

'Why didn't you write?'

'Sorry?'

'Why didn't you write?'

'I did.'

'One letter?'

She did not look at Eric as she spoke, concentrating instead on cutting her scone and spreading a delicate portion of jam on each slice. He laboured to defend himself with talk of the difficulties faced when away in such a different world, but he knew the explanation was tenuous. If he wasn't convinced, how could Vera feel any different? He put down his cup, looked out on to the street, and spoke quietly, grateful for the seclusion of their table.

'I met a girl in Blackpool called Kitty...'

Vera recoiled, and he knew immediately his choice of words had been unfortunate.

'No, no, nothing like that,' he said, resuming his stare out of the window. 'She was a WAAF who volunteered when her boyfriend joined the RAF to become a pilot. I heard the other day he'd been killed in a training accident. She's now a widow at nineteen...'

'Oh dear...'

The sound of a spoon striking the insides of a china cup filled the void that followed.

He continued, 'I've noticed most of the other RAF lads have this attitude of indestructibility... "it'll never happen to me"... "I'm going to live forever"... but me?'

He picked up his cup and swilled the remaining tea around with a gentle movement of his hand.

'... I can't think like that. When I start operations, I'll be praying to God before every mission knowing full well it might be my last...'

'Please don't talk like that Eric.'

He turned around and looked straight into her violet eyes, eyes that had softened.

'It's the reality of war Vera. There are no certainties. It just seems wrong to subject anybody to the constant worry of receiving that dreaded telegram.'

He poured himself another cup of tea and swigged it down like a thirsty navvy. There was silence for a short while, until Vera spoke.

'I understand...' she said, leaning forward and kissing him on the cheek. 'I understand... goodbye Eric... and good luck.'

She rose from her chair, grabbed her coat, and placed a florin on the table.

'No, I insist.'

He handed the coin back to her, which she grasped, reluctantly. And after one final intense but impenetrable gaze into his eyes, she left the tea rooms, the same puny doorbell sound signalling her departure.

231

CHAPTER 23

Mr Butler drew near, his hair newly greased.

'Whitfield... my office.'

A reprimand was on the cards for the young clerk, now trailing respectfully behind as he was ushered into the spacious room by the manager. The silence inside was unexpected, the walls and glass thick enough to mute the sound of typewriters, comptometers and adding machines. Mr Butler's chair, set at a height that towered above the visitor's seat in front of his desk, enabled him to speak down to his staff in both the physical and figurative sense.

'You're not like your brother are you?' he said, puffing on a pipe that rested in the corner of his mouth, a pillow of smoke rising slowly towards the high ceiling.

Billy didn't answer the question, instead looking around the room, his eyes fixing on a row of metal filing cabinets, army green in colour with small beige labels above brass handles.

The manager continued, a great, big draw on his pipe followed by smoke billowing out of his nostrils like a cartoon dragon.

'Let me help you out with a few facts. I've been checking your brother's records and between his start in September 1938 to his leaving date last July, do you know how many times he was late?'

Billy didn't have a clue but knew not to guess.

'I will give you the answer... never... not once.'

He sucked on his pipe to allow time for Billy to digest this impressive statistic before switching to the third person approach.

'So what about William Edgar Whitfield, how many times since 27th July 1942 has he been late for work?'

Billy again knew to stay quiet.

'I'll tell you something,' resumed Butler, staring over half-moon spectacles with menace, 'it's easier to count the times he's arrived on time. Once? Twice? Who knows? But I'll tell you one thing, I wouldn't need more than these to count.'

He held up a palm with five outstretched fingers.

'This is simply not good enough Whitfield. Your timekeeping is appalling and unacceptable. My father had a saying, "punctuality is next to godliness", and he was not wrong.'

Billy wanted to contradict him, believing the expression was "cleanliness is next to godliness", much safer ground for Billy. He might be late on a regular basis, but he was always well-scrubbed. However, he avoided any insubordination by sensibly remaining silent.

Mr Butler then nervously flattened his greasy hair to an equally greasy scalp before locating a file on top of his pending tray and saying, 'I must inform you Whitfield that I am placing a record of this interview on your file and hereby warn that it may be used for future reference. Now, do you have anything to say?'

He didn't and returned to his desk feeling lucky to still have a job.

One o'clock and the now daily visit to the Liverpool Boy's Lunch Hour Club in Williamson Square could not come quickly enough. The soup and bread were an especially comforting combination today, washing away the bitter taste left by his dressing down earlier in the morning. And he really enjoyed the tiddlywinks football, and the shove ha'penny, winning at both, although he lost his frame of snooker. For all too brief a time, the drudgery of the workplace disappeared.

He was about to go back when the supervisor at the boy's club, 'Baldy'

Crompton, made an announcement about plans for Easter.

'Can you gather round boys? I have some news.'

Keen eyes shone beneath small, round spectacles, perfecting his unwitting portrayal of a mad scientist. Billy's final tiddlywinks football match was halted, the young club members bunching together to listen to what Baldy had to say.

'Some of you may be aware that in Lord Street there is another lunch time club.'

Billy wasn't.

'This,' said Baldy, 'is the Liverpool Girl's Lunch Hour Club.'

Girls?

'And we have decided to come together for an Easter dance, and you are all invited.'

Dancing? And girls? Billy was interested… and so were the other lads. All of a sudden, tiddlywinks football had lost its appeal. The final game was postponed.

Arriving back at the office he checked the clock, thankful to see there were five seconds to go before the two o'clock chimes, a relief compounded when Mr Butler opened his door to peer in his direction. Billy's attention returned to the large batch of invoices on one side of his desk. He had already spent a few hours trying to reconcile these documents to a ledger entry and was out of balance by £60. He added and re-added the batch, still unable to find the difference. Reluctantly, he stood up and approached Mr Butler's office, knocking on the door.

'Come in,' the manager shouted.

The man in charge didn't try to disguise his scorn when he saw it was Billy.

'Yes Whitfield, what is it?'

At least his earlier anger had been replaced by something more wearied, removing much of the intimidation.

'It's this batch,' he said, holding up the offending documents. 'I can't get them to balance. They're out £60.'

'Right,' said Butler, getting up from his chair. 'Follow me young man.'

The official was taking the bull by the horns, showing the junior how it should be done. He sat in Billy's seat and started checking the tally roll against the invoices.

Halfway through the task, he let out an exclamation. 'That's it... there's your £60. You've added that one as £10 and it should be £70.'

He showed Billy the culprit. It was a document handwritten by the manager himself.

'But doesn't that say £10 Mr Butler?'

'No! It doesn't!' said Mr Butler indignantly. 'Miss Graham, can you come here a moment?'

'Yes Mr Butler?' said Edna, her attractive face casting an encouraging glance in Billy's direction.

'How much is that invoice for?'

She examined the paper.

'I'd say £10.'

He grabbed it back.

'Of course it isn't, that's a seven not a one.'

'In fairness, your sevens do tend to look like ones,' she said, again flashing a momentary smile at Billy.

Butler was in a corner, trapped, and there was no escape.

'Never mind... let's all get back to work.'

It was a small victory for Billy but an important one, all thanks to Edna's intervention. He went home that day feeling better about work than he had expected.

****

235

It was Easter Saturday, two days before Billy's fifteenth birthday, and the Liverpool Boys and Girls Dinner Hour Club Dance was taking place. He had not rested on his laurels since Baldy Crompton's announcement of the event, organising a few ballroom lessons at Sexton's in New Brighton. The dance was close to the city centre in a church hall, either side of which bombed-out buildings starkly demonstrated the fickleness of fortune. Billy was one of the last to enter the good-sized room in which a violin, piano and drums trio were set up on a small, raised platform ready to provide the entertainment. The boy and girl tribes had already separated into two distinct groups, the males lined up against a wall where tea was being served, the females on a dangerous looking dance floor of wooden planks and protruding nails. This alarmed Billy. After getting used to Sexton's French polished surface, this rough and ready version was likely to create mayhem for his newly learnt footwork.

The band started playing the usual mix of Victor Sylvester numbers, with Glen Miller and the Andrews Sisters playing no part in the repertoire, just as well for a novice like Billy. The prospects of a dance that involved throwing a partner over your head and catching her on the way down would have taken ambition to the extreme. He was happy to stick to the waltz, the quickstep and the foxtrot, or at least variations on these staples.

The girls, handbags on the floor at their feet, were dancing in a circle, but the lads remained fixtures at the side, gawping helplessly at the females. It was going to take a courageous male to make the first move, one that risked humiliation if spurned when asking for a dance. This was not going to be Billy, and he was silently thankful to see one lad break ranks and successfully negotiate the hand of the prettiest girl in the room.

Billy finished his tea and returned the cup to its saucer. He glanced around to see a growing number of boys and girls waltzing and one girl on her own, swaying along watching the others. He didn't hesitate and walked

236

purposefully towards her.

'I'm Billy, would you like to dance?' he said, mustering as much charm and self-assurance, clearly uncomfortable bedfellows, as he could.

'Thank you,' she replied. 'I'm Irene...'

She was a shy, petite blonde, Billy fervently hoping her confidence would transform when they started dancing, and she didn't let him down. The musical trio were playing a foxtrot, a challenge for any novice, but his diminutive partner led him better than Mrs Sexton, and he quickly relaxed into a kind of daydream. The soft skin of Irene's hand, the firmness of her back, the brush of their bodies against one another, conspired to create moments of wonder and joy. Moving around the room with ease, he enjoyed another dance with her, before she exchanged partners, Billy doing likewise to enjoy a quickstep.

A short while later he was sat down and enjoying another cup of tea as the trio and dancing continued in full flow. He recalled his crush on Rita in Bridgnorth, but this was different. He was not religious like Eric, but today he knew how Adam felt. He had discovered Eve.

CHAPTER 24

Eric's next destination, RAF Innsworth on the outskirts of Gloucester, had opened early in the war as No 7 School of Technical Training, specialising in courses for engine and airframe fitters and mechanics. By 1943 it had expanded to incorporate the Record Office relocated from London, a fully equipped RAF hospital, and No 2 WAAF depot providing Recruit and Trade training for female personnel. The station roll call had grown to reach over 4,000.

The geography of the area was in stark contrast to Blackpool. In place of the sea, the beach, the promenade and the guest houses, there were green fields, open spaces, and hundreds of wooden billets. The huts covered the whole of the site and extended far beyond the eye line, Eric unlucky to be based in one some distance from the ablution blocks and bathhouse. The experience was more like Filey but with the discipline a few notches down, the informality of staying in digs with Mrs Kay having toned down the exposure to the rigidity and regulation of air force life. The return to an RAF base with its boundaries and guards served to heighten his isolation from the everyday world, though it did facilitate a focus for his studies. This included practical training and theory tutorials, many a repetition and reinforcement of things learnt at Blackpool. Within a few months, he could strip a radial aircraft engine, rebuild it, and run a successful test. Unlike wireless operations and the dreaded Morse code, flight mechanics was a subject for which he had a greater natural aptitude. All in all, he was now far more optimistic about making the grade.

Leave passes, although more commonplace than at Blackpool, remained difficult to obtain. Even when granted, it created a challenge for Eric to get home in good time before having to plan his return journey. Consequently, he made it back to Wallasey just once in the five months based there. He also had to face the disappointment of missing the 1943 Cheltenham Gold Cup, a cancelled event he had planned to attend. Yet it wasn't a case of 'all work and no play makes Jack a dull boy'. The place was teeming with WAAFs, and so female company was never a problem, some of his course mates taking things a bit further. Eric relented. He and Vera may have gone their separate ways, but the bombardment of warnings by his seniors about the dangers of venereal disease kept a lid on such extra-curricular adventures. He remained happy to be the friendly AC2 who played the piano when it came to a singsong.

On the day of Eric's final examinations in May, rumours filtered through of a successful mission by the Avro Lancasters of 617 Squadron to destroy a number of German dams. News of the accomplishment provided a timely boost and helped relax the nervous trainee. The exam consisted of written papers and an oral test in which various parts of an engine had to be identified, piston pins, connecting rods, front ball bearing, crankshaft, muffler, full throttle needle, engine mount, intake manifold and - guaranteed to create a snigger from the youngest trainees - breather nipple. There had been a few tricky moments, but he felt more chipper than after the wireless exam last January. And he had good reason. His mark improved to 68%, passing out of RAF Innsworth with a promotion. He was now AC1 Eric Norman Whitfield, a First Class Aircraftsman, proficient in the understanding of airframes, carburettors, magnetos, electrics, instruments, Merlin engines, radial engines, in-line engines, hydraulics, propellers, and aerodrome procedures.

Delighted with his new competencies, new status, and new rate of pay, he received confirmation of a transfer to RAF No. 4 School of Technical Training at St Athan near Cardiff, the service's one specialist unit for flight engineers. Such was the volume of men being trained, there was a month's wait before Eric could start the course. This was the RAF, and so the logical step of extended leave was ignored. Allowed home for a mere few days, he was recalled to spend the rest of the time based at the recently formed Air Army Corps in Middle Wallop, Hampshire, shadowing the maintenance and engineering crew looking after the RAF aircraft supporting the Glider Pilot Regiment. For a few weeks, Eric was effectively in the army, although finally in the middle of July, he was dispatched to St Athan.

****

Eric was more than impressed with No. 4 School of Technical Training. The place was vast and his first training base that had an actual runway with real aircraft taking off and landing. There was an east camp, a west camp, a dummy runway to fool the enemy, giant hangars, brick-built workshops, equipment stores, and a large amenities building with swimming pool, cinema, chapels, and gymnasium. This was impressive enough, but there was still enough room to house the living accommodation for over four thousand instructors and trainees, the billets a step up from the usual, each having their own latrine and showers.

'Awrite, mah name's Dougie McVitie.'

The voice may have been stereotypically Glaswegian, but the look of its owner was quite the opposite, dark hair, dark eyes, and olive skin an unusual partner to the dialect.

'Eric Whitfield.'

They shook hands, Eric continuing to place his clothes and belongings carefully into his locker. Dougie was in the next bed.

'Thes is a braw place dornt ye think?'

'Definitely.'

Eric wasn't too sure of the question, but he gave a confident answer.

'Ah bit ye ur thinkin' Ah dornt look Scottish?'

'Well, I erm...'

Eric didn't want to offend.

'Mah faither is Maltese... Mario... he feel in love wi' a Scots lassie, mah mammy.'

'Mario McVitie?'

'His surname was Vitti, sae he jist added the Mac.'

Dougie was a clear indication of the RAF casting its net ever wider to recruit servicemen, his broad accent the antithesis of the 'plum in the mouth' Eric had expected to find everywhere.

'Where have you been transferred from?' said Eric.

'Nowhaur, I've been haur.'

Unless 'nowhaur' was some remote Scottish outpost, Eric assumed he meant nowhere, and that he had done the preliminary and intermediate sections of the flight engineer's course here at St Athan.

'So you must know your way around this place then.'

'Aye... don't panic mucker, Dougie'll shaw ye th' ropes.'

The Glaswegian with the Mediterranean good looks then joined Eric in unpacking and filling his locker.

Following a brief induction and tour for those new to the camp, the trainees met up to discover the aircraft chosen as their specialism. The three options were the Short Stirling, the Handley Page Halifax, and the Avro Lancaster. Eric recalled the exchanges with Wing Commander Thompson at RAF Cardington about the new bomber that was going to win the war. This had indeed turned out to be the Lancaster, and everything seen and heard since had reinforced Eric's desire to work on it. To be allocated to a Stirling or Halifax would be a major disappointment.

Eric heard a list of names that included 'McVitie' and ended with 'Whitfield'.

241

'You chaps will work on the Avro Lancaster.'

Eric was delighted that fortune was on his side, and he celebrated with Dougie and the others by retiring to the dining room for a meal that didn't quite maintain the high standard of RAF cuisine, after which they ended the day in the cinema watching *For Whom the Bell Tolls* with Gary Cooper and Ingrid Bergman.

Dougie's verdict on the movie was unequivocal.

'It wisnae as good as th' book.'

Eric was surprised.

'You've read the book?'

'Aye, I've reid aw Hemingway's, though ah prefer *A Fareweel tae Arms* an' *Tae Hae an 'Huvnae.*'

'Ta?'

'*Tae Hae an 'Huvnae.*'

'Of course.'

Dougie sounded like a Clydeside docker but was certainly well read, and Eric soon discovered he was not just an expert on American novelists. He proved to be no slouch when it came to the Avro Lancaster.

****

By now it was apparent that the further Eric progressed in his training, the less severe the discipline he encountered. The standards at St Athan were as stringent as anywhere else, but the regime was distinctly more adult. The marching, the running, the inspections, the parade ground drills remained a constant, but the need for a bawling NCO to bully and cajole the men into shape had disappeared somewhere along the way. He had to concede that the training had worked. The enforced discipline from the early days had evolved into an effective form of self-discipline.

Enjoying a break in the billet, Eric read a few letters, including one from Reg Wilson, his friend from the days at Filey and Blackpool. Reg was now a qualified wireless operator for 78 Squadron at RAF Breighton in the East Riding of Yorkshire, assigned to a crew primed and waiting for their first operational sortie in a Halifax bomber. But for Eric's switch to flight engineer training, that could have been him, the thought inducing a reaction that was part envy, part reprieve. Reg's letter finished with two pronouncements. After getting a special leave pass, he had returned home to marry Gwen, an enclosed black and white wedding photograph portraying the occasion as far from ostentatious, Reg in uniform, Gwen in a simple dress carrying a small posy. The second piece of news confirmed that number one child was on its way. Reg Wilson, the Ludlow wonder, was certainly a man of action.

'Let's go an' gie close tae a real aircraft,' said Dougie, suddenly jumping to an upright position from his bed.

'Aye,' said Eric, slightly concerned that one week with his Scottish counterpart was already impacting on his own accent and vocabulary.

It was time for the trainees to visit the tethered airframe of a Wellington bomber, testing the engine at full throttle. The noise was deafening, Eric taken aback by the power of the mechanical marvel before him. And this was the Wellington, now supplanted by the majesty of the four engine bomber. Eric exchanged a knowing glance with Dougie, noting that the Scotsman was equally awestruck. They moved next to a salvaged cockpit to simulate the environment of pre-flight checks, take-off, in flight duties, and landing. He was still yet to fly for real, but this hands-on experience was emphatically whetting his appetite. The thought of Reg at 78 Squadron was now weighted heavily in favour of envy rather than reprieve.

The final lesson of the day was a study of the Lancaster's instrument panel, each trainee preparing their own diagram of the controls, switches, dials, levers and regulators. Eric's drawing was unsurprisingly flawless in

243

terms of scale, perspective and legibility, Dougie's messy in comparison, though the man knew his stuff and was able to answer any question about the workings of the aircraft. He was by some way the star pupil, even if the tutor required regular Scottish to English translations.

After dinner, Eric and Dougie ambled to the St Athan theatre to watch the BBC Symphony Orchestra in concert, the ensemble having relocated from the capital due to the Blitz.

Striding past one of the large Bellman hangars, Dougie said to Eric, 'Dae ye ken whit th' orchestra will play tonecht?'

'Not sure... something classical I suppose.'

'It's nae a question. I ken th' answer... they ur playin' Elgar's *Pomp an' Circumstance.*'

'Elgar?'

'Aye, but it's nae a patch on *Enigma Variations* or his *Second Symphony.*'

Dougie was at it again, surprising Eric with the depth of his knowledge, this time in music. They crossed the road to the wide pavement running alongside the amenities building, a red brick structure with a stone entrance shaped like the letter 'M'. Inside, its interior lacked the ornate features of the typical provincial theatre or picture house, but the auditorium was a good size and had seating for a few hundred, enough to accommodate the RAF servicemen and WAAFs looking to entertainment as a means of relaxation or escape.

Dougie dragged Eric to a couple of empty seats near the front, a short distance away from the orchestra members already in position. The house lights lowered as the lead violinist walked on to the stage, quickly followed by the conductor, a mad professor archetype, the audience no doubt trusting that the music man had more control over the strings, woodwind, brass and percussion than his hair.

Pomp and Circumstance began with gusto, Eric startled to see two flailing arms conducting the piece in wild abandon. Regrettably, the limbs belonged to Dougie McVitie. Elgar's trademark ability to compose stirring and rousing music was backfiring spectacularly for those sat within the vicinity of the inspired Scotsman, now lost in a performing trance. He came within a whisker of landing a right hook on Eric's chin and nearly decapitated him with an elbow that jerked back and forth like a piston cased inside a Merlin engine. This was more boxing ring encounter than theatre concert, and in the end, Eric had to tap his colleague on the shoulder to calm him down. To the intense relief of Eric and those at one end of the second row, his conducting duties were duly suppressed for the remainder of the performance.

Walking back from the theatre, the warm breeze of a July evening gently brushing his face, Eric looked forward to something less dangerous than tonight's sparring match... perhaps a session in the decompression chamber or the parachute simulator. He had met some colourful characters during his time in the RAF, Reg Wilson and Fanny Kay springing to mind, yet nobody could match the sheer eccentricity and unpredictability of Dougie McVitie, the man with Maltese roots raised on the banks of the Clyde.

'Ah still think they shood hae played his *Second Symphony*.'

Not for the first time to time that evening, Eric had to dodge a flailing arm.

CHAPTER 25

A short while after Eric arrived at St Athan, the RAF enjoyed a real boost to its morale. Under the leadership of Arthur Harris and endorsed by Winston Churchill, Bomber Command stepped up its campaign to area bomb key German cities, the principal way Britain was taking the war into enemy territory. US Eighth Air Force planes joined the fray for the first time with daytime sorties, the RAF concentrating on night missions, and with the port of Hamburg selected as a primary target, four major raids were undertaken over the course of ten days, destroying much of the city. The home newspapers celebrated, declaring 'Hamburg is Target for More Than 2,500 Tons of Bombs'. Word spread within the base that the success was due to an initiative called 'windows', thousands of aluminium foil strips dropped to jam and neutralise German radar defences. The information bolstered Eric's inner judgment that he had chosen well in volunteering for the RAF.

A few days after the Hamburg raids, he was resting on his bed, pleased to have a free evening. Today had been a tiring one, the sessions physical. This had included a cross country run battling the humidity of a thunderstorm; decompression training to replicate the loss of oxygen at altitude; and parachute practice minus the aircraft, though thankfully not at 22,000 feet.

Dougie, who had only just got round to sorting his mail, handed him a letter.

'Ah think thes us yoor's. It's got mixed up wi' mine.'

'Thanks.'

The writing was a woman's hand. Eric held the envelope up to his nose, the faint scent providing another clue. He opened it and started to read.

Dear Eric,

Reg Wilson

It is with deep sadness and a heavy heart I write to inform that during a mission to Hamburg on Thursday 29th July, Reg's aircraft was shot down over the city. All crew members are missing, presumed dead. I am holding on to the faint hope he has survived and is now a Prisoner of War, but I have been told this is an unlikely scenario.

In his final letter, to be sent in the event of his death, he writes about you Eric. He says how much he admired your calm, considerate personality and how much he valued your friendship. Indeed, he looked back on Blackpool as the best time of his life. He also refers to your shared faith and asks if you would pray for the loved ones he leaves behind.

As you know, we were recently married, and although our time together was destined to be short, I feel blessed to have met and shared my life with a man as wonderful and full of 'joie de vivre' as Reg Wilson. Although I have enormous pride at the bravery shown by my husband, I hope you will forgive my inability to see his loss in the context of the war at the moment. I am still coming to terms with everything, and being two months pregnant, you will understand how this compounds my sorrow and makes it challenging to think straight.

I am so sorry to have to disclose this terrible news to you, but it serves as a reminder for us to keep Reg's flame flickering through our shared thoughts, memories and reminiscences.

May God protect you, Eric, in the days and months ahead.

I remain sincerely yours,

'Bloody hell...'

Eric didn't normally swear, but the expletive was involuntary in the light of the devastating news. The 'missing presumed dead' had to be interpreted as 'dead'. If Reg's aircraft had come down over the target, he'd have stood no chance, even if managing to parachute clear. The initial jubilation at the success of the Hamburg raids had been tempered by news of the devastating loss of life. The bombings had wreaked devastation on Germany's second largest city with a firestorm developing due to a lethal combination of high temperatures, dry weather, incendiaries, and bombs dropped. Reg would have fallen from the skies into a burning hell.

'Bad news?' said Dougie.

'Yes,' he replied, his eyes fixed on the bed frame as he struggled to assimilate the news. 'It's a pal from Filey and Blackpool... wireless operator in 78 Squadron... bought it over Hamburg... he was twenty one.'

'Ah Jesus Christ...'

Eric ignored the blasphemy. It was the least important thing. His head was a whirl as Dougie patted him on the back and left for the picture house. He re-read the letter in the ludicrous hope the words might say something different. Of course, they didn't. Reg Wilson, that irrepressible young man from Ludlow with the singing accent and fiery red hair had gone, forever, a man with so much ahead of him, with such a zest for life, a man in love. He thought of Gwen and leant across to his locker, locating a small bundle of photographs held together by an elastic band. He retrieved the snapshot from their wedding day. The first time he saw the image he had been struck by its everyday ordinariness. It hadn't appeared to be a wedding photo. Yet now the overriding perception from the picture was one of unabandoned joy, of two young lovers without a care in the world, happy to be together... till death us do part. Tragically, the parting came sooner than either had imagined.

A wave of pity washed over Eric at what might have been, indeed what should have been. There was a very good chance that Gwen, such a pretty and vibrant young woman herself with bounding vitality, would never be the same again. Then it occurred to him. This whole situation vindicated what had happened between him and Vera and was precisely the thing he wanted to avoid, a wife without a husband, a child without a father. He went to return the photograph to the elasticated bundle but stopped, placing it instead against a tumbler on top of his locker. He lay back down on his bed, head resting on the pillow, and stared at the apex ceiling of the billet.

Hamburg.

On hearing about the successful bombing raids, his reaction had been one of satisfaction, one of pride. His organisation, the RAF, and moreover, his section, Bomber Command, was making a real difference. The land armies and naval vessels were struggling to establish inroads into destroying the enemy, but the lads in the skies were truly showing the way. Reg's demise, however, had confirmed a change in his thinking. He tried to remove the image of the firestorm from his head but failed. There would have been many ordinary families in Hamburg that succumbed to the call of mortality the same night as Reg, and though he attempted to counter-balance these thoughts with recollections of the Liverpool Blitz, he found himself questioning the validity of his place in Bomber Command. Would he have the stomach for the fight?

He sat up on the edge of his bed and glanced around the billet, his only company Bob the Snorer, who true to form was asleep and making the noise of a foghorn. Eric stood up and left the hut for some fresh air. Walking past the rows of identikit accommodation and the sergeant's mess, he ended up alone in the parade ground and glanced up towards the heavens. The thunderstorm had done its job, the air now fresh, the sky clear, a faint twinkle of the first evening star visible to the eye. The solitude and peace helped unclutter his thinking. He could not allow the naturally strong emotions from losing a pal to impact on his attitude to the war in general. He remembered the chaplain in Filey answering Reg's pertinent questions about the legitimacy and ethics of warfare and recalled the answer from Ephesians.

'For we wrestle not against flesh and blood, but against principalities, against powers, against the rulers of the darkness of this world, against spiritual wickedness in high places.'

Adolf Hitler and his Nazi party were the current rulers of the darkness in this world, soaked in spiritual wickedness. The recollection served to remind him that many of the answers he sought were to be found in the bible. He returned to the billet to fetch his copy and then made his way across the camp to the amenities building.

The chapel inside the same building as the cinema was quieter than the billet with no Bob the Snorer to affect the seclusion. As with the auditorium, there was nothing lavish or elaborate about this place of worship, but it successfully purveyed an air of spirituality, aided by the lit candles flickering to the sides and in front of the modest altar. He walked to the front and kneeled down, closing his eyes to pray. The prayer was easy, the inspiration provided by Reg in his final letter.

As he stood up, he heard the door open. It was the chaplain.

'Good evening,' he said.

'Hello Padre.'

This was a typical church man, full of kindness, tolerance and benevolence, older than the average, but carrying off the necessary gravitas and holiness with ease.

'May I ask what brings you here at this time?'

'I heard today a good friend of mine has been killed in action.'

'I see.'

'In his final letter he asked if I would pray for those left behind... so that's what I've been doing.'

'That's very worthy of you. Your friend chose well.'

'Could we talk a little Padre?'

'Certainly... shall we sit on the front pew?'

Their positions at the front of an absent congregation and before a non-occupied lectern seemed a little strange but appropriate nonetheless. Eric took out the bible from his jacket pocket and opened it from the back, the hand-written page headed 'Warfare' displayed first.

'I started this when I was at Initial Training,' said Eric. 'I search the Holy Book for references to explain the conflicts and contradictions that war and fighting bring and then write them down. You can see helpful verses from Ephesians, Corinthians, Philemon, and Chronicles. But hearing today about Reg and thinking about the impact of our bombing campaign on ordinary families in Germany, I'm struggling to accept we're doing the right thing. What would be your advice Padre?'

'What's your name Sergeant?'

'Whitfield.'

'Christian name?'

'Eric.'

'Well Eric, I think the best thing to read is Corinthians Chapter 10. May I borrow your bible?'

Eric handed him the book which the chaplain flicked through until he found the page he was seeking. In common with every other vicar or church man he had met, the chaplain read from the Holy Book as though in St Paul's Cathedral, projecting his voice so that people at the back could hear.

For though we walk in the flesh, we do not war after the flesh, for the weapons of our warfare are not carnal, but mighty through God to the pulling down of strongholds, casting down imaginations and every high thing that exalteth itself against the knowledge of God.'

The chaplain closed the bible and returned it to his visitor.

'Thank you,' said Eric, sliding the book into his pocket.

'You see Eric, the fascism formulated and practised by Hitler and his Nazi Generals is that high thing that exalteth itself against God, and the real weapon used to fight this tyranny is not the gun or the bomb, but the might of God. Nobody in Bomber Command wants to kill civilians, the targets are military or industrial, and although it can and does happen, you have to remember that 'we do not war after the flesh'. God is on our side, your side Eric. I'm sure of it.'

'Thank you Padre... that's... very helpful.'

Eric left the chapel to return to the billet where Bob the Snorer had moved on to his repertoire of farmyard noises. Eric retrieved his black and red pens from his locker and sat up in bed. He re-opened his bible at the handwritten 'Warfare' pages and proceeded to copy Corinthians 10 Chapters 3, 4, and 5 under a heading called 'The Means of Warfare.'

Once complete, he lay on his bed and closed his eyes, thinking of Reg and wondering about his last seconds. He hoped that death had been instantaneous, flying one moment and blown to Kingdom Come the next. If crash landing, he wondered what might have gone through his head but quickly discarded the deliberation. It was all too close to home for comfort. And then, quite suddenly, a rage towards the enemy grew from within. He didn't need a bible passage to come to terms with the morality of warfare. The Nazis were the aggressors and the sole reason why the remnants of Wireless Operator Reg Wilson were now scattered over Northern Germany, leaving behind a litany of grief in its wake. He vowed to commit this moment to an indelible section of his memory, to be recalled in an instant when required, branded until his dying day. He would throw himself into his RAF training with renewed vigour. This war with its madness and destruction had to end. Area bombing was a key strategy in defeating the enemy. At the very least, he would do it for Reg, the friend he would never see again but whose voice would play through his head, as much a guiding light as the Lord... a saviour with a countryside twang.

****

Mid way through the course at St Athan, the soon-to-be flight engineers were sent to the factories building the bombers. The Avro works were generally in the north west of the country, and so the Lancaster trainees were dispatched to Woodford Aerodrome near Stockport. Eric and Dougie stayed in a somewhat posh detached house off Woodford Road, from where they caught the bus to the factory on the first morning. The main works were housed in a gigantic, hangar-sized structure brightly illuminated by natural light streaming through the glass panels of its vast roof and through its windows running the full length of the building. It would have been an impressive spectacle if empty, but with rows of aircraft under construction, it was nothing short of awe-inspiring.

Eric's first glimpse of a Lancaster had been at St Athan, when he had not quite appreciated its bulk from his position on the other side of the airfield. Astride this factory floor, however, he could see the aircraft was an absolute colossus. And there was more than one, probably near thirty. A visiting flight engineer called Jessop greeted Eric and Dougie. He was to be their guide around the four engine bomber.

The trio paced across the factory floor and climbed a ladder to a portable inspection platform to be confronted by a gigantic starboard wing and one of its Merlin engines, each blade on the giant propeller taller than the average man. Walking down narrow planks to inspect other parts of the aircraft, Eric was struck by the machine's ability to reconcile two mutually exclusive factors. The Lancaster was incredibly robust yet aesthetically exquisite. His friend agreed.

'I'll teel ye somethin' fur free...' said Dougie to Jessop, 'she's a beauty an' a beest.'

He was not wrong... a beauty and a beast.

'Shall we take a look inside?' said Jessop, a well-spoken, jaunty man with natural enthusiasm.

'Aye...'

They were taken to a part of the factory lined with completed bombers and duly climbed into the main fuselage of one through its rear door. In terms of dimensions, the interior was a different story from the outside with cramped and restricted conditions. To reach the front, they had to duck as they stepped over the top of the bomb bay and then crawl past the front wing spars, a task not far removed from an obstacle course. For over eighteen months, Eric had been bombarded with information pertinent to serving as an aircraftsman, but at no stage had there been any clue as to these constraints. It was a sobering moment, imagining a fully crewed flight and having to manoeuvre through such tight confines to locate an escape hatch and parachute to safety.

When they reached the main cockpit, Eric was surprised at the expanse of the Perspex canopy, one that provided superb visibility from all angles. Those new to the aircraft would have been mesmerised by the instrument panel, a complex array of dials, switches and levers, but this was a section he knew well from training. His note books had many hand-drawn incarnations of the layout before his eyes, although seeing it within the context of the overall flying machine was still an exhilarating sight. He gazed at the pilot's raised seat on the port side and at the adjoining space where he would sit as flight engineer, as good as flying the plane in many ways. It was some piece of engineering this Avro Lancaster.

They heard a noise from behind. Someone was joining them on board.

'Excuse me.'

It was a female voice.

'Ah jist need tae replace a fuse.'

A Scottish female voice.

Dougie moved quickly to investigate. Eric heard his greeting, even broader than his normal inflection.

'Awrite quine, aam Dougie frae Glasgee.'

'Aam Margery, th' electrician.'

Eric and Jessop exchanged amused looks and moved through the fuselage towards the bomb aimer's position whilst the two Scots took up in animated conversation about their capital city. Dougie had a few rough edges to his personality, but his Mediterranean good looks were his saving grace, Margery already falling for him. She was more of a Celtic archetype, pale skin, blue eyes, and a red tinge to her blonde hair, attractive in her own right. Her clothes, utilitarian and practical, did her no favours, but Eric was bowled over by the sight of this pretty girl in overalls working on the electrics of such an engineering marvel. Before the war, such an image would have been inconceivable. It made him think of his last conversation with Vera in the tea shop when she had talked about her own frustrations of wanting to do more to help the war effort. At the time, he hadn't really appreciated the point, but now he could see it.

It was time to disembark for a lesson on 'fuel', although not before Dougie had arranged to meet up with Margery for a trip to the cinema.

Late the following evening, Dougie and Eric were on the way home to their digs, the streets dark and quiet, the evening warm, calm, contrasting with the unsettled weather prevalent during the previous few days.

'Aam sorry mucker,' said Dougie.

He took out some minor frustrations by kicking a small stone from the pavement into the gutter. The night had ended in disappointment for him, notably due to the guardian accompanying Margery to the pictures.

'That's alright pal.'

Eric's magnanimity did him credit. He would have been within his rights to give his friend 'down the banks' for arranging a double date with Margery and her 'friend' who had turned out to be her chaperoning mother.

'Ne'er mind. I've got 'er name an' address, sae Ah can write tae 'er.'

Dougie's disconsolate reaction suggested he was normally successful in such pursuits, a case of 'you can take the boy out of the Mediterranean, but you can't take the Mediterranean out of the boy'.

The attacker came out of the blue, jumping on Dougie and punching him to the ground. Before Eric had time to react, the Scot was kicked a couple of times before the aggressor turned into a silhouette disappearing into the dark of night and shouting 'Bloody I'tie' as he ran away. Dougie had been mistaken for an Italian. Yet the unprovoked assault was perplexing. Why would someone from Italy be walking down a Woodford street dressed in RAF uniform?

'Are you alright Dougie?'

He sat up and wiped blood from the side of his mouth.

'Aye… the bastard.'

'Do you need this?'

Eric offered a handkerchief.

'Thanks mucker.'

Eric became indignant about the whole Italian issue, but Dougie cut him off.

'At wisnae abit Italy. He was Margery's boyfriend.'

'Her boyfriend?'

'Aye.'

'Then why…'

'She only tauld me afar…'

At least it explained why Margery had brought her mother. It was a tough lesson for Dougie and his lothario ways, but he'd bounce back, no doubt. In fact, he had already dusted himself down, ready to resume his walk.'

'Aye,' he said, 'I've got 'er name an' address, sae Ah can write tae 'er.'

Dougie was not a man to give up.

CHAPTER 26

It had been his brother's idea. Home a few weeks before, Eric had noticed Billy at a loose end and suggested he try visiting a youth club. Seacombe Methodists on Brighton Street was the obvious choice and had since become the highlight of his week. The venue was a standard hall attached to a chapel with brick walls, hard floors, and a spacious main area with a high domed ceiling into which all voices created an echo. On the inside, close to a door leading to the kitchen, a group of chairs were positioned around two tables joined together as one. Tonight it was a Beetle Drive.

Billy was sitting next to his friends, Johnny Williams and Ronnie Rose, and opposite raven-haired identical twins, Norma and Eileen, both attired in the same grey dresses, shoes, and hair ribbons. Their slightly dreary appearance, as ever encumbered by clothes rationing, was in direct contrast to their natural demeanours that were lively, even vivacious, the sisters adding a spark to a game that involved only paper, pencils and dice. Johnny and Ronnie were equally sprightly, with quick, keen minds and friendly dispositions. In his short time at the club, they had become his best friends. Billy Whitfield, the young man who learned to be independent during his time in Bridgnorth, was breaking out of his previous, solitary world.

Billy threw the dice.

'Oh no…' he moaned.

It was a five. He needed a six to draw the beetle's body and get his insect creation underway. The other players already had a body, a few legs, a head, and the odd eye, but his paper was blank. The dice went around the table until his go again.

'Come on Bill,' said Johnny, 'give it a good shake.'

He cupped the dice within two closed palms and blew through the gap between his thumbs, shaking it like an overexcited Brazilian playing the maracas. It did the trick.

'Six!'

He was off the mark. He could draw the body.

A few rounds later, he had caught up with the others, his beetle shaping up nicely, not just in terms of the requisite parts, but in its artistic appearance. Billy's wasn't just a squiggle of a wing or an antennae, he pencilled in the outline before adding in shading and detail. His creation was taking shape as a piece of art in itself. In the end, Billy was pipped by Norma, or it may have been Eileen, when needing just a front leg, but his beetle had stolen the show, and he was asked to finish it.

'Can you draw people?' said Ronnie with a flash of his permanent, broad smile.

'I've never tried.'

'What about me?'

'Alright Ron, let's have a go.'

Ronnie Rose was a little older than Billy, his features more adult, his razor blade already in active use. He was a good model for Billy's first portrait and willingly swivelled his chair to one side to give the new artist a side profile to sketch. It was a tad easier than the beetle, not requiring a six to start for a kick-off, and even when Johnny with his brushed back hair and healthy complexion stood behind to assess the work as it progressed, he was not distracted.

He handed the finished drawing to Ronnie.

'There you are.'

His friend assimilated the results, and for the briefest of seconds his grin faded, yet he was quick to recover.

'I can definitely see it looks like me,' he said, failing to suppress a modicum of disappointment, as though he had expected Gary Cooper and had been given Will Hay.

Billy's creation was a caricature of his pal, the forehead protruding excessively, the nose twice its actual size, the chin correspondingly diminished. Yet it was him alright, and the others thought it was great.

'What about drawing the girls?' suggested Ronnie, his magnanimous smile reappearing.

'Do Norma first,' said Eileen without hesitation.

Her sister's expression was blank but gave Billy his first clue as to which twin was which. His latest model had a small scar on the left side of her forehead. He made a note.

Norma took to the role of Billy's artistic muse with less natural enthusiasm than Ronnie, and she had good cause. Johnny took up the same position behind the artist but this time let out an occasional nervous grunt. The others soon found out why. The twins were pretty girls, dainty featured, with smooth, pale skin and full heads of hair. Unfortunately, Billy's sketch of Norma had echoes of the Wicked Witch of the West. Her button nose had grown like Pinocchio's, distorting into a crooked form, and the minor scar near her temple had been exaggerated to something from *Lady Frankenstein*. Billy had a talent for drawing, a talent for drawing the male gender. As for the fairer sex, a commission to paint the Queen of England was a distant proposition.

Ronnie, sensing the potential damage to their relationship with the girls, wasted no time in creating a diversion.

'Anyone for table tennis?'

This was safer ground, Norma and Eileen choosing to watch rather than play. First match was between Ronnie and Billy, an opportunity for the latter to flaunt his playing technique, which involved grasping the handle of the bat as though a fountain pen. It looked the part, and

Ronnie's conventional grip seemed to hand over the initiative to his innovating opponent.

The game started well for Billy, winning serve and the first five points without reply. He was running his poor challenger ragged, forcing him into difficult returns from shots driven over the net with devastating top spin. Ronnie battled to sustain his Cheshire Cat grin throughout, and with the score on 9-20 and receiving serve, Billy needed one more point to take the set comfortably. His opponent's service was text book average, with no spin, disguise, and bouncing at a height that screamed to be thrashed back over the net. He met the ball as sweetly as WG Grace in his prime at Lords and waited for the crack as it hit the table on the other side of the net to leave the playing surface like a missile. Regrettably, there was not so much of a crack as a scream.

Billy in his excitement had mistimed the shot. Norma, still recovering from the bruising sketch, had another type of bruise to contend with, one infinitely more painful. The ball had struck the scar on her forehead and made her cry, Ronnie quick to put down his bat and soothe her distress. Billy was left standing there like a lemon, muttering.

'20-10... my serve.'

****

Another good thing about the youth club was football. Following his exertions as an evacuee against the muscled might of Bridgnorth Grammar School, Billy had not played a great deal since returning home. The war had wreaked havoc on the game with leagues suspended, players off serving their country, and organised matches few and far between. Yet the importance of the sport had intensified as a consequence. On the mud-soaked fields of the homelands, in the deserts of North Africa, and under the scorched midday sun of the Far East, eleven versus eleven regularly kicked a ball to seal the game's status as the great sporting pastime. And with the help of Seacombe Methodists, Billy resumed his playing career.

The first match was against Egerton Grove on Leasowe Road playing fields. Old Charlie from the youth club, the self-appointed manager, promised to bring along the shirts and was as good as his word, struggling with a large canvas bag as he tottered towards the group of keen footballers gathered outside changing rooms seemingly modelled on a Victorian public convenience. Charlie plonked the bag down and took a few deep breaths to recover before pulling out a succession of white short sleeved shirts and a blanket, which on closer inspection turned out to be the goalkeeper's jersey, presumably as modelled by Gulliver in the Lilliput FA Cup Final. Billy tried it on. It was enormous.

'Crikey Charlie, where did you get the goalie top?' said one of the lads.

Old Charlie had a habit of wheezing when he spoke, as though fighting for his last breath, his words intermittent.

'It was... the one... worn by... Fatty Peacock.'

He gave no further information about Fatty Peacock, but this was obviously a giant who had enjoyed his food as much as his goalkeeping. Billy looked comic and wanted to remove the garment but had no alternative, certainly not wanting to wear his work shirt. So he rolled up the sleeves and tucked the jumbo jersey into his shorts.

The game kicked off, things starting quietly for Billy, at least on the playing side. Most watching were clustered around the halfway line, leaving barren, empty spaces behind each goal, apart from one boy at the Seacombe end... one boy and his rattle. It was most likely a Christmas present that had gathered dust and garnered the smell of mothballs due to the football postponements, but today was the young man's chance to let rip. At the slightest sign of any action, a clicking, thunderous clatter invaded the quiet. The opposition centre forward tried a shot from outside the box that trickled like an earthworm five yards wide of the target, cue

262

excitable rotation of the rattle from the youngster. A cross from the tricky winger floated over the goalmouth as high as a barrage balloon to go out for a throw-in on the other side of the pitch, cue even more noise.

In the second half with the score at 3-2 to Egerton Grove, Billy made a series of outstanding saves despite the restrictions of Fatty Peacock's jersey. One in particular saw him leap like a salmon to stop a certain goal, a save so impressive that applause rang out from spectators and players alike. Ironically, it was the one time in the ninety minutes that the lad with the rattle was too stunned to shake his prized Christmas gift.

This was the moment Billy realised he wanted a career as a goalkeeper. He already knew the clerical world was not for him, a point reinforced repeatedly by the nit-picking Mr Butler, and regardless of any duty to serve his country, he no longer fancied joining the Navy. Draughtsman would now be relegated to second choice. Once the war was done and dusted, Billy Whitfield was going to be the next Vic Woodley or Harry Hibbs.

Two quick goals from Seacombe, including a screaming header scored by centre-half Johnny Williams, turned the game on its head. The last ten minutes produced an onslaught on Billy's goal, but his further heroics kept the opposition out. When the referee blew for full time, the keeper was mobbed by his teammates, the boy behind the goal using both hands to crank up the volume from his rattling, wooden pride and joy.

'Flamin' 'eck Bill, where did you learn to play like that?' said Johnny.

'Just practice I suppose.'

'You're a natural.'

Billy was five feet something but left the pitch feeling ten feet tall. And at that height, even Fatty's shirt was going to fit.

CHAPTER 27

Despite its momentous contents, the small piece of paper still looked innocuous. Eric re-read it for the umpteenth time, satisfaction radiating from within.

Results of Ab Initio Courses and Remarks
FLIGHT ENGINEER COURSE
No 4 S. of T.T. R.A.F. St. Athan
Type of Aircraft: Avro Lancaster
Examination Result: 68.9%
Passed
Date: 6th September 1943

He folded the document in half and returned it to the locker at the side of his bed. A few days had passed since receiving the news, and today was his passing out parade, after which he was off to the Heavy Conversion Unit at RAF Lindholme for the final leg of his training before operations proper. He checked and re-checked his uniform to confirm the required perfection, leaning forward to see his face shining back from ridiculously polished toe caps before leaving the billet to join the others.

An NCO immediately made his presence felt, and within seconds the highly disciplined group formed a perfect line to march in faultless synchronicity towards the parade square. Following a period of unsettled weather, temperatures had returned to their seasonal norms, today's thermometer pushing 80°F. As Eric stood to attention, his posture upright, his stance rigid, droplets of sweat formed between the collar of his shirt and the back of his neck, the overheating an inevitable consequence of the uniform's thick weave. It may have been an uncomfortable moment for the young man from the banks of the River Mersey, the sun blazing down without mercy, but it was unquestionably a proud one. He was now a qualified flight engineer, promoted to the rank of Sergeant, the minimum for aircrew. He had even received a salary increase, his weekly wage up to ten shillings a day. His outward demeanour and behaviour did not betray him, but on the inside Eric was bathing in waters of deep self-satisfaction.

A visiting Air Commodore, leeching authority, breeding, and deportment, inspected the rows of impressively turned-out servicemen, to a man pristine in appearance and self-controlled in manner. He beamed approval then moved back to re-join the other senior officers. Eric heard his name and stepped forward to receive his coveted flight engineer brevet and sergeant's stripes. After a firm salute, he resumed his place in line. The ceremony continued, Dougie McVitie amongst the next batch of names called out, giving Eric time to reflect on his progress to date in the Royal Air Force.

He had come a long way from the raw recruit that volunteered well over two years ago. He was now a trusted specialist on the Avro Lancaster, making up the final piece in the jigsaw that was a Bomber Command Air Crew. At an Operational Training Unit some place somewhere, a pilot, navigator, wireless operator, bomb aimer, and rear gunner had already formed into a five man team working on twin engine bombers. They would now be transferring to the same Heavy Conversion Unit as Eric where they would seek out a mid-upper gunner and flight engineer to add to the group. Eric would be ready to join them. He wondered about this unknown band of brothers that by all accounts would become the closest friends he would ever have. He looked forward to meeting them.

Pride notwithstanding, Eric was relieved when the parade formalities concluded, although it came a few seconds too late for one poor beggar at the other end of the line, the heat getting too much as he slumped to the floor, adding additional poignancy to the 'passing out' label. The dazed lad was quickly dragged from view so as not to spoil the spectacle of professionalism for the Air Commodore and other dignitaries. Eric, along with those that had stayed on their feet, then undertook one final march along the concrete pathways and roads of the No.4 School of Technical Training, St Athan.

There was still time for one last conversation with Dougie back in the billet before leaving the camp. The Maltese Scot had been posted to another HCU, and so the two friends were about to go their separate ways.

'Sae th' honeymoon is ower.'

'Sorry?'

'Th' honeymoon... things ur gonnae gie sticky frae noo oan.'

Dougie's accent was getting broader by the day.

'Sticky?'

'Aye... up in them planes riskin' life an' limb.'

His tone was neither overly serious nor overly dramatic. He was simply making a statement based on the realities. In fairness, Eric was not alone in hiding from such truths. He was riding high and getting ready to do his bit.

'Speak for yourself Dougie... the honeymoon's just beginning for me.'

He would one day look back on those words and consider them rather foolish and naive. But for now, he remained gung-ho and bid his friend a fond farewell to leave the wooden hut for the last time. He was just about to close the door, when Dougie shouted across the room from his bed. He was holding up a letter, much like Neville Chamberlain with his piece of paper signed by the German Chancellor.

'She wrote back,' he said.

'Who?'

'The Scot's lass frae Woodford.'

'Good for you.'

It seemed to be another RAF love story in the making, like that of Reg and Gwen, though he sincerely hoped for a happier ending.

He saluted, Dougie returning the gesture, and then departed for the next stage of his war adventure.

****

RAF Lindholme near Thorne and Doncaster in South Yorkshire, home to the 1656 Heavy Conversion Unit, was another highly populated base with over two thousand servicemen and a few hundred WAAFs. It enjoyed a typical Bomber Command airfield layout, located in a rural setting of largely flat, green fields, its centrepiece a triangle of runways that permitted take-offs and landings from six different directions. Five Type-C hangars, their corrugated walls large enough to house a vast number of Lancaster bombers, together with thirty six dispersal pans were scattered across the base, while two bomb stores, built to accommodate the wide range of munitions and fire-power, were positioned at a distance away from the main airfield. There was also an administrative block, sick quarters, and sites for the living and communal areas.

Eric's time at Lindholme was destined to be different for one very good reason. To date it had been words, theories and simulations that had dominated training, but from now on it was for real, his feet finally leaving the ground. He was going to fly in an actual aeroplane.

This was Eric's first day at the base, and he was on his way to the Sergeant's mess, a rectangular brick-built building with double-door entrance the colour of petrol blue. He walked in to join the queue for food, glancing around the room. Six uncomfortable wooden chairs accompanied each table covered in a white tablecloth with condiments sat in the middle. The dish served up today was the staple for airmen returning from a night raid, bacon and eggs, an indication that training extended beyond the obvious. Eric was handed an empty plate by the chap

267

in front of him.

'Thanks,' he said, offering the hand of friendship. 'Eric Whitfield.'

They shook.

'Alec Bowland… good to meet you,' the young man replied, a mild Midlands accent discernible, 'everyone calls me Ginger.'

They moved along the line, Eric appraising his neighbour. The trimmed hair was a shade of ripening carrot, his face etched in puzzlement, though friendly and benevolent. His brown eyes, an unusual shade for his colouring, sparkled with friendliness. He appeared to be a man steeped in trustworthiness, and Eric immediately took to him.

They headed with their plates of fried food and cups of tea towards a vacant table, the two men sitting across from one another. Ginger painstakingly set out his cutlery, plate, cup, and napkin in front of him prior to tucking into his dinner, providing further insight into his personality.

'I'm a flight engineer Ginger. What about you?'

'Mid-upper gunner.'

'Ah… so you'll be looking for a crew like me,' said Eric, dipping a slither of bacon into the perfectly runny egg.

'Yes, that's right.'

'Where are you from?'

'Coventry.'

His geographical placement had been accurate.

'Coventry? Goodness… I suppose there's no need to ask why you volunteered for this.'

'That's right.'

In November 1940, the Luftwaffe had dispatched more than five hundred bombers to the British city to destroy its factories and industrial infrastructure, in the process blitzing residential areas, monuments, and the cathedral that had stood since the 14th century. Eric recalled the impact of the Liverpool Blitz on his own decision to join up, yet compared with Coventry, the Mersey Estuary had got off lightly. The city and towns he knew were intact, whereas the heartland of Ginger's upbringing had all but disappeared, inducing even this obviously mild-mannered young man to answer the call to action pulsing through his veins.

Eric discussed his own background and RAF experiences at Cardington, Padgate, Filey, Blackpool, Innsworth, Middle Wallop, and St Athan, making him appreciate the length and ardour of his journey to take to the skies, the lack of accomplishment regarding the latter providing almost comic irony. Ginger's training had been more straightforward with no protracted wait as a reserve and no mid-training switch from one discipline to another. Consequently, the man from Coventry was a year younger than Eric, a mere nineteen years of age, undoubtedly amongst the youngest serving with Bomber Command.

As he mopped up the last of his yolk, Eric experienced a sense of *déjà vu*, eating bacon and eggs with others in RAF uniform, listening to a newly encountered, flame-haired serviceman about his life and his hopes for the future. Last time it was Reg Wilson just over a year ago at Padgate. Poor Reg was now dust. Where would Ginger, or he for that matter, be in twelve months' time? It was not a question that required an answer, especially not now.

Eric was about to fly.

CHAPTER 28

The de Havilland Mosquito was unique within the canon of RAF World War Two aircraft. Although powered by Rolls Royce Merlin engines, the similarities with the Lancaster ended there. Unlike the mighty metal machines rolling out of the factories of Avro, Bristol and other manufacturers, the Mosquito was made of wood. Yet against the expectations of many, the plane had become a great success. Labelled the 'Wooden Wonder', it had the handling capabilities of a fighter plane, a top speed that could outpace any enemy fighter, and a seat in the front this afternoon for Sergeant Eric Norman Whitfield's inaugural flight above the fields and open spaces of the South Yorkshire countryside.

Eric followed the pilot through a hatch underneath the plane to climb into the cockpit. The first time he boarded a Lancaster, he had been struck by the lack of space, yet compared with the Mosquito, the Avro was cavernous. The de Havilland had just enough room to seat two men, and whilst the control panels reflected the dials and switches required by a modern design, the layouts were simpler than those scorched into Eric's memory bank from the hours and hours of training on the four engine bomber. In a few weeks' time, his role would be far from passive, but today's circuits and landing was close to a leisure flight, his only task to listen and observe. He made himself comfortable, adjusted his flying jacket, and readied himself for what lay ahead.

The man at the controls, Pilot Officer Nelson, indicated to Eric he had the go ahead for take-off. Scrolling through a series of scrupulously well-rehearsed pre-flight checks, the routine culminated with a press of the ignition switch to start and warm up the engines. The chocks were then cleared by ground crew, permitting the Mosquito to taxi forward, the pilot then straightening the tail wheel until positioned at the far end of the south east runway. Eric heard familiar phrases as the airman outwardly aired his final checks.

'Trim... elevation... nose heavy as required...'

'Rudder... slightly right...'

'Aileron... neutral...'

'Props... max rpm...'

'Fuel... cocks fully on...'

'Flaps... up...'

'Radiators... open...'

The man at the controls opened the throttles slowly, and with the twin engines nicely synchronised, there was no discernible swing as the aircraft raced along the runway, the Merlins and wind combining to crank up the decibels. When the plane reached take-off speed, the pilot pulled gently back on the control stick to raise the airplane clear of the runway and begin its climb towards the clouds. Eric felt exhilarated, seemingly forced back into his seat as the Mosquito continued its ascent until straightening out and banking left. Through the cockpit window he had a bird's eye view of the Lindholme base and noticed in particular the runways intersecting to create the letter 'A'. He was also surprised at the extent to which the buildings and structures of the base were diffused over such a large area. The mess halls, sleeping quarters, shower blocks, latrines, and medical buildings formed a collection of oblong dots peppering the meadows delineated by a criss cross of country lanes. Trees were sparse other than one distinct area of ash woodland enjoying the last throes of late summer bloom before nature tinted brown over green for the change of seasons.

After a few circuits, and with a long, straight strip of runway in view directly ahead, Eric heard the pilot articulating over the intercom the final checks for landing.

'Fuel... check tanks...'

'Radiators... open...'

'Brakes... off... check pressures...'

'Wheels... down and locked...'

'Props... 2850 rpm on final...'

'Flaps... full on final...'

It was a text book landing, smooth and gradual, Pilot Officer Nelson demonstrating his undoubted flying skills assembled from a vast bank of experience in theatres a thousand times more challenging than that faced today. The skipper was a terse, no-nonsense type of man, drenched in self-assurance and confidence, ideal attributes for the person in charge of your first foray into the air. As they stepped outside the Mosquito and on to the concrete of the dispersal pan, he spoke bluntly to Eric.

'Sergeant Whitfield... you have to appreciate that is as easy as it will get. You will never enjoy a flight as much as that one. From now on, your every second on an aircraft will require absolute concentration and application. This de Havilland has a pilot's check list of one hundred and twenty eight items, and you don't need me to tell you that the Lancaster has over two hundred. And as for flying on active operations, you will need to double your efforts to concentrate and perform a professional job when anti-aircraft flak and enemy bombers are doing their utmost to blast you out of the sky. Understand?'

'Yes sir.'

'Good.'

It was a sobering message, yet one that had little impact on Eric's state of mind. He was ready to make the first entry in his flying log book and could not shake off the feeling of jubilation. He had been bitten by the flying bug and was not seeking a cure.

****

During his first week at Lindholme, Eric logged more than ten hours flying experience. His new colleague, Alec 'Ginger' Bowland did likewise, the friendship between the calm, equable Wallaseyan and the softly spoken young man from Coventry quietly blossoming. Both men were now ready to join forces and find a crew of five to make up the required seven personnel for the four engine bomber. It made sense to do this together, as a ready-made flight engineer and mid-upper gunner pairing was an attractive proposition to any crew looking to boost its numbers. And so it proved.

The process for crewing-up was remarkably informal. Given the strict discipline enforced by mouthy NCOs in the early days of square-bashing and training, Eric was surprised to discover a process in which they were sent to a hall and told to get on with it. It was a blind date without the complication of romance.

Eric and Ginger toured the sterile room, long tables with tea urns, cups and saucers the only embellishments. The two men poured hot drinks and then strolled past groups of uniformed men spread across the floor, some laughing, some in deep discussion, all drinking tea. This was not the easiest thing to do, but when Eric spotted a huddle of five men in the far corner, he immediately liked the look of them. They seemed relaxed and comfortable with one another.

He indicated with a nod to Ginger.

'What do you think about trying those boys?'

His friend shrugged.

'Alright.'

They approached and were given an immediate friendly welcome. It was handshakes all round and somewhat telling that each man's introduction stated the Bomber Command role before their name.

273

'Pilot... Flight Sergeant Peter McIntosh...'

'Navigator... Sergeant Don Lincoln...'

'Bomb Aimer... Sergeant Charlie Balderstone...'

'Wireless Operator... Sergeant Arthur Trotter...'

'Rear Gunner... Sergeant Barrington Haynes...'

The newcomers followed suit.

'Flight Engineer... Sergeant Eric Whitfield...'

'Mid-Upper Gunner... Sergeant Alec Bowland... everyone calls me Ginger.'

The approaching pair were duly invited to make up the numbers, Eric delighted to be part of this newly formed Avro Lancaster crew. His gut feeling that these men were good friends was likely in part to their common status. This was a group of non-commissioned officers, an obvious advantage in establishing a quick rapport. Pilots, navigators and wireless operators were often sourced from the officer classes, and though the RAF was far less hierarchical than the Army or the Navy, separate mess halls, medical and other facilities were still the norm.

A casual glance at the ensemble in their standard issue air force blue garments would have found little to distinguish them from one another. Yet such a nonchalant assessment was deceiving. On closer inspection, this was a collection of very different individuals and personalities who would use these differences to create a whole bigger than the sum of its parts.

Eric conversed mostly with Peter, known as 'Mac', the pilot. A well-spoken twenty year old from Edinburgh without a trace of a Scottish accent, he was undeniably officer material and a very handsome looking man. His brushed-back mid-brown side part had a tendency to flop forward, something he corrected habitually with his left hand. Symmetrical features portrayed a kind, compassionate expression, his eyes, a deep shade of hazel, revealing a man of undoubted intelligence. Considering the importance of the pilot/flight engineer axis, Eric could not be happier with the outcome.

As for the other men, Don the Navigator with his jet black hair, wide smile and equally wide gap between his two front teeth, seemed to be the oldest of the crew, probably in his late twenties. His deep voice, words articulated with crystal clear clarity, radiated competence, and he appeared an outstanding choice as the man to guide them to and from enemy territory in the dark of night.

Charlie the bomb aimer was jovial, cheerful, and good-humoured. He was Wigan born and bred, the same place as George Formby, and but for the absence of a gormless grin, he was his double, a man tailor-made for maintaining the morale of any group. Arthur the wireless operator, big ears and receding fair hair was a local, at least while stationed at Lindholme. He hailed from Doncaster and was a typical Yorkshireman with a friendly but gruff nature.

That left Barrington, the rear gunner with wavy blond hair, bright blue eyes, and skin tone liable to turn a shade of pink in company. Hailing from a small village in Essex, he was diminutive, not much more than five feet two, and had probably stood on tiptoes at his medical to sidestep any minimum height requirement. Eric noted that Ginger and Barrington were already comrades, the two comparing notes on all manner of things, a clear case of gunners sticking together.

The seven man crew sealed their affinity with further handshakes before leaving the hall, Ginger and Eric heading to collect their things, as they were to move into the same billet as the other five. It was not lost on Eric that, from this moment on, the crew of Pilot Peter McIntosh, Navigator Don Lincoln, Bomb Aimer Charlie Balderstone, Wireless Operator Arthur Trotter, Rear Gunner Barrington Haynes, Mid-Upper Gunner Alec 'Ginger' Bowland, and Flight Engineer Eric Whitfield would sleep, work, train and play together. He fought to suppress the thought tunnelling its way to be heard that one day they might all die together.

CHAPTER 29

'Boxing?'

'That's right.'

'Isn't that a bit dangerous?'

'Not really... we wear big gloves that are quite soft at the end, so they don't hurt that much.'

'Oh dear... I don't know why you can't just do a beetle drive or play table tennis.'

'I'll be alright mum, don't worry.'

Billy's mother was not so sure. Old 'Wheezing' Charlie from the Seacombe Methodist Youth Club had set up a boxing ring for later in the week, and a certain William Edgar Whitfield was chalked-in to fight Kenneth Potter in a bout.

'Ted, have you heard what they're doing at Billy's youth club?'

Ted Whitfield had returned from a half hour visit to the outside toilet. He slumped into the deep cushions of his favourite seat, exclaiming 'deary me' as a small blast of flatulence invaded the air.

'Ted!'

'Eh, what's that?'

'Billy's going to be boxing at the youth club.'

'Is he?'

'Yes.'

His dad smiled, the prospects of an encounter involving his younger son and the Queensbury Rules clearly meeting with his approval.

'I'm wearing gloves,' said Billy, 'big ones as well.'

'He'll be alright,' said Ted, dismissing his wife's concerns with an outward flick of his right hand. 'It'll do him good... toughen him up a bit.'

'I'm not so sure.'

Eva was unconvinced but conceded.

'Any chance of a cup of tea around here?' said Ted.

'It's brewing.'

'Bloody hell...'

Ted had a few virtues, but patience was categorically absent from the list. He checked the time on his silver pocket-watch attached to his waistcoat.

'Just in time,' he said with deep satisfaction.

'What's that Dad?'

'Just in time for ... *It's That Man Again!*'

His announcement was accompanied by uncharacteristic theatricality. Ted was something of a dour man, but he liked his radio comedy and *I.T.M.A.* was top of the tree. Named after Adolf Hitler's tendency to appear in every newspaper headline in the lead up to war, the light-hearted show was a major factor in maintaining the morale of the ordinary people. Billy thought it amusing, but his dad consistently chuckled his way through each half hour episode, particularly when the various catchphrases were aired.

"Don't forget the diver"

"I don't mind if I do"

"I'm going down now sir"

"I go I comeback"

"This is Funf speaking"

"After you, Claude - no, after you Cecil"

'I don't mind if do,' mimicked Ted, laughing into his tea.

The broadcast that followed *I.T.M.A.* proved an effective antidote to the mirth, the BBC Northern Orchestra performing Mozart's *Requiem*, but

Ted was soon back on form, engrossed in his newspaper and grumbling inaudible comments into his chest.

Billy chose the moment to climb out of his chair and stand by the birdcage. Suspended at head height from its stand, it presented the perfect eye line for a fledgling boxer, and his gaze met that of Percy the canary-coloured budgerigar. Billy started dancing on his feet, dodging, weaving, and jabbing. He was Joe Louis or Tommy Farr. An upper cut and a few body blows thrashed the air in front of the bird, but then he stumbled on his dad's shoe, fell forward, and collided with the metal cage that began to swing like a galleon in a stormy sea, the poor budgie fluttering within its confined space as if pursued by a tomcat.

'Bloody hell son... what are you playing at?' groaned Ted, his voice climbing an octave. 'Stick to the real thing son for God's sake.'

'Did you ever box dad?' said Billy, dusting himself down.

Ted looked up to the ceiling, dredging a memory or two from times gone by.

'I was a flyweight... a skinny, lanky bugger. And I'll tell you one thing son, those pork chop rations your mother picked up from the butcher's last week had more meat on them than me. But I was fast, nippy, with quick feet. The other boxers struggled to get near me, cos' I moved out of the way before you could say Jack Dempsey.'

'Did you have a good fight record?'

Did I buggery... lost every flamin' one.'

The memory failed to provide a crumb of comfort for Billy. If he was to do well in the ring, he would have to rely on something other than inherited traits.

Apart from its position in the middle of a long connecting corridor, the boxing ring looked the part, Old Charlie having done a sterling job setting up ropes to approximate the regulation dimensions. The floor was less authentic, there being no spring in linoleum-covered tiles, but with low lights and the smell of sweat - Charlie's toil had soaked his shirt - the atmosphere was authentic. It was time for Billy to put on his gloves and get changed, although obviously not in that order.

By the time he was ready, a crowd had gathered around the ring... that is if you can call Ronnie, Johnny, Norma and Eileen a crowd. Billy relaxed when he saw his opponent. Stripped of clothing layers, Kenneth Potter was a thin, weedy type, with arms more like branches of a baby willow than the trunk of an English oak. This was just as well, Mother Nature having failed to bless Billy with a strong upper body or muscular frame.

Despite no referee or bell to signify the start, Billy's head transported him to the Liverpool Stadium. He imagined beating the broad muscles of his chest with his gloves, grunting animal noises, and clenching a gum shield, as the paying spectators bayed for blood, the fighter inside responding with a savage attack of leather on skin. The reality was somewhat different. The young boxers held their giant gloves up to cover their faces, so much so they couldn't see where they were going, and at one comical point they were facing away from one another while bouncing on their feet. The first punch of sorts was eventually thrown by Billy, and it scraped the edge of Kenneth's chin, not a killer blow, but a scoring point nonetheless. A second punch made a similar impact before his slight opponent swung a wild left hook that made him lose his balance and fall to the floor.

Johnny in the corner started counting to ten, but Kenneth managed to get back to his feet and carry on. As the pattern continued with landed punches as scarce as petrol and bananas, Billy's advantage was becoming evident. He may have lacked power and strength, but he was blessed with quick reflexes, witnessed most notably in his goalkeeping. Poor Kenneth had neither muscle nor rapid reactions and was lumbering towards an inevitable defeat. Billy relaxed into his role as vanquisher, his mind returning to the Liverpool Stadium with the crowd urging him to go for a knockout. He obliged and swung a right hook that struck his opponent square on the jaw.

'Bloody hell Billy,' shouted Johnny, 'what a punch!'

His friend's outburst brought the fighter back from the Stadium to Seacombe Methodists, and he was perturbed to see the stricken Kenneth stumbling backwards, his eyes as wobbly as his legs. Billy moved quickly to catch him before he fell, words of apology gushing forth.

'Get a stool and some water,' Billy called to his pals.

Fights 1 Wins 1, Billy Whitfield had the perfect record, yet he didn't feel like a winner. He felt terrible. Young Kenneth was never going to be a boxer, but neither was he. He lacked the killer instinct, and regardless, not every opponent would be as hapless as this. Percy the canary-coloured budgerigar had given him a more testing duel. As Johnny mopped his brow and helped remove his gloves, Billy concluded this was a good time to retire.

He withdrew to wash and change, returning ringside just in time to see Ronnie Rose climb over the ropes for his fight. His opponent was a lad rarely seen at the youth club, but the boxing ring had induced his return. Previously known as Vic, those sizing up his ripped muscles knew this was about to change to Big Vic. Billy felt for his friend Ronnie. A year older and a few inches taller than either him or Johnny, these attributes had matched him with a Samson rather than a Delilah-esque Kenneth Potter. For the first time since meeting him, Ronnie's permanent smile was displaced by a grimace, albeit one disguised as a rueful grin.

He then watched a race rather than a boxing match, Ronnie dashing around the ring with Big Vic in pursuit. Billy's friend was quick, but after couple of minutes of arduous sprinting, he was caught by a beauty and knocked to the 'canvas'. In truth, the punch had missed, something obvious from Billy's position, but he couldn't blame his pal for taking the easy way out. Johnny obligingly counted to ten in double quick time to bring the contest to an end, Billy certain that here was another fighter about to announce his retirement from the ring.

About ten minutes after the boxing had finished, Norma, Eileen, Johnny, Ronnie and Billy gathered around a table to drink some damson flavoured lemonade, a speciality of Charlie's wife. Although not quite on par with cream soda or dandelion and burdock, the concoction was not bad at all.

'I used to pick these in Bridgnorth,' said Billy.

'Pop bottles?' said one of the twins.

Billy noticed the little scar on her forehead and remembered this was Norma. Her scar-less but otherwise identical sister Eileen was now chatting with Billy's friends.

'No, damsons,' said Billy, 'in the summer holidays... I earned money fruit picking.'

'Is that where you were evacuated, Bridgnorth?'

'Yes... to a farm with no electricity or running water.'

'That sounds terrible.'

'It was difficult at first, but I got used to it. By the end I didn't want to come home... Did you go away?'

'Yes, we went to Aberystwyth. We were living in Liverpool at the time and that's where most of the children were sent.'

'Did you like it?'

'Ye-es,' the stretching of the syllable suggesting mixed feelings. 'I liked it, but Eileen was less sure. We stuck at it for about six months.'

'I was away for fifteen.'

'Gosh... you must have enjoyed it.'

'I did.'

Billy took a sip of lemonade, the scent of damsons drifting from his glass to carry him back to filling baskets of fruit on a warm September day in rural Shropshire. Bridgnorth already seemed a long time ago, and he couldn't see when he'd get there again. The thought saddened him, the sudden onset of melancholia an unforeseen surprise.

Old Charlie drew near the table to bring him back to the present moment.

'How's the... lemonade?' he panted.

'Great.'

'Very nice.'

A treat.'

The universal acclaim pleased the old man.

'I'll tell... the wife... the good news... later.'

Sometimes, Charlie's delivery was that of a dying patient attempting to reveal their final words in a race against the ticking clock of mortality. He was about to leave, when he made one final announcement.

'The boxing... it's been... a real... success. But I've a... new idea.'

'What's that?'

'Wrestling.'

'Wrestling?'

He nodded.

No sooner had Billy hung up his gloves that he was thinking about practising his Boston crab. One thing was certain. His mum would not approve.

CHAPTER 30

The Heavy Conversion Unit course at Lindholme was scheduled to last twelve weeks, Eric's crew now past the halfway point. Mornings involved ground school lessons, the men immersed in tutorials of pre-flight checks, starting, running up, aircrafts, airfields, landings, overshoots, feathering propellers, fire drill, cross-wind, ditching and emergency procedures. Afternoons were taken up with flying practice at Air School, and after some early frustration when Eric spent much of the time watching from afar while a flying instructor accompanied the pilot, navigator and wireless operator into the air, the crew had recently undertaken their first solo flights as a seven, performing the undemanding circuits and landings routine followed by a more challenging three engine landing task. Today, however, was an interesting one. They were again going solo, but this time it was bombing practice, albeit performed in the anodyne setting above the Yorkshire countryside with no anti-aircraft flak, no bright illuminations from searchlights, and in place of enemy fighters, just a few high flying birds.

Eric was sitting next to Pilot Flight Sergeant Peter 'Mac' McIntosh in the Lancaster's cockpit, the two crew members close to finalising their pre-flight checks. He had been alarmed earlier to see a slight tremor in Mac's hands when he signed to confirm inspection of the aircraft, and the same tremble was now visible as he pressed switches and turned dials. The genial chap with the floppy hair that Eric had come to know was a very different proposition from the man alongside him this afternoon. Fortunately, on completion of the checks and with the engines powering into life, Mac

283

recovered his composure to manoeuvre the four engine bomber along the taxiway and on to the runway, achieving a smooth take-off without any hitches. They were in the air.

'Good work Engineer,' said Mac.

'Thanks Skipper.'

It was a feature of Bomber Command that crew members referred to one another by their roles when flying, enabling late replacements to operate effectively without knowing the full names of their colleagues.

The flight went well, including the dummy dropping of shells co-ordinated by Charlie, the bomb aimer somewhat incongruously carrying out his duties with the same cheerfulness as George Formby. Away from the rigorous routines, practices and professionalism of their flying duties, the seven individuals within Eric's crew enjoyed exceedingly cordial relations. It was now evident that performing their tasks aboard the four engine bomber served only to heighten their compatibility and ease with one another, Eric reflecting with satisfaction that things had worked out rather well.

With the runway in sight, he awaited the sound of Mac's voice to work through the landing checks. But there was nothing. He turned to see his pilot staring ahead in a daze.

'Mac!' he shouted, for once discarding the normal protocol of calling him 'Skipper'.

The pilot responded quickly to the call, the indoctrinated training taking over, starting with a warning to his crew to get ready for landing. When the speed of the aircraft had reduced to 150 knots, he and Eric dealt with the flaps, undercarriage, rpm control levers and harness before the wheels made contact with the concrete. It seemed to be a steady manoeuvre, but the rear of the Lancaster was affected by swing, and for a few nervous seconds, Mac battled to keep the four engine bomber on a straight course, ultimately managing to bring it to a halt at the edge of the runway, inches away from the adjacent soft turf. No words were spoken, but Eric, for one, was glad to be on *terra firma* safe and well. His pilot had struggled today. He hoped it was a one-off. There would be far sterner tests ahead.

The following evening, a Saturday, the lads each took an RAF issue bike from the base and cycled to nearby Hatfield for a drink, a routine outwardly encouraged by those in command on the grounds that young men working this hard earned the right to play equally hard. Some public houses near to a Squadron base operated a two-tier service, the lounge for officers, the bar for NCOs, but Nobby the publican at the Black Bull would not countenance such exclusion, rank making no difference in his eyes. In fairness, Eric had discovered this attitude prevailed throughout Bomber Command itself. His initial impressions when crewing-up had proved misleading, officers and non-commissioned personnel mixing and socialising with surprising informality, despite the best efforts of established norms for segregated facilities at the base.

Leaning against the scuffed wood of the bar at the Black Bull, Eric downed most of his first pint of mild in one, surfacing to gasp for air with deep satisfaction. He was standing next to Mac who mirrored his colleague's actions.

'I wasn't really on top form yesterday Eric,' he said suddenly, sipping more cautiously this time from his glass.

'Can't say I noticed old chap,' said Eric, uttering a few words of denial, his deceit finding refuge in the jargon of the stiff upper lip.

Mac was brutal in his self-assessment.

'I'm sorry my friend, but you're wrong. I had the shakes and a momentary seizure of dread coming in to land.'

'We've been working hard Mac… it's bound to catch up at times.'

'Perhaps,' he replied, brushing his hair back with increased vigour.

A few pints later, he had regained his normal composure and

disposition, but the disclosure had unnerved Eric. Fortunately, Flanagan and Allen were on hand to provide a welcome diversion.

Unbeknown to Eric's crew, Saturday evenings at the Black Bull ended with a walk upstairs to a small function room in which Nobby played the piano and sang a few out-of-tune songs, the clientele tolerating his discordant performance thanks to the availability of beer and spirits beyond normal opening hours. Around their table, drink flowed like Niagara Falls, and Eric lost count of the number of pints he downed, although he did manage to remain the most compos mentis of the group. Mac had adopted a permanent stupid grin, the gap in Don's teeth had widened as he mirrored his pilot's look, and Charlie had unknowingly perfected the gormless expression of his doppelgänger film star from Wigan. As for Arthur, his whopping ears glowed so red; he had become a potential target for enemy bombers. But it was the gunners who were about to steal the show.

Ginger, the measured, carrot-topped young man from Coventry unexpectedly stood up and then walked - though not in a straight line - towards a compact podium next to the piano. The step up to the raised floor was not much more than six inches, yet Ginger laboured to achieve the task, having to lift one leg at a time with both hands as though made from the best mahogany. When he was loosely upright, he swayed slightly from side to side and held up his hand. Nobby stopped singing, much to the relief of the others in the room. Even for those who thought he sang in tune, his performance was tiresome, the publican's musical repertoire not extending beyond about 1910.

Ginger abruptly announced with an uncharacteristically loud voice, 'My name is…'

There was a pause.

Arthur filled the gap.

'Ginger Bowland yer' daft bugger!'

'No!' said Ginger, his retort adamant, 'my name is... Chesney Allen... and I want to...'

He tried to say the word 'introduce' but the result sounded very different. He gave up.

'... here's Bud Flanagan!'

Barrington Haynes, the little man with the theatrical name, took to the stage to join Ginger, loud applause and raucous cheers greeting his entrance. A tall, well-built man, well over six feet and rumoured to be the local constable, rushed across to hand 'Bud' an overcoat and hat, both about three sizes too big for the pocket-sized gunner. He put them on, and everybody fell about laughing. He looked ridiculous.... too ridiculous even for the Crazy Gang. The only people in the room with a straight face were 'Bud' and 'Chesney'.

Ginger, now subsumed by his show business alter ego, once again adopted a loud, slurring voice.

'We s-shall now s-s-sing, 'Run R-Rabbit R-Run'.

'I can't play it,' said Nobby.

'I can,' said an alcohol-fuelled Eric, sweeping the publican off the piano stool and launching into the opening bars.

There followed a painfully funny rendition of the hit song with an adapted chorus of 'Run Adolf Run' creating audience participation in the form of singing and howls of laughter. During the next number, 'We're Going to Hang out the Washing on the Siegfried Line', Bud pulled down his hat to completely cover his eyes. This was getting too much for some who banged their tables in appreciation, and when the pocket-sized performer fell off the stage at the end of the song, a few suffered paroxysms of laughter so strong, events almost called for medical attention. There was even time for a genuine sing-a-long with the final choice of 'Underneath the Arches,' a performance that concluded with Bud shouting 'Oi!!' It had been a memorable occasion, one that Eric

287

pledged to cherish and recall, perhaps at those darker moments that inevitably lay ahead.

The journey back to Lindholme was almost as comical. The singing continued as they cycled down the country lanes, slowly, haphazardly, and, for Ginger and Barrington, painfully. Another RAF opportunist had nabbed Barrington's bike outside the Black Bull, leaving him to get home via a 'seater' on Ginger's crossbar. It had gone reasonably well until the final stretch when overtaken by a supplies vehicle. In moving to the side of the road, the inebriated Ginger veered off and deposited the off-duty gunners into a hedgerow laced with nettles. The others knew they shouldn't laugh but couldn't help it.

The seven eventually crawled back into the billet for sleep, hugely thankful that the days of waking at 6.00am with a sadistic NCO banging two bin lids together as a wakeup call for a cross country run belonged in the past. It was one of the perks for an aircrew in Bomber Command.

****

The weeks went by at the 1656 Heavy Conversion Unit, and as Eric's crew awaited details of their posting to an operational squadron, the training continued with lessons in the mornings and flight training in the afternoons. Around this time Bomber Command was moving centre stage in the fight against the enemy. Emboldened by the success of the Avro Lancaster, Commander-in-Chief Arthur Harris launched the Battle of Berlin in November 1943, convinced the war would be over within months via a strategy of sustained bombing raids on the capital city.

The HCU planners duly aligned the practical and theory tutorials to deliver these aims, preparing and enabling seven men aircrews in minute detail to carry out area bombings from day one. High above the clouds on a daily basis, they practised flying, wireless operating, map reading, radar, air-to-air gun firing, day and night aerial combat, evasion, corkscrew flying, baling out, night bombing, and affiliation exercises with other aircraft including the Spitfire, Hurricane, and Mosquito. The bombing runs included dropping live 10lb bombs from 20,000 feet over uninhabited terrain, such procedures vital for practising the communications during this critical part of a mission. It gave them a taster for the real thing, though only a taster. On live operations, they would be releasing ammunition four hundred times more powerful, the massive bomb bay of the Lancaster permitting a bewildering quantity of explosives and incendiaries as cargo.

Looking back, Eric now considered Mac's loss of nerve an aberration. Today he was a confident and capable pilot, the 'skipper' of a crew blessed with exemplary teamwork, skills, and expertise. For his part, Eric had developed into an expert on the mechanical workings of the Lancaster. His knowledge extended to the running of the engines, fuel systems, hydraulics, pneumatics, electrics, fuses, radar shutters and all manner of instruments housed in its cockpit. Wing Commander Thompson had been right. In many ways, he was as important to flying the aircraft as the pilot. The original prime motivation for joining the RAF, to better himself, was coming true. The future was bright, even if tinged with a few dark thunderclouds.

As November made way for December, Eric's long training journey was nearing its end. Sat in the billet with Arthur, Ginger and Barrington, the men awaited the return of Mac, Don and Charlie from the briefing that was to reveal their first squadron posting.

'I reckon it'll be somewhere in Lincolnshoyer,' said Ginger, the mention of a rival county bringing an extra Coventry-cum-Warwickshire twang to his words.

'Mebbee, but 'cud alsa be in God's own country,' said Arthur, staying loyal to his beloved Yorkshire.

'Essex?' said Barrington.

'Be'ave lad.'

The door opened, allowing a cool blast of air to penetrate the warmth of the quarters. The others were back, and Mac wasted no time in imparting the news.

'It's 103 Squadron chaps, Elsham Wolds, start date 11th December.'

'I told you it would be Lincolnshoyer.'

Arthur grunted in reply.

'I've heard the local girls are something else at Elsham, much prettier than Lindholme.' said Charlie, teasing his colleague in their continuing minor Battle of the Roses.

'I'll tell thee, there's nowt prettier than t' Yorkshire lass.'

The banter continued, the quips protecting the crew from any thoughts about the significance of the moment. The rehearsals and preparations were just about done. They were now ready for the opening night proper.

The seven left the billet for the Sergeant's Mess. After eating, things developed into a bit of a sing-a-long, although the lack of beer meant there seemed little chance of Ginger and Barrington reprising their memorable Flanagan and Allen double act. Yet a few minutes later, the gunners were standing on top of a table about to relive their now infamous Black Bull performance. There was, however, more poignancy than comedy on this occasion. A giant cheer cast its way to the rafters and then faded to be replaced by the melodic refrain of 'Underneath the Arches'. Everyone joined in. This time, any tears were not sourced from beer induced mirth. For many, this was a moving, affecting moment that reached out to the universal theme of friendship, a genuinely affecting moment.

Walking back to the billet a short time later, Eric considered the song a fitting end to his training. He was now ready to go to war.

CHAPTER 31

Although with 103 Squadron for over a week, the crew were yet to go on an operational sortie, the commanders seeing fit to keep Flight Sergeant McIntosh and his team stationed at Elsham Wolds while assessments continued. Watching from the sidelines, the inherent danger of Bomber Command had already been brought home to the new intake with tragic immediacy. Two days after their arrival, fourteen aircraft left the base for a major raid on Berlin, Eric, Ginger and Barrington joining a small group at the side of the runway to wave off planes as they departed.

A mist descended towards the ground as the first bombed-up Lancaster roared past at 16.22, its engines generating a deafening noise that shook the bones of the well-wishers huddled together on the turf. The next plane sped along the concrete six minutes later, followed quickly by a spate of aircraft at 16.30, 16.31, and 16.33. The same was happening at the myriad of airfields in the east of England, hundreds of pilots navigating beyond the clouds to rendezvous with a main stream heading for the enemy coastline.

576 Squadron shared Elsham Wolds with 103, and so further planes were leaving from the other side of the base around the same time on the Berlin raid. At 16.37 the next aircraft passed Eric, his group waving as enthusiastically as for the first. He watched, still in awe of this mechanical marvel as it disappeared into the clouds, its navigational red lights fading into the settling dusk and haze from the mists. One minute later at 16.38, just as the next crew taxied into position; an enormous explosion shook the ground. The sky to the east was suddenly bright orange interspersed

with reds, yellows and black smoke.

'Jesus...'

More than one of the onlookers blasphemed in horror, their initial suspicions confirmed later. Flight JB670 from 103 had collided with a bomber from 576 Squadron, a matter of seconds after take-off. The crews would have stood no chance, fourteen men and two bombers lost in an instant. It was a sobering moment, and the farewell greetings from the runway crowd to the aircraft that followed until the last at 17.00 were blessed more with prayers than enthusiasm.

Perversely, Elsham Wolds was one of the lucky places that evening. By the time the bombers returned from their mission, the mist had turned into thick fog, and many aircraft and men were lost as the landing routines and practices descended into chaos. Elsham was spared the pea soup and incurred no such weather-related losses, although one flight failed to return, the crew shot down over Berlin by a night fighter. The day - later coined 'Black Thursday' - had been a baptism of fire for Eric's crew. It may have been observed from the safety and security of the squadron base, but as a portrait of life in Bomber Command and its inherent dangers, it painted a stark and vivid picture.

A few days later, a further thirteen aircraft left the base to bomb Frankfurt, one failing to return. Eric's crew would have to fly thirty non-aborted operational sorties to complete a tour, after which they would be posted to a training base as instructors before another tour began. Statistically, the odds on a crew finishing their term were not great; a reality reinforced by the flights lost on the Berlin and Frankfurt raids. These were the truths that the young men with side caps, brevets and sergeant's stripes had to face, armed with either the innocence of youth, the arrogance of youth, or as in Eric's case, a pledge to trust in the Lord.

Things finally happened on Christmas Eve. Although not sent out as a rookie crew, Mac, Eric, Ginger and Barrington were dispersed amongst other bomber teams as replacements for the next assault on Berlin. The capital was the least favourite destination for bomber crews, the German defences such that each new sortie to the city became more hazardous than the last. Mac was to fly second 'dickie' as an eighth crew member, while the others were to carry out their duties in full, each man allocated to separate aircraft. This was not what Eric had anticipated. Despite their lack of experience, he trusted his crew mates, and to be sent out on his first bombing raid with a bunch of strangers was a little disheartening. But the professional flight engineer within rallied, and by the time he was drawing his flying kit and parachute from a friendly, smiling WAAF, his attitude was one of calm professionalism. He had a job to do, a job he had trained for, a job he could and would do well.

He met the other six members of his crew when boarding the vehicle that transported them to their Lancaster sat a mile away at its dispersal pan. Although names were exchanged, it didn't matter for the flight. His skipper, Warrant Officer Gregg was another Scot, and another north of the border type with little hint of an accent. He was an experienced pilot on his second tour, a fact that reassured Eric and helped him appreciate the benefit of sharing a first mission with someone 'long in the tooth'. The one person who went out of his way to be friendly was the rear gunner, a Canadian called Ernie. This was often the case. The man with the worst job of all at the back of the plane, exposed in temperatures of minus thirty odd degrees, was invariably the chirpiest.

As their synchronised watches ticked past midnight for the start of the day before Christmas, Eric completed sections A and B of his Bomber Command Flight Engineer Log in readiness for take-off. The first of the engines powered into life, starboard first, and soon all four Merlins were exercising their considerable motorised muscle. The pilot shouted the first to the last pre-flight checks before starting to manoeuvre the vast bulk of the Avro along the taxiway using brakes, rudders and judicious bursts of power to stay within its narrow width of fifty feet. Turning on to the active runway, there was a wait until a flash of green from the Aldis lamp gave the signal for the skipper to open up the four engines and release the brakes. Full power and take-off boost increased the rpm, and as they powered along the runway Eric called out the escalating airspeeds.

'100 -105 -110...'

The throttles were held wide open against the stops and the aircraft lifted from the concrete to become airborne, one of the most perilous moments of the flight. Any mechanical problem now for a bomb-laden plane was likely to be fatal. Thankfully, the pilot and Eric had achieved a straightforward take-off, the Avro gradually climbing to its safety speed, its undercarriage and flaps up. The flight engineer breathed a little easier. Above the clouds, the Lancaster joined layers and rows of bombers in the main stream, the first indication of aircraft close by the turbulence that rattled their fuselage. Eric glanced through the Perspex of the cockpit, awestruck by the sight of these fellow four-engine leviathans of the sky, a true vision to behold. The necessary radio silence continued over the North Sea, the plane gradually ascending to its cruising height of 22,000 feet where the fur-lined boots and other protective attire fought a losing battle to protect the crew from the freezing cold temperatures. It was a harsh reality that the Lancaster had no internal heating.

At ten minute intervals, the skipper communicated with the crew via the intercom, ensuring everything was going to plan. As flight engineer, Eric's job was to monitor the instruments and dials in front of him and to the side of his sliding chair, checking fuel consumption and ensuring optimal performance from the engines. He confirmed to his skipper that all was well. The wireless operator exchanged Morse code signals about wind speed with operations on the mainland and fed this information back to the navigator who altered their course accordingly. Although the plane was now flying over enemy territory with the gunners on constant lookout for fighter planes ready to attack at a moment's notice, the journey out remained uneventful.

Nearing the target and in preparation for releasing its cargo of destruction, the bomb aimer took up his position above the bomb bay. He then checked the selector switches and began the search for red target indicator flares deposited by the Pathfinder flights at the head of the main stream. Leaning over to see what lay beneath, Eric viewed the ground ablaze, incendiaries and exploded bombs showing no respect or regard for buildings and architecture. Yet there was no sound to accompany the sight, no sound other than the constant drone of their four Merlin engines.

The moment had arrived for JB487 to add fire to the fire. The bombs were fused and selected, the master switch turned on, and the bomb doors open. Around them shrapnel from anti-aircraft guns pelted the shell of the Lancaster, the crew all hoping to avoid a direct hit. The pilot and bomb aimer continued to co-ordinate the precise positioning of the aircraft over the target, and against the odds it was held level and straight while the 'bombardier' called out the final few adjustments.

'Right... right... steady... steady... BOMBS GONE!'

The action of releasing its bomb load compelled the Lancaster to rear up like a frightened stallion, but as the pilot banked immediately to the right, a sudden explosion penetrated the roar of the engines, shrapnel pummelling the airframe, turbulence hindering any pretence of a level ride. The views accorded by the Lancaster's canopy, nose cone, and turrets provided front row seats for all but the navigator and wireless operator to witness the carnage. A fellow bomber had been scorched out of the Berlin sky by an anti-aircraft shell that had landed on the bulls-eye.

'Some poor bugger's got the chop,' said the skipper, as casual as a man looking for his socks, before adding more poignantly, '...seven new souls heading for the gates of heaven.'

Eric said nothing.

'There but for the grace of God go I,' he thought.

There was no time to dwell on such matters. They were still in mortal danger, the expected fighter planes yet to make an appearance. Moreover, they all had a job to do. Eric checked the tanks and calculated the fuel required for the homeward journey. There was more than enough. Leaving the German capital behind with the fires fading into the distance, the return flight over enemy countries offered no respite. But when JB487 eventually left the Dutch coast to cross the North Sea, the crew could finally relax a little.

The first signs of dawn were appearing on the western horizon, a flaming orange infiltrating the industrial greys and blacks of the fading night. It was December 24th, the absurdity of Father Christmas and his reindeer navigating the skies they had left behind in Berlin not lost on Eric. There was none of the fog that had blighted returning crews on 'Black Thursday', and so the final part of the journey passed by without incident, the aircraft landing on the concrete of Elsham Wolds at 7.33am. They had been in the air for just under seven hours, seven challenging hours, but it was done. Eric had flown his first operational sortie... one down, twenty nine to go. With the image of the downed bomber replaying through his mind, he recognised the thought as one to discard with haste.

The same vehicle that had dropped the crew at the dispersal pan just before midnight collected them for de-briefing in the interrogation room, where they enjoyed a well-earned cup of tea drenched in rum, after which it was off to the mess for the staple returning meal of bacon and eggs. Warrant Officer Gregg was not exactly effusive in his praise for Eric's contribution, but that didn't matter, the flight engineer taking deep pleasure from a sense of self-satisfaction. For a first timer, he knew he had done well.

It was left to Ernie the Canadian rear gunner to provide the acknowledgement, shaking his hand warmly and uttering, 'Well done buddy, you did a great job.'

It was a small thing, but it meant a lot to Eric.

Sat at one of the tables in the mess were Mac, Ginger and Barrington, all safe and well after their own sorties. Eric wished his crew of the night well, and joined his friends.

'Morning gents,' he said. 'We've earned this, don't you think.'

'You're not wrong there,' said Ginger, his carrot-coloured hair showing signs of perspiration. 'How'd it go for you?'

'We were lucky... no fighters... and just after we dropped our bomb load, right in front of us, we saw another Lancaster buy it, hit by flak.'

Eric tucked into his food. It had never tasted so good.

'What about you Ginger?'

'We had a close shave with a Messerschmitt, but we lost him... otherwise no problems. Barrington saw some action though.'

'Did you?'

'Yes,' said the little man from Essex. 'It was another Messerschmitt... appeared out of the blue, right behind us in my line of fire. I gave him a blast and shouted to the pilot to corkscrew, and thank God he was quick in his reactions. A second's delay and we might have all gone for a Burton.'

Eric was aware that Mac was quiet, reflective.

'And you Skip?'

'It was alright.'

That was it... no elaboration, no anecdotes, no stories. And much as he tried, Eric failed to get anymore out of the man who had flown second dickie.

Separated for the Berlin Christmas raid, the crew were back together again, returning to their billet to catch up on sleep. In the few minutes before Eric closed his eyes and drifted off, he reflected on the magnitude of the night's experience, the images, the pictures, the sounds, a jarring juxtaposition to the quiet peace and solitude of these sleeping quarters. He picked up his bible and turned to the hand written pages headed 'Warfare' and silently read his own flawless script.

'We do not war after the flesh, for the weapons of our warfare are not carnal, but mighty through God...'

And then he slept.

CHAPTER 32

1943 was drawing to a close, and although the war had turned in favour of the Allies, its impact on the home front had tightened. Christmas and the season of goodwill was not going to be a time for excess, and Billy's modest presents of chocolate and oranges from his mum and dad reflected this, although the frugality of Yuletide in Bridgnorth two years earlier had been ideal preparation for such low expectations. He looked at the rusted frame of his bicycle leaning against the shed in the yard and quickly set aside any thoughts about the lucky ones riding a new two-wheeled pride and joy this morning. He finished the last segment of his Jaffa, put on his coat, gloves, and bike clips, and set off for a spin. Billy had bought the bike a few months ago for a guinea from a junk shop on Poulton Road. It was close to a death trap, its wheels wobbling like raspberry jelly, its fickle brakes either shuddering in anger or quivering in protest. But it got him around, and it was coming in useful this Christmas Day morning for some fancied fresh air.

Careful to avoid potholes in the roads, Billy safely navigated his way to Egremont Promenade where he took in the familiar sight of the Liverpool Waterfront. His daily journey to work presented the same view, and so it was far from novel, yet today's seasonal calm presented a different perspective, and he perceived anew the 'Three Graces', the Liver, Cunard and Port of Liverpool Buildings, survivors of the Liverpool Blitz, the latter already fading into the distant past. It was a mild day, and gazing up to the clouds, he thought of his brother now flying Lancasters in airspace nowhere near as benign as that above the Mersey today. The reports of the bombing raids in the newspapers, on the wireless, and at the cinema, had been universally optimistic yet unable to mask the number of casualties sacrificed. Eric's letter, received only two days ago, had reassured his mum, though its impact had been transient, the apprehension etched upon her face quickly reappearing. Thankfully it was Christmas Day, its distractions a welcome relief from the worries and the stress.

Billy climbed back on his bike, promptly slipping off the seat and on to the crossbar, his testicles taking the full impact, literally bringing tears to his eyes. Marginally recovering, he rode gingerly along the prom towards New Brighton before turning round and cycling home.

As he walked into the kitchen through the back yard door, his mum, always wary of the bike, said, 'Any flat tyres today?'

Tempted to answer, 'No flat tyres, but two flat cobblers,' he resisted and muttered, 'no... all fine.'

He began to help his mum set the table.

It was around 3 o'clock, the last sprout eaten, that Billy, his mum, dad, nan, and aunt were all sat around the wireless listening to the Christmas broadcast of King George VI.

'And once again from our home in England, the Queen and I send our Christmas greetings and good wishes to each one of you the world over. Some of you may hear me on board your ship, in your aircraft, or as you wait for battle in the jungles of the Pacific Islands or on the Italian peaks...'

After the word 'aircraft', his mum emitted an unintentional slight cough.

'Some of you may listen to me as you rest from your work or as you lay sick or wounded...'

That could be me thought Billy, gently massaging his testicles under the table, thankfully out of view of his family. The King continued to deliver his message, slowly, awkwardly, attempting to coat every syllable in reassurance.

'…I hope that my words spoken to them and to you may be the bond that joins us all in one company for a few moments this Christmas day.'

The adults in the room signalled their endorsement, the monarch succeeding in bringing seasonal comfort to the front room of this terraced house and presumably countless others throughout the Empire.

'Do you know anyone who has met the King or Queen?' said Billy, the question posed to all present.

Shoulders were shrugged.

'We met his brother when he opened the Mersey tunnel,' said his mum.

'Don't mention that traitor in this house Eva,' said Billy's nan.

Old Mrs Beecroft was a lady of few words, but the mention of the abdicating King Edward VIII had made her speak out.

'He was only a bloody dot in the distance, said Ted, pulling an uncomfortable collar away from his Adam's apple, 'that's hardly meeting him.'

Eva shot a disapproving glance in the direction of her husband, as Hilda turned off the wireless.

'It's a pity Eric isn't here to play the piano,' said Billy's aunt.

The others agreed. Family sing-a-longs had not been the same since he left for the RAF. Billy was helpless to offer any alternative. He was not especially musical and, moreover, had never been afforded the opportunity to learn an instrument. A few hundred miles away in Lincolnshire, Eric was probably pounding the ivories to accompany a chorus of booming and shrill voices, but in Barrington Road, the Christmas cheer was deflating to the noise of a ticking clock and full stomachs.

Billy let out an involuntary laugh.

'What are you smirking at?' said his dad.

'Nothing.'

The sight of people slumped around a table of Christmas food had triggered the memory of the Ebenezer Scrooge play in Bridgnorth when

Tiny Tim had enjoyed a few minutes of sprightly athleticism, leaping across the table in a frantic hunt for food. Billy looked out of the window, remembering his time as an evacuee. He had seen many of his peers from that time around and about, but he wondered about some of the characters he had left behind, George the farmer, his glamorous wife Rose, their daughter Patricia. Perhaps she was still getting a lift to work in the Jaguar. Then there was Miss McDonnell, his teacher, and Trampy, undeniably his smelliest ever friend. Billy had enjoyed living in the Shropshire countryside and still missed it today.

Whilst daydreaming his time away, everyone other than Billy had settled into easy chairs to enjoy a nap, the ticking timepiece now joined by the sounds of snoring and flatulence, his dad naturally responsible for the latter. It was still light outside, and although tempted to go for another dice with death on his bike, he decided against it... for the sake of his cobblers.

CHAPTER 33

'Double top to win,' said Ginger.

Eric steadied his feet, leant forward, perfected the line of his dart to just below the 20, and unleashed his throw. It hit the metal of the board and jumped back, missing Barrington by a few inches.

'Damn.'

The farm workers laughed heartily. The game was taking place at the Dying Gladiator pub in Brigg, the errant flight engineer handing back the initiative to their agricultural opponents. Three games later, and the lads from 103 Squadron had lost by three sets to two.

Eric checked his watch. It was time to visit the chip shop. He was mobilising the rest of the crew, when Mrs Clarkson spoke up.

'Where do you think you're going?' said the landlady.

'The chip shop,' he replied.

'Oh no you're not,' she said robustly, pointing at two of the farmhands. 'You two can go and bring some food back for these boys. They can eat here'

The lads from the farm were not happy and protested, but Mrs Clarkson was having none of it, lifting the hinged part of the wooden counter and walking through to confront them. She was less than five feet tall and alongside their muscled bulk appeared ridiculous, but she was demonstrating that on the inside she was a giant.

'Now listen,' she lectured, 'you'll be here this time next week, playing darts and drinking beer, but these brave, young souls will be up there fighting the enemy and risking life and limb. They might not get the chance to come here again. And so when I ask you to go and fetch their fish and chips to eat in here, I expect you do it, no questions asked.'

Shamefacedly, they conceded, departing shortly with a fish and chip order for the losing RAF darts team. It was a bittersweet moment for Eric and the crew. To witness the old lady's support was heart-warming, yet she had also chosen the moment to reinforce the frailty of their fate... bittersweet indeed.

Three quarters of an hour later, Eric wiped the grease from his mouth, downed the final dregs of a pint, and waved goodbye to Mrs Clarkson, the parting gift an unmistakable stench of salt and vinegar to linger in the bar long after their exit.

Catching the last train from Brigg to Barnetby Le Wold, the seven friends picked up their blue Elsham bikes at the station and cycled back to the base, wasting no time in going straight to the mess where a New Year's Eve party was already underway. A sea of young, carefree people greeted them as they entered, a large group getting ready for a photograph. The backdrop to the image was a collection of Christmas decorations as faded as autumn leaves, but the joy and exuberance from the smiling faces was never going to be diminished by such tired adornments.

It was a night off from piano accompaniment for Eric, one of the officers more than proficient at the keys, freeing him to enjoy the rest of the evening and even the odd dance. With the clock ticking down to midnight, he waltzed with Gloria, a WAAF from the Radio Section. The steps were his old speciality, and as he glided around the floor, Vera suddenly burst into his head, catapulting him back to the Grosvenor Ballroom in Wallasey. A surge of melancholy threatened to engulf him, until New Year came to the rescue, time literally on his side. The countdown had begun.

'10... 9... 8... 7... 6... 5... 4... 3... 2... 1...'

'Happy New Year!'

Everyone cheered, embracing one another with handshakes, pats on the back, and if lucky, a kiss on the cheek from a WAAF, the luckiest of all enjoying one on the lips. 1944 was seconds old, and the revellers struck up 'Auld Lang Syne', the singing hearty and enthusiastic, everyone joining in full belt with the chorus. Eric's arms were interlocked between those of Mac and Gloria, and he was aware of being unusually sober for the occasion. Yet he was not alone. The crews had been stood down from operations for the last couple of days but expected the resumption of sorties any time now, a level of sobriety therefore more than wise. Ironically, it was a night he could have done with a few drinks. Spared from the Berlin raid two evenings ago, he was coming to terms with the news that JB748, the Lancaster he had flight engineered on Christmas Eve, had failed to return. The latest information suggested that Warrant Officer Gregg and five of his crew had survived and were likely prisoners of war. The rear gunner, however, that friendliest of friendly Canadians by the name of Ernie, was dead, no doubt blown to smithereens from the vulnerability of his turret. Could it be true that only the good die young? It seemed so unjust. But for the fickle hand of fate, Ernie and his friendly manner would be here now, enjoying the festivities with all these other smiling faces.

'Auld Lang Syne' ended with the usual 'All the best for the New Year' utterances. The WAAFS and ground crew had the normal span of twelve calendar months in their minds, but the lads from the aircrews, Eric included, preferred to focus on the short-term and the next mission. And that would be later in the day.

For the crew of Flight Sergeant Peter McIntosh, the New Year was irrefutably making a grand entrance. The weather forecast for later in the day was favourable, and they had been slated for the evening's sortie. Mac,

305

Don and Charlie returned from the briefing to confirm Berlin as the target, Arthur, Barrington, Ginger and Eric greeting the news with the expected lack of enthusiasm. Berlin's defences were getting stronger by the day, and as a destination for the team's first joint operational sortie, it was some way down the wish list. Nonetheless, a bolt of electric excitement accompanied the trepidation. They had trained for many months, years even, and this was their destiny, the austere wireless man from Yorkshire issuing the rallying call.

'Come on lads... let's get at 'em,' said Arthur.

The remainder of the day was a combination of preparation and rest. Despite no hangover from the previous night, Eric was nonetheless grateful to catch a few hours sleep in the afternoon. They would depart near midnight and fly for seven or eight hours. It was going to be long day.

Attired in heavy layers of battledress that incorporated three pairs of gloves, long pants, flying boots, leather, silk and wool, it was close to 11.00pm when the aircrew of ND363 climbed into their Mark III Lancaster, the latest version of the aircraft, the men quickly settling into their tasks. Eric helped strap Mac into the pilot's seat, took up his own position beside him, and commenced the internal and cockpit checks. Hearts were now beating faster, but everything remained calm, ordered, as if just another training exercise. The start and warming up of the engines, however, signalled a change. Mac began to lose concentration and give wrong instructions, Eric having to correct his skipper and remind him of the next procedure. It was taking every ounce of his concentration to keep things on track.

'Engines set to 1200 rpm Skip.'

'What's that?'

Eric added urgency to his tone.

'Engines at 1200 rpm Skip.'

'Right... erm... thanks Engineer.'

'Radiator shutters Skip?'

'What's that?'

'Radiator shutters open?'

'Yes... radiator shutters open.'

And so the distracted preparations continued.

The Lancaster was fully bombed up, carrying 1 x 4000lb cookie, 48 x 30lbs, 630 x 4lbs, and 90 x 4lbs type 'X' incendiaries. It was a very heavy load, one that the Avro was designed to handle, but one that required a diligent and meticulous approach at the controls. Eric was in text book mode, but Mac was struggling, and the consequence of this misdirection became apparent when the aircraft taxied towards the runway.

'The rpm is falling Skip,' said Eric. 'Less than 1000... 900... now 800,' he said, frantically checking the instruments.

Mac failed to respond and continued to open the throttle, but the power was not there, as though climbing a steep hill with a load too heavy for the engines. In aviation parlance, the pilot had 'bogged' his aircraft, the Lancaster coming to a halt on the taxiway. One thing was evident. They would not be flying tonight.

Back in the interrogation room, the de-briefing was taking place about seven hours earlier than expected. Eric knew why the bogging had occurred. Mac had lost his nerve again. Yet it was inconceivable to give chapter and verse to those in command. Accusation of LMF, or Lack of Moral Fibre, was the greatest of all fears for aircrew serving in Bomber Command. If found guilty of such 'cowardice', the individual was literally stripped of his stripes in a public ceremony designed for maximum humiliation and then dispatched for re-training where the cruelties of a sadistic NCO could be vented with valediction. Mac was a good man, deserving of his absolute loyalty. Eric made up his mind. He would fall on his sword for the skipper.

The others had little to answer, but pilot and flight engineer, responsible for getting the plane off the ground and into the air, were about to be questioned with some ardour. The flight commander, a man Eric did not recognise, presumably a flight lieutenant deputising in some capacity, was sat on a wooden chair behind a wooden trestle table. One glance into his eyes was enough. He was unambiguously the disagreeable type, sympathy and understanding anathema to his vocabulary or personal attributes. His face creased into a scowl as he spoke.

'At this very moment, somewhere over continental Europe, eleven Lancasters and seventy seven men from this squadron are taking the fight to the enemy, flying to Berlin. Meanwhile, your aircraft is sat on a dispersal pan over there, going nowhere, thanks to the ineptitude of its crew. So...' he spat, his eyes shooting from Mac to Eric and back to the pilot, 'pray tell me what the Dickens happened?'

'Well...' said Mac, reaching out to find the right words.

Eric rescued him.

'It was my fault, sir.'

The flight engineer's peripheral vision picked up a quick turn of Mac's head towards him.

'What's that Whitfield?'

'I had the fuel mixtures too rich, sir... we lost power as a consequence.'

The flight commander turned to Mac, eyebrows set deep.

'And what do you have to say McIntosh?'

Mac didn't answer at first, but after an exasperated glare from the officer, he uttered, 'I think Sergeant Whitfield is probably right, sir.'

'Is he... well then Sergeant Whitfield, this is simply not good enough. The RAF has invested a huge amount of time and resources into your training and to fail in such a deplorable way is utterly unacceptable. I will not tolerate mistakes on my watch again'

The flight commander turned back to the disconsolate pilot.

308

'And one more thing Flight Officer McIntosh...'

'Yes sir?'

'Your crew will fly on the next mission. Weather permitting, this will be tomorrow night. You understand?'

'Yes sir.'

'Right... now be off... the pair of you.'

Mac and Eric sidled out of the interrogation room to walk back to their billet in the dark of night, neither man uttering a word. But about ten yards away from their quarters, Mac halted Eric, pulling him back by the arm.

'Eric? I... I just wanted to s-say...'

'You don't have to say anything Mac. Let's start afresh tomorrow... a new dawn and all that stuff...'

'Good idea... good idea.'

Twenty four hours later, the crew were back in ND378 preparing for yet another raid on the German capital. They had just started the pre-flight checks inside the aircraft.

'Eric?' said Mac, quietly.

The flight engineer was immediately put on alert. His skipper had not called him 'Engineer.' Eric reciprocated the informality.

'Yes Mac?'

'I can't read this?'

'What do you mean?'

'I have some kind of double vision.'

'Try blinking a few times.'

'I've tried everything, but it's still blurred.'

The same unfeeling, stand-in Flight Commander was likely to be in the control room this evening. Eric knew this was not going to be easy. An aborted mission for the second successive night, regardless of a medical reason, was going to be explosive, unlike the fully bombed-up load of the

Lancaster about to be abandoned at its dispersal point again.

Don pulled back the curtain in front of his navigator's position.

'Everything alright Skip?' his words articulated with the clarity of a radio announcer.

'Mac's a bit of double vision,' replied Eric. 'He's having trouble reading the checklist and instruments.'

After a brief consultation with the others, the crew concluded they had no choice but to abort the flight. Don took the lead and contacted the control room, the authority of his voice over the airwaves keeping a lid on any LMF suspicions. The sortie was called off.

Exiting the Lancaster prematurely and travelling back to the main buildings was a case of *déjà vu*, the journey quiet, almost funereal. Eric's stomach lurched at the sight of the same flight commander's unsmiling demeanour. Fortunately, Don acted assertively and insisted Mac get urgent medical attention, the pilot immediately whisked away to see a doctor. The rest of the crew stayed behind, waiting patiently and drinking tea, singularly devoid of any rum on this occasion.

Mac was back surprisingly quickly.

'Alright Skip?' said Ginger, concern etching a shade of pink to his complexion, a colour mismatch with his hair.

'Fine thanks... the doc wants me to go for further tests, but I can see alright now.'

The news was a relief to them all, but the real test was still to come. Next up was the de-briefing with the flight commander, the same venue, the same austere environment, the same stern and unsympathetic stance. The difference tonight was the presence of all seven crew members fielding the enquiries.

'Let me start by saying I don't enjoy this,' said their interrogator.

For a moment Eric thought a shadow of humanity was being cast by the unsmiling officer. He was wrong.

'That is... I don't enjoy reporting back to HQ that one of my aircraft has failed to take off again. If it's mechanical incompetence on the part of the ground crew, then that's the Station Commander's territory. But if it's for reasons linked to the aircrew, it casts aspersions on my capabilities as a leader, unfair aspersions.'

The crew knew to stay quiet, any compulsion to take a stand or challenge the officer's attitude rightly quelled. He leant across and picked up a sheet of folded paper, briefly scanning its contents. His stare returned to Mac.

'Double vision?'

'Yes sir.'

'Very convenient... very convenient... one of those things you can't see or touch... or prove.'

Indignation and frustration was undoubtedly growing within the crew, instinctively loyal to their skipper, but the officer's inference troubled Eric. He had covered for Mac last night and recalled the incident at the Heavy Conversion Unit. Something was not right, notwithstanding this evening's medical cause.

'I can't afford another incident like this during my watch, and so from today you are temporarily stood down from operations, pending further enquiries. Now go back to your billet.'

The aircrew returned their Irvin sheepskin flying jackets to the lockers before walking back to their sleeping quarters, most lighting a cigarette before venturing out into the cold wind.

'E's a right sod in't he?' said Arthur, rubbing his hands together to help stay warm.

'In Coventry they'd call him a twonk,' said Ginger.

Barrington added, 'he'd be a twerp in Essex.'

'I can't tell you what they'd call him in Wigan,' said Charlie. 'I might get court marshalled!'

311

They all managed to laugh, even Mac. It provided some much needed relief from the mounting anxieties.

Eric looked at his watch. It was 1.30am; the other 103 Squadron crews now well on their way to Berlin.

'Whooaaa!' said Ginger, almost swept off his feet by a sudden gust.

They were glad to get inside the billet, despite its feeble attempts to stay warm from the January cold. It was not long before weather conditions outside had become a gale, creating challenging conditions for returning bombers. Eric lay on his bed listening to the wind and rain, glad to be inside. He wondered about those now in enemy skies and who might get the chop tonight. He concluded there was only one certainty in that regard. It would not be them... and all because of a bit of double vision.

CHAPTER 34

The only other bombing raid for 103 Squadron in the first two weeks of the year was a mission to the port of Stettin near the Baltic Sea, a combination of weather and the moon's phase delaying further action. The suspension of Eric's crew from operations had largely gone unnoticed, but in the end failed to matter. By mid-January, they had been transferred up the road to 166 Squadron in Kirmington to replace a missing aircrew, the Elsham Wolds command unquestionably pleased to discard this 'problematic' group of men.

The day they departed, the team fractured, Charlie Balderstone forced to stay behind at 103 to join another crew that had lost its bomb aimer. The other lads felt for the Wigan man, his ever-present grin unusually absent in the final hours when saying goodbye to his pals. Although forewarned, the extent of the bond between crew members had surprised Eric. They had only known each other for a short while but were already the best of friends. Saying farewell to Charlie had been an unexpected wrench. He was going to be badly missed. In the days since their abandoned Berlin missions, Charlie, more than anyone, had maintained spirits within the team, a man who instinctively cheered things up. They awaited his replacement with understandable apprehension.

Ready for a new beginning, the crew's first day at Kirmington provided an inauspicious start. The Commanding Officer of the Squadron, leading from the front, had piloted a Lancaster on a mission to Brunswick, one of nineteen aircraft leaving the aerodrome for the enemy coastline late the night before. It had not been a successful operation, and sadly, his was one of two crews that failed to return. This was a serious blow, and Eric wondered if they had jumped from the chip pan into the fire. He need not have worried.

The following day, the officer in charge of 'B' Flight, Squadron Leader Fred Powney was re-posted to command 166 as Acting Wing Commander, immediately gathering aircrew personnel together in one of the mess halls. Powney, a charismatic Canadian with the archetypal, dashing good looks that romantics expected of a Brylcreem Boy, recognised the importance of an instant boost to the morale of his charges. Eric, Mac, Don, Arthur, Ginger and Barrington joined the other groups to form an audience for the new leader who walked into the room at a brisk pace, his muscular frame and positive demeanour effortlessly conveying self-assurance and poise.

'Good morning gentlemen,' he said, his manner cheerful and optimistic. 'As you know, Wing Commander Craggs is missing after the Brunswick raid. To lose a man of his standing is undoubtedly a major blow to the Squadron, though I have every faith he is presently making his way across enemy territory to engineer an escape back to Kirmington. Nonetheless, it is essential that we don't let this news affect our spirits. There is no other way. For those new to me, wondering who on earth is this guy, let me fill you in on some of the details. I am Acting Wing Commander Fred Powney, originally from British Columbia, Canada. I started flight training in England before a posting to 27 Squadron in India to fly Wapitis over Waziristan in the Northwest Frontier Province. Last year I was repatriated back here for heavy bombing training, which has led to this. I am extremely proud to be your Squadron Commander, and I promise you that I won't let you down, in the same way I know you won't let me down. And finally, today you are all stood down from operations. I suggest you use the opportunity to enjoy some well-earned rest and relaxation... thank you gentlemen.'

314

Eric had already made up his mind. Here was someone to look up to, a natural leader of men, one of the rare examples in the RAF where the officer was both authoritative and approachable. Maybe his North American background gave him an advantage over the home grown types. Regardless, Eric was pleased with the outcome. Perhaps the tide was turning in their favour after all.

Back inside their Nissen hut, the outside cold easily penetrating its corrugated steel exterior, the crew were congregated around the combustion stove in the centre of the room. To a man they expressed satisfaction at the appointment of Fred Powney, Mac especially animated and affirmative. Eric experienced a sudden surge of optimism, certain they were on the verge of their first operational sortie as a collective. He was not wrong.

****

Five days later, the Squadron was detailed to attack Berlin, seventeen aircrews selected from 166 including Eric's. This was it. After the false starts at Elsham Wolds, the McIntosh crew were ready to chalk up their first bombing raid. In place of Charlie Balderstone, Sergeant Joe Penfold had been assigned as the bomb aimer. Joe was a bespectacled, studious, acutely intelligent man, slight in frame, yet able to oversee the release of nearly twenty four thousand pounds of bombs and incendiaries.

The now familiar routine on the day of a mission ensued; the checking the aircraft in the morning; the briefings in the Operations Centre as to target, route maps, and weather forecast; the pre-flight meal of bacon and eggs; the requisition of parachutes and Mae West life jackets from the WAAFs on duty; the donning of flying clothing including the Irvin jackets and fur-lined boots; the transport to the bombed-up Lancaster at the dispersal pan; the exhaustive list of exterior and interior pre-flight checks;

and the taxiing to the end of the runway ready for take-off.

This raid was starting early, their flight W4996 having a scheduled leaving time of 16.21. Eric was pleased to note his fears about Mac's nerve had long evaporated, a new found level of self-assurance from his skipper evident since Wing Commander Powney's pep talk. With the Aldis lamp flashing green in poor visibility, their aircraft moved forward along the runway and built up speed until its imposing bulk lifted from the concrete towards the clouds, confidence and certainty flooding Eric's physiology. Their departure had gone as smooth as Savile Row silk, and such was the good feeling; he had yet to resort to prayer, confident that no such ecclesiastical help was required tonight.

On the journey over enemy territory, the gunners, Ginger and Barrington, occasionally warned their skipper of Luftwaffe fighter sightings but no combats developed. As they neared their target, Mac and Eric exchanged a rueful smile when viewing the significant cloud cover obscuring Berlin, the subsequent attack consequently rather scattered, although they did hear one large explosion. Turning for home, the sortie had gone without a hitch, but there would still be time for concern and disquiet to invade the optimism of the crew. Eric checked their fuel consumption and identified an issue.

'Skipper?' said Eric through the intercom.

'Yes Engineer?'

'Bit of a problem… fuel calculation suggests we have enough for 310 miles but still 350 to go.'

'Navigator?'

'Yes Skip?'

'Can you double check our position?'

'Will do.'

A few minutes later, Don admitted to navigating the incorrect journey home. Without corrective action, they would run out of fuel before the dry land of Blighty. Eric's training kicked in. He reduced their flying speed to optimise fuel consumption, the revised computation giving them just enough in the tanks to make it back to Kirmington. There were some nervous moments as the Lancaster neared the Lincolnshire airbase, the dials screaming louder and louder that they were close to bone dry, but the screech of tyres on the runway was a more than welcome sound, and when the aircraft taxied to a standstill at 00.07, close to half an hour later than other returning crews, spontaneous applause rang out amongst the group.

Of the seventeen 166 Squadron Lancasters that had left the aerodrome earlier, three returned early due to engine or oxygen failures, one bombed a last resort target, and another failed to return. The latter put a slight damper on the euphoria, but the sense of satisfaction at a job well done remained. The corner had definitely been turned.

Eric fell asleep at 3.00am, waking five hours later to the startling news that the crew were slated for another sortie later that day. Notwithstanding the success of last night's bombing raid to Berlin, it was a daunting task to rise to the challenge of a second mission within twenty four hours. The day's preparation was the same as yesterday, although the apprehension about Berlin was avoided when the evening's target was confirmed as Magdeburg, home to significant German oil refineries. The take-off time allocated to W4996 was 20.04, second to last of sixteen aircraft to depart.

It was during the pre-flight checks that Eric noticed Mac start to prevaricate; querying all manner of instrument readings with Operations Control and slowing things down to such an extent there was an increasing likelihood they would miss their scheduled slot. The Lancaster eventually left Kirmington at 20.34, half an hour late. The race was on to catch up with the tail end of the main stream, and by Eric's computations, this was just about feasible. However, his skipper proceeded to fly the aircraft, not in the required straight line, but in a slight zigzag. Eric kept his counsel even when obvious they would not reach Magdeburg at the required concentration time. Mac duly informed the others of the failure and turned the bomber round to fly back to the squadron base. The aircraft was in perfect working order with no flak or fighter damage necessitating a bomb drop over a secondary target, and so with their 'tail between their legs', the still bombed-up, aborted mission returned early to the flat lands of Lincolnshire, landing at 01.13.

No words were spoken on the way to the interrogation rooms, but when Eric found himself alone in the mess with Ginger, eating the obligatory but welcome bacon and eggs, the subject was raised, quietly, confidentially, the mid-upper gunner speaking first.

'What did you make of tonight?' he said.

Eric, armed with knife and fork, played about with his food. He was thinking. Eventually, he broke his silence.

'Well… I think the last thing Mac wants to do is let any of us down, but tonight…'

He dropped his cutlery on to the plate.

'… tonight was different. He was in control, but he deliberately delayed our take-off and made sure we didn't catch up with the main stream.'

Ginger's eyebrows lifted in surprise.

'You mean…'

He struggled to form the words.

'Listen Ginger…' said Eric, conspiratorially checking for eavesdroppers, 'I'm going to tell you a few things, but you've got to promise to keep them to yourself.'

The gunner's expression changed from alarm to solemnity, his eyebrows lowering.

'Of course,' he said quietly.

There was nothing salacious about his response.

'One day at Lindholme,' Eric resumed, 'when we were on a dummy

318

bombing raid, Mac bottled it, and I had to snap him out of it. You might recall a bumpy landing where we ended up on the edge of the runway.'

'That's right, I remember.'

'Things settled down after that, but our first aborted mission at 103 was due to Mac. He was all over the place with the checks and the procedures, and that's why he bogged the plane. At the debriefing, I knew I'd have to take the blame to protect him from that upstart in charge.'

'I can see why you did that.'

'But the next night with the double vision…' Eric paused.

'You think he made that up?' said Ginger.

The flight engineer shook his head. 'I don't know what to think… I'm just a bit uneasy... because of everything else.'

'We had the Berlin sortie… that went well.'

'I know but… when we had the fuel problem, I could see him tightening up… I'm worried about him Ginger. He's a really good lad… but he's in trouble… and that means we are as well.'

'What do you think'll happen now?'

'Not a lot... if this was 103, he'd be having his stripes torn off as we speak.'

'And a couple of other things a bit more painful.'

They both chuckled at this welcome light relief. It was a prompt to finish their food, now going cold.

'Mac's lucky we've got Fred Powney,' said Eric. 'I don't think he's the type to hang someone out to dry.'

The gunner was nodding in agreement when Mac walked in with Don, Arthur, Barrington, and new boy Joe.

'Everything alright Skip?' said Ginger.

'Yes thanks…' the pilot replied, flicking his hair back, the mop immediately flopping forward to cover one side of his forehead, '… the Squadron Commander has taken full responsibility… says he should never have sanctioned us to be out two nights in a row.'

'Bloody right he shouldn't,' said Arthur, grumpily. 'That girl needs more of a rest than one bleedin' night.'

The wireless operator was referring to the Lancaster, though Fred Powney had clearly meant the crew and Flight Sergeant McIntosh in particular. The mission had, for the first time, truly dented Eric's morale. Although feeling better for sharing his thoughts with Ginger, he had major concerns over his pilot's ability to lead the group, yet to challenge his capability would be almost treacherous.

The men from W4996 hung about to await the return of the other crews, the denial of sleep and rest a self-imposed penance for the abandoned raid. Every Lancaster landing was greeted with understatement, the tired, weary aircrews welcomed back with a 'well done' but nothing more, their achievements far too commonplace to be considered heroic.

When Eric heard that another crew had failed to return from the sortie, and that many of the 166 bombers had witnessed aircraft shot down, the news compounded his pessimism. It didn't help that some voices within the Squadron were spreading a rumour that the bomber offensive strategy was not succeeding as expected. The loss of men amongst aircrews was building. Life suddenly appeared as fragile as a delicate piece of crafted crystal, death robust, persistent, something to which most had hardened, though not Eric. He knew what he had to do. Making his excuses, he headed back to the Nissen hut. There he took out his bible, turned to the hand written pages headed 'WARFARE', read a little, and then prayed.

CHAPTER 35

'Can I have a word mum?' said Billy.

Eva Whitfield was on her hands and knees scrubbing the kitchen floor with disinfectant. She stopped for a few seconds and looked up at her younger son.

'You'll have to wait till I finished this.'

'Oh… alright,' he conceded with a dejection his mum picked up on.

'Come on then… what is it?'

She stood up and walked through to the lounge, sitting down at the dining table. Billy joined her and passed her an envelope.

'Mr Butler gave me this yesterday,' he said.

'Who's Mr Butler?'

'My boss at GEC.'

She read the letter. It was a final written warning on company letterhead threatening to terminate the employment of William Edgar Whitfield should he continue to be late for work.

'Oh Billy,' she said, unable to mask her exasperation, 'sometimes you're hopeless.'

'I just need to get up earlier.'

'Of course you do… I've been saying that for years. But I can't drag you out of bed these days. You've got to start doing things for yourself.'

There was a very real chance of losing his job at GEC. Butler had stressed that a number of ex. employees were ready to return to work having been invalided out of the services. Billy's habit of turning up late continued to be a source of acute frustration and annoyance for the manager who was rapidly running out of patience.

A knock at the door interrupted their discussion.

'I'll get it,' he said, jumping at the chance of a diversion.

The bad part was over. His mum knew about the letter.

It was early evening and dark, but he was still able to make out a silhouette of a tall man through the glass in the front door. He walked slowly and opened it.

'Hello Bill.'

This was a surprise.

'Eric...'

His brother was in the same RAF uniform as the last time he saw him, but he looked different... not as scrubbed... if he was to use one word, it would be tired.

'You get taller every time I see you,' said Eric. 'You must be nearly as tall as me now.'

'Five feet nine.'

'There you are.... erm... can I come in?'

Billy's daydream was broken up.

'Yes... Mum?' he shouted. 'It's Eric.'

At the other end of the hall, the brothers heard their mother trying to stir their dad.

'Ted... wake up... it's Eric!'

The sound of a groan, a fart, and a 'bloody hell' evidenced him coming round. Eric had travelled light, and so it was just him and a small kitbag that made an entrance at the door and into the lounge.

'Hello Mum... Dad,' he said, quickly finding an armchair into which to ease himself.

'I'll make a pot of tea,' said his mum.

There were no embraces, no kisses on the cheek, no histrionics, just the idea to indulge in a spot of tea making, the great British refuge.

'How's it going son?'

Ted Whitfield posed the question as he blinked his way into the present from slumber.

'Not bad…. not bad,' replied Eric.

This briefest of responses was good enough for his dad. Small talk to accompany the tea ensued, shading all from the shock and drama of any meaningful discussions about Bomber Command.

'Your Auntie Ada's hoping to come up from London in a few weeks…'

'Auntie Hilda's courting… he's a gentleman called Bert…'

'Poor old Maisie in number 7… she lost her husband…'

'We're lucky this weekend… we've a nice piece of brisket…'

Billy was glad to make an excuse and get on his bike to head for the youth club.

About fifteen minutes later, he was getting ready for a game of table tennis with Johnny Williams, the pair warming up with a few shots across the table.

'Our Eric's back home on leave,' he announced, as he returned a tricky serve.

'Is he?' said Johnny, stopping play. 'Did he tell you about the RAF and flying the bombers?'

'Not really.'

'Didn't you ask him?'

Johnny was incredulous.

'I don't think he wanted to talk about it.'

'You still should have asked him, yer' daft blighter.'

'Maybe.'

But he knew he hadn't been daft. His brother was home for peace and quiet, a break from Bomber Command. If he didn't want to talk about things, that was fine with him.

They started playing the best of three, though Billy's mind was not on the game. He was thinking about Eric and the time he cycled to Bridgnorth in the summer sun. The brother he greeted earlier on the front step was the not the same man, his vitality and strength diminished. He wondered if the change was temporary.

'0-5... change of serve,' said Johnny.

'Eh? Have we started?'

****

It was the following Sunday, Eric alone in Barrington Road ruminating about the last few days in Wallasey. It had not been especially enjoyable. After the fiasco of the latest abandoned sortie, Wing Commander Powney had given the crew a leave pass, but the opportunity to catch up with family and friends had come at a bad time, concerns about his skipper at the forefront of his mind. Moreover, the intensity of Bomber Command, with the inherent and very real perils of the night raids, made it near impossible to embrace the humdrum and everyday existence of the world at home. If the Liverpool Blitz had still been in full swing, things may have been different, but life on the banks of the Mersey in early 1944 seemed a million miles from the combats over enemy skies and the infernos of the German cities and ports 20,000 feet below. Eric was finding it difficult to adjust. It might have helped if Len was around, but he was settling down to life far away in the forces, as were all of his peers. He decided to go for a walk.

This was the first RAF leave break in which he had consciously left the air force blue uniform hanging in the wardrobe, not wishing to invite discussion from passing strangers unable to grasp the realities facing those in the bomber squadrons. He walked along the streets, past the rows of terraced houses, the only trace of war the occasional bombed-out residence, its fallen brickwork and masonry long since tidied away. He kept his head down, glad of a hat and coat now that dark grey clouds above had surrendered to heavy rain. He quickened his pace and found shelter in the archway of a familiar building. It was the Oakdale Mission, home to the bible classes he used to attend. He glanced towards the ground and the turn ups on his trousers. They were sodden. He leant down to squeeze the material, draining the rainwater over his shoes and on to the tiled step, but as he straightened up, the noise of a bolt behind made him jump. He turned to see the door open slowly and was taken aback at the sight before him.

'Vera?'

'Oh... it's you,' said the shocked voice, its familiar tone, gentle, female.

'Yes... it's me.'

He was struck anew by the beauty of the girl he had not seen for almost a year, the almond-shaped eyes a dark shade of amethyst, the shine of her ebony hair, the delicate, perfectly smooth skin. Yet for all the physical perfections, her most arresting qualities were sincerity and natural warmth. She was that rare example of someone beautiful on the outside yet even more so within.

'Eric... you're... erm... very wet.'

'I know... I got caught in a bit of a downpour,' he said, looking out towards the road. 'It seems to have calmed down a bit now'.

'What on earth are you doing here?'

'I don't know... I'm back from leave and needed to get some fresh air. I went out for a walk and without thinking ended up here... on this step.'

A crack of thunder made Vera jump, before a fresh downpour began to drown out their words.

'Do you want to come in until it goes off?' she shouted.

Eric thanked her and gladly took shelter inside the church hall.

'I've turned the boiler off,' she said, 'but it should still be warm enough.'

325

'How come you're here on your own?'

'Miss Finch had to leave early, and so I agreed to lock up. Did you want a cup of tea?'

'Are you sure it's not too much trouble?'

'Of course not.'

While she filled the kettle and lit the stove, Eric stood at the door to the kitchen, glancing around the main hall.

'It only seems like yesterday I was here,' he said, 'with Len making a fool of himself.'

Vera laughed, 'Ah, poor Len... or was it Derek?'

'Do you remember when he reckoned 'The Lord's My Shepherd' was about Jesus working as a hill farmer?'

'That's right.'

They both laughed, paving the way for Eric to experience a momentary yearning to return to more innocent times. But it quickly passed.

'Has Margaret said how Len's getting on?' he said, 'I haven't heard from him lately.'

'Fine... I think he's on an aircraft carrier somewhere in the Mediterranean.'

'That's good.'

Len would be alright, he thought. He was one of life's survivors, indefatigable, even in the face of the enemy.

The rain outside was hammering against the windows, endorsing the decision to take sanctuary inside. In all honesty, the weather was an irrelevance. As soon as he set eyes upon Vera, he wanted to be with her, to spend some time together. He had found it impossible to talk to his family about what was going through his head, but Vera was different, and the urge to confide in her was getting stronger by the second. There was a small table with chairs in the kitchen, and when the tea was ready to pour, they sat down on opposite sides to drink from their china cups. They started with the small things.

'Are you still at the bakery?'

'Sort of... I'm working at the flour mills on the Dock Road.'

'Sounds like hard work.'

'It's more boring than hard. When I was called up, I fancied joining the WAAFS, but I knew I couldn't leave Mum on her own with the girls, so I opted for Buchanan's.'

'How is your mum?'

'She's a lot better thanks.'

'Is becoming a WAAF still out of the question?'

'Funny you should ask, because no... Sylvia's seventeen now and can help out at home... so... I've applied.'

'Have you?'

'Yes.'

'You'll be great Vera. The boys will love you on the bases!'

She smiled, as much with her eyes as her mouth, and then looked away coyly as she asked a question.

'Have you met a WAAF while you've been away?'

'No... some of the lads are going steady, but not me.'

Eric took refuge in a sip of tea.

'What about you? Is there a GI who has stolen your heart?'

She threw back her head and giggled.

'No! I'm afraid there aren't many eligible bachelors round here at the moment.'

They stopped talking for a few seconds and stared down at the cups on the table, Eric lost and distracted, thinking about the irony of his current situation. The overriding reason for distancing himself from Vera had been the uncertainty of their future together; a factor vindicated by the fates of poor Reg and Gwen. Yet now, as he looked death in the face on an almost daily basis, the doubts about waking up tomorrow alive were fuelling his desire to get close to her. He had thought the only true antidote to the fear of mortality was God and the power of prayer, but he was beginning to appreciate a more powerful force, the force of love. It suddenly all made sense. Even the bible agreed. He recalled Corinthians 13:4-8.

'And though I have the gift of prophecy, and understand all mysteries and all knowledge; and though I have all faith, so that I could remove mountains, and have not love, I am nothing.'

On cue, he felt the soft, warm skin of Vera's hand cover his own. He glanced up.

'You look really tired Eric.'

'Do I?'

She nodded, the precursor to an outpouring from the RAF man.

'It's not easy you know...' he said.

Vera tightened her grip.

'The main difficulty,' he continued, 'is our pilot... he's struggling to cope. We've been selected as a crew on four sorties yet only completed one, and then we nearly ran out of fuel.'

He talked about the realities of Bomber Command, Vera heeding his words patiently without uttering a sound. By the time he had no more to say, the hall had turned cold, and although the rain was nowhere near as heavy, the place was getting darker by the minute.

'Would you like to dance Vera?'

'Dance?'

'Yes.'

'But there's no music.'

'It doesn't matter.'

He stood up and led her by the hand to the main hall to stand in front of the empty class. There was enough space here for a waltz. The pair went into hold, and as Eric began to hum the melody to 'Underneath the

Arches', a slow dance followed, the couple slowly revolving in small circles across the wood block floor.

'De-de-de de de-de,
De de de de de-de,
De-de-de de de-de de de-de-de de...'

They drifted into a dream world, the humming deteriorating into an intermittent drone, their hold collapsing to leave them leaning against one another for support. Vera's head was now resting on his shoulder, and a surge of sadness and regret about what might have been threatened to wash him away. There was now virtual silence in the room, yet still the Flanagan & Allen tune played in his head. The same song that had made him cry with laughter at Ginger and Barrington's double act was now threatening to make him cry again, a lump in his throat making it difficult to swallow. Vera, however, succumbed, her restrained weeping characteristically tender. He held on to her as tightly as he could, and she the same, the young dancers protecting one another from the weight and the worries of the troubled world, if only for the briefest of moments. They swayed gently until the song and the dance gradually faded away.

Eric and Vera stood there, facing one another and holding hands.

'Thank you for the dance Vera.'

'No... thank you,' she said, dabbing her eyes.

'I've been thinking,' he said.

'About what?'

'About the future?'

'And?'

'Well... not to think about it... to take one day at a time.'

'I understand... live for the day and let the future take care of itself.'

'Yes... that's basically it.'

'I'd just say one thing. On one of those days when you wake up, would you remember to write this time,' she said.

329

'I will... I promise.'

The rain had stopped. It was time to go home.

Eric settled down for the remainder of his leave. He came to appreciate how much he had needed the break, his chance encounter with Vera key in changing his outlook. And so it was a reinvigorated Eric on the platform to Lime Street Station awaiting his train back to Lincolnshire. He had kept the goodbyes to his dad and brother routine and was determined to do the same with his mum and nan standing next to him. But there was one thing he wanted to say.

'Mum?'

'Yes Eric.'

'About Billy...'

'What about him? Oh his lateness... I've already told him he needs to get up...'

'No Mum... not that.'

He put his hand on her forearm, an unfamiliar tactile act.

'I know he's only sixteen next month, but make sure you get him in a reserved occupation. Don't let him join up.'

'Oh... and what job do you think?'

'Maybe an apprentice draughtsman at Cammel Lairds... he has a genuine talent for drawing. I think it could be the making of him.'

Eric's comments had unnerved her, not because of Billy, more the inference about himself. But he had to say it. Seeing at first hand the dispensability of young life in Bomber Command, he wanted something different for his brother. Moreover, he did not want his mum to end up losing both of her children.

A soldier next to them opened his newspaper, revealing its front headline, a bullish celebration about the latest RAF bombing raids on Berlin.

'Don't believe everything you read in the papers… there's a lot of propaganda out there you know.'

Despite his original intentions, he leant over and kissed his mum on the cheek and then his nan before picking up his kitbag to walk to the awaiting train.

He had only taken a couple of steps, when he heard old Nan Beecroft say to her daughter, 'I don't think we'll see him again.'

He ignored the comment and picked up the pace to find a seat in the compartment. He looked back once and waved.

CHAPTER 36

The return from leave of Eric, Mac, Don, Joe, Arthur, Ginger and Barrington to Kirmington coincided with a two week period when the squadron was stood down from operations. During this time, the commanders took advantage of the moon's phase to train six new crews up to operational standard and re-train Eric's group. Finally on 15th February, 166 Squadron were detailed to attack the enemy, the accustomed dismay greeting the news that the target was once again Berlin.

In the first sortie for the Peter McIntosh crew since the late take off and abandoned mission of nearly a month ago, the pre-flight checks, preparations, and subsequent departure were mercifully uneventful. At the cruising height of 20,000 feet, there were no Luftwaffe fighters, no searchlights, and only moderate opposition from ground to air defences. It made what was about to happen all the more perplexing.

They had been in the air for two and a half hours, now deep over enemy territory when without warning Mac banked the Lancaster sharply to the left, and then left again, before straightening up.

'Navigator here Skip... are we on a change of course?'

Don was more baffled than anyone but stayed true to his regular, calm persona. The pilot glanced across to Eric and shook his head from side to side.

'Sorry boys,' he announced, 'I can't do this... we're heading back to base.'

No-one in the crew challenged him, but they were all thinking the same. This was almost certainly to be interpreted as LMF, lack of moral fibre.

There was no greater shame within Bomber Command. Peter McIntosh would be stripped of his rank and humiliated, his only compensation this was not the 1914-1918 Great War when such actions were considered a Court Marshall offence that warranted death by firing squad.

The homeward journey was as uneventful as the outward leg, the return to base a sombre occasion, the only communications those necessary to navigate and land the aircraft successfully. After the briefest of interrogations, tea laced with rum, and a somewhat indigestible plate of bacon and eggs, the rest of the crew were informed that Pilot McIntosh had been taken off flying duties, and that they were to return to their billet until further notice.

****

The daily routines continued without Mac, without any news of his fate, and without operational sorties for the crew. However, a few days on and it was a return to action for some of the group, Eric, Ginger and Barrington, the men instructed to crew up with a Flight Officer Stamford for an evening raid to Leipsig. Twenty two aircraft left the base, JB649 departing at 11.45. It proved to be a busy night for the gunners with large numbers of enemy fighters in action. On more than one occasion, Eric heard the voices of Ginger and Barrington over the intercom, 'Corkscrew to starboard skipper, corkscrew to starboard.', certain they shared his own silent gratitude that an experienced Flight Officer was at the controls to take the necessary evasive action in shaking off the ME 110 in pursuit. They bombed the target at 04.19 and made it home by 06.55, thankful not to be one of three 166 Squadron aircraft that 'bought it' on the mission.

There was little rest for the men the following day, the same crew selected to fly with Stamford on a raid to Stuttgart in the evening. In contrast to Leipsig, this was a routine sortie with no enemy fighter action encountered and no aircraft from the squadron lost, the first such incidence since Eric had arrived. He ended the day hoping for a few more raids like this one.

****

A few days later, the lads were sat in their billet passing the time, Barrington having forty winks, Don doing a crossword, and with no sense of the supreme irony involved, Joe reading Agatha Christie's *Death in the Clouds*. Eric, Ginger and Arthur were playing cards.

'Twist… twist… bugger… I'm bust.'

Arthur was out.

'Hey chaps,' said Don from his bed, 'can anyone help with this one… 10 across… 'Not the Rear End'… eight letters… A-blank-blank-E-four blanks?'

'Arsehole,' said Arthur, deadpan.

The others laughed.

'What's funny?' said the offended Yorkshireman.

'Arsehole is the rear end,' said Don, his well-modulated intonation on the colloquialism making it sound all the more funny.

'Anterior.'

The door to their sleeping quarters had opened. Standing there, looking healthy, refreshed, uniform immaculate, was a certain Flight Sergeant Peter McIntosh. Eric glanced straightaway at his sergeant's stripes. They were still there.

''Not the Rear End', eight letters beginning with A, Anterior,' Mac explained.

This was more than a surprise and the others reacted by gaping and saying nothing until Barrington woke up, rubbed his eyes, and uttered an everyday, 'Morning Skip,' as though he was just back from the baker's.

334

It broke the ice and the others raised themselves to shake the pilot by the hand. At a personal level, they were all delighted to see him looking so well. The lack of information about his welfare had led them to speculate all manner of things, none of them good. The returning airman invited his colleagues to sit down. He wanted to explain the situation.

'I've been away the last few days having a few tests and assessments on the recommendation of Wing Commander Powney. And to cut a long story short, I'm transferring to a specialist unit, which unfortunately I'm not able to talk about… I'm sure you understand.'

The rest of the crew nodded. Eric had been right about Fred Powney. The Canadian had not only managed Mac's unsuitability for Bomber Command with sympathy and humanity, he had spotted untapped potential in the young Scot and facilitated a solution to use his undoubted talent and intellect for the rest of the war.

'The thing is…' said Mac, hesitating with a familiar sweeping back of his hair, 'I know I've let you down.'

'You haven't let anyone down Skip.'

It was Ginger who spoke up, and his conviction was shared by the others who chimed in agreement. They all knew first-hand the demands placed on aircrews, but pilots were subject to particular pressure and stress. To some, it was water off a duck's back to take to the skies and attack the enemy, but for a sensitive, intelligent soul such as Mac, it was never going to be easy. In that sense, Eric concluded, his friend had displayed enormous courage to persevere, a courage now reciprocated by the leadership of their Commander. And a final act of bravery and valour was still to come.

'Listen chaps, even if I haven't let you down, I feel I owe it to you and to myself to finish on a high. So… with one of the Flight Commanders flying second dickie, I will be piloting JB649 this evening on a sortie to Schweinfurt with you chaps as my crew.'

Notice of selection for a bombing raid was not ordinarily greeted with enthusiasm, but today they were all pleased. It was a chance to put the difficulties of their aborted and abandoned missions behind them. Consequently, the normal level of apprehension that accompanied the build up to a night raid was missing.

For 166 Squadron, Operation Schweinfurt started badly. One Lancaster failed to depart, one crashed on take-off, another collided with a fellow four engine bomber in the main stream, and two had to return to base due to navigational difficulties. For the remaining fourteen, including Eric and his colleagues on JB649, the mission proved otherwise straightforward and uneventful, Mac transformed in terms of confidence and competence. After a successful bomb drop over the smoking target, the crew returned home at 5.00am having been in the air for nearly nine hours.

That ought to have been it for Mac, ready now to transfer to his new section. But he insisted on one more flight, this time without the calming presence of a flight commander. In acknowledgement of the new found confidence in their skipper, none of the lads, Eric included, experienced or voiced any concerns about the plan. The raid came the next evening on 25th February, a sortie to the Bavarian town of Augsburg, home to the U-Boat diesel engine factories. They left Kirmington in daylight with conditions of good visibility and enjoyed a trouble free route, reaching the target for Joe Penfold's 'Bombs Gone' pronouncement to occur at 22.59. Although the flight engineer spent most of his time reading dials and instruments, part of his remit was to support the gunners and bomb aimer in scanning the skies for fighters, and it was Eric who spotted the enemy aircraft first, adrenaline shooting through him at the speed of a bullet.

'Corkscrew to port skipper... enemy fighter ahead... corkscrew to port,' he shouted.

Mac responded with lightning reactions, diving down sharply to the left, the Lancaster demonstrating its surprising manoeuvrability for such a giant of an aircraft, while tracer from the gunners in their turrets tore through the air in the direction of the German plane. The skipper then straightened out the aircraft only for Ginger to spot another fighter, this time above.

'Corkscrew portside Skip... corkscrew portside...'

Again, Mac's actions were almost instant, expertly losing height and modifying their direction. Flak blasted around them, the exploding fragments clattering the fuselage and provoking some uncompromising turbulence. Additional firing from the turrets momentarily overpowered the drone of the four Merlins, Eric quick to note the engines continuing to perform well, clearly having escaped any damage so far in the attack. Joe warned of another Lancaster only 500 feet below them, Mac once more adjusting the height and position of JB649 to keep them safe. There were a few more tense moments that followed but soon the crew breathed a little easier in the recognition they had survived the assault.

Glancing back over his shoulder, Eric watched Augsburg recede into the distance, the city a concentrated mass of fire, smoke rising towards the sky. The incident with the fighters had been the ultimate test of skill and nerve for Mac in his first combat engagement with the Luftwaffe, and he had succeeded far beyond the crew's expectations, his pride, dignity, and honour intact. They returned to Kirmington at 2.40am, mission complete, a happy ending for the crew, but still an ending. With Mac leaving for pastures new, the rest were unsure as to what the future held. Would they get a new pilot, or would they be farmed out to other aircrews as late replacements? Eric feared the latter.

****

Snow fell in Lincolnshire on the first day of March, though it failed to stop 166 Squadron sending fifteen aircraft on a successful mission to

Stuttgart, Eric flying with an aircrew led by another pilot, Flight Sergeant Mycroft. They were the last sorties from Kirmington for a couple of weeks, the inclement weather cancelling planned night raids on four subsequent evenings. When the snow cleared, it was the moon's turn to delay operations, and it wasn't until the 15th that night bombings resumed with another attack on Stuttgart, one that Eric sat out, although Ginger, Joe and Arthur took part, albeit on different aircraft.

The crew was providing a flexible source of manpower for other aircrews in need, and it had become evident that Mac was not going to be replaced, an ideal arrangement for those in command but dispiriting for Eric and his colleagues. They had even transferred to different billets. Eric, Ginger and Barrington now shared sleeping quarters with the crew of Flight Officer Stamford, the men with whom the flight engineer had flown recent sorties to Leipsig and Stuttgart. The collective bond that bound Stamford's group of seven was plain to see, unquestionably helping them cope with the extraordinary demands placed upon their young shoulders, something denied to Eric's crew because of its fragmentation.

For his next sortie, there was another pilot with whom to share the Lancaster cockpit, a Flight Sergeant Fenner. The target for the raid was Frankfurt, and with Barrington for company as rear gunner, the mission was a straightforward affair. The snows came and went until four days later, Eric and the same crew augmented by Ginger Bowland experienced another uncomplicated bombing raid to the same city. Although impossible to be blasé about a tour of operations, the sorties were becoming almost routine. Returning to their living quarters in the early hours of the morning, Eric, Ginger and Barrington lay on their beds and quickly dropped off to sleep.

Eric emerged a few hours later from a fitful slumber to see Ginger sitting at the end of his bed.

'Morning Eric.'

'Ginge...'

'It doesn't look good for the other lads,' he said, his carrot hair messed up like Stan Laurel.

'What's that?'

'The Stamford boys haven't returned.'

Eric glanced across to the other side of the billet and took in the row of empty beds, the tell-tale sign that aircrew and bomber had been downed by the enemy during last night's operation. The hope at these times was always the same; that they had parachuted to safety and were now attempting to escape from the clutches of the Germans or were at least safe and well as Prisoners of War. Given the rumoured one in five chance of escaping a stricken Lancaster, the hope was often forlorn.

His eyes for the first time spotted the photograph by the bedside of his fellow flight engineer Henry, the man for whom he had deputised last month. It was a family snap, probably his mum, dad, brothers and sisters, all now at home blissfully unaware of the bad news. Henry was a larger than life character with a booming laugh, and their sleeping quarters would be quieter without him. Eric had woken to the new day after a pitiable three hours sleep and now wanted nothing more than the lost engineer to walk in and tell one of his terrible jokes. He would laugh with all his heart. Later on, squadron personnel known as the 'Committee of Adjustment' would arrive to carry out the sombre task of removing all personal effects to be sent to the families of the missing. The family photo would need a new home.

'Do you ever think it might be you next?' said Ginger, his expression downcast.

It was too early for a question like this, and Eric was not in the mood to tackle it.

'Not really,' he said, lying back down on the bed and turning around.

He tried, without success, for a little more sleep. And things were about to get worse. A letter arrived early that morning from Margery, Dougie McVitie's Scot's lass in Woodford. In echoes of the fate that befell Reg and Gwen, he read that the larger than life Glaswegian with the Mediterranean good looks was no more, killed on the recent Augsburg raid. Death was now so commonplace, so every day, that Eric might have been excused for reacting to the news in a cold, sterile way, but Dougie had been such a rich, larger than life character, his demise appeared all the more devastating and difficult to accept. He tore the letter until little more than confetti, sprinkling the paper into the coke stove. Eric had reached a new low point.

****

There was no respite for the aircrews of Kirmington, the bombing raids continuing night after night, the schedule only impacted by lunar or meteorological interruptions. On 24th March, Eric, Ginger and Barrington flew sorties to Berlin on what was a bad night for 166 Squadron, four aircraft lost on the raid when miscalculated homeward winds sent many aircrews off course. Reuniting safe and well in the early hours, the friends encountered a stronger feeling of relief than usual. They had survived another game of Bomber Command's Russian roulette.

Two days later Eric was mobilised for a raid to Essen, accompanying Pilot Officer Bridge aboard ND621. Returning to the billet from their Lancaster's pre-inspection, he browsed through his Operations Log Book, surprised to see he had flown with seven different pilots. The majority of flight engineers served their squadron with the same man at the controls, but Eric's log told a very different story. He also noted this would be his fifteenth sortie, the halfway point on a tour, though not for him, the abandoned and aborted missions with Mac not counting towards the target. There was still some way to go.

After a short sleep, Eric left with Ginger and Barrington to attend the pre-flight briefing. There were only two bikes outside the hut that afternoon, and so Barrington being a little chap readily agreed to ride on Ginger's crossbar. The memory of Flanagan and Allen and the cycle ride back from the Black Bull in Hatfield flooded through Eric's head as he followed behind them. On cue the pair in front began to sing 'Run Adolf Run', Barrington stretching his short legs in time to the music, a rare moment of light relief amongst the underlying trepidation and apprehension that dominated the day of a sortie.

The briefing was routine with no real surprises, and the ritual continued with a walk to the mess for the pre-flight bacon and eggs. Ginger and Barrington were already at a nearby table tucking in to their food and enjoying a laugh with Arthur when Eric joined them.

'Ayup Eric.'

'Hello Arthur, how's it going?'

'Not bad lad.'

Arthur may have been the same age as Eric, but he tended to adopt the persona of an old man whittling wood and chewing on tobacco.

'I'm with Bridgy tonight,' said Eric, 'what about you?'

'Owens... an' a couple o' Canadian lads.'

The flight engineer turned to Ginger and Barrington.

'What about you boys?'

'Vince Perryman,' said Barrington, mopping up the last dregs of food on his plate with two fingers.

'I'm told he's a good pilot,' said Eric.

'Vince the Prince,' added Ginger. 'We paupers are in safe hands tonight.'

The exchanges led to a quick chat about Mac. No-one had heard anything since his departure. Other news included Don's transfer to the Pathfinder Force, Arthur suggesting he was now actually working for the BBC as a continuity announcer. With hot tea swilling around their stomachs and washing down the fat, the friends stood up and wished one another 'good luck' for the night's sortie.

It was a Sunday, and so Eric paid a quick visit to Kirmington's chapel, a typically unpretentious and makeshift RAF House of God with pulpit, chairs, and lit candles. It may have been far from the ornate majesty of Westminster Abbey, but in its own modest way, the place was an equal in terms of holiness. There was no service taking place at this time, Eric sitting down alone on a front row seat before removing his side cap, lowering his head, and closing his eyes to pray.

He called upon God to take care of his family and friends, notably Mum, Dad, Billy, and last but not least, Vera. He prayed for the aircrews, for Ginger, Barrington, and Arthur, and he silently mouthed the text from Ephesians written with such care and precision on the 'Warfare' inserts of his bible.

'Put on the whole armour of God that ye may be able to stand against the wiles of the devil.'

Eric got to his feet and left the calm solitude of the chapel for the decibels of anti-aircraft fire and four Rolls Royce Merlin engines generating 5,000 rpm at 22,000 feet.

Essen with its tank and artillery factories was a shorter haul than other German targets, and after a relatively short and successful five hours in the air, Pilot Officer Bridge with Flight Engineer Whitfield alongside returned in their Lancaster at 1.05am, the personnel in the interrogations room chalking up the return time for ND621. A routine end to the flight ensued with Eric and the rest of the crew making their way to the building for debriefing.

Inside there was the familiar bustle of intelligence staff, officers, and aircrews drinking tea, smoking cigarettes, and answering endless questions. Those that had spent the evening at Kirmington looked smart and manicured, unlike the returning men whose demeanours and appearance reflected the rigours of flying at altitude with an absence of comfort and lack of protection. This was especially true for the rear gunner, positioned at the back of the aircraft with part of the Perspex canopy usually removed to give the necessary clear lookout for enemy fighters. Eric searched for the darkened face of little Barrington but failed to spot him. He looked across to the schedule of aircrews on the blackboard. Nineteen had been marked as departed but only eighteen as returned. His stomach lurched. The gap was against Flight Sergeant Vince Perryman, the Lancaster on which Ginger and Barrington had flown.

He checked his watch. There was still plenty of time for the aircraft to make it back. If stricken in some way, Operations Control would still be in the dark because wireless messages were never risked until close to the English coast. It was perfectly feasible that the bomber had developed engine difficulties, reduced height and speed to run on a lean mixture of fuel, and set course on a slow but safe journey to Kirmington. They could also have diverted to another airfield as a result of a navigational error, but he was unable to shake off the nagging fear that this was something serious, so much so that he lingered around until most of personnel in the interrogations room had left for the mess or for their beds.

Wing Commander Fred Powney was still present, sitting next to a WAAF from Intelligence. Eric approached the pair.

'Excuse me sir, any news on LL749?'

The Canadian had a pencil in his hand that he was bouncing on the table. He stopped and looked Eric in the eye.

'Have you friends in the aircrew?'

'Yes sir… the two gunners.'

'Listen Sergeant, I suggest you go and get some sleep. You've had another tough night, and I'm sure you know there's nothing you can do here that will make any difference.'

'Yes sir.'

The Squadron Commander's message was brusque yet couched in understanding and sympathy. Eric thanked him and cycled back to the billet, the air sharp and penetrating on the journey. The Nissen hut, always austere and unwelcoming from the outside, was tonight as cold and sombre on the inside. It was empty, the combustion stove lifeless, all beds unoccupied. The personnel effects of Flight Lieutenant Stamford and his crew had been removed with replacements yet to fill the empty spaces. As he braved the chill to turn off the lights and take refuge under his RAF issue blankets, he made a conscious effort to avoid looking at the beds of Ginger and Barrington. He picked up his bible and torch from the side of his bed to take solace from a holy chapter or two.

CHAPTER 37

Billy looked at the time in horror. It was 9 o'clock. He had overslept. The one day his mum was out on an early errand, and he had fallen back asleep. He rushed out of bed and started to dress as quickly as he could, but when he fell backwards on to the floor trying to pull up his socks; he stayed there staring at the lined paper peeling at the edges of the ceiling. What was the point in hurrying? The damage was done. He was going to be at least an hour late, so why bother breaking his back? He reverted to his normal routine, doing everything at the pedestrian pace that suited his early morning physiology.

During his tardy commuting journey, there was no escaping the time, the giant clock hands of the Seacombe Ferry terminal and the Liver Buildings bookending his trip across the river. As he walked up Bold Street to the GEC building, Billy was acutely aware of his record breaking achievement. Even he had never been as late as 10.30 am. It was a mild, early spring morning, yet Billy was feeling hot under the collar, the discomfort intensifying when he pictured the scene of a purple-faced Mr Butler as chair of the welcoming committee. He took one last deep breath, turned the corner, and walked through the revolving doors into the grand reception of the General Electric Company, taking the lift to his floor.

A quick glance through the glass revealed Butler to be at his desk, so Billy sidled in, exaggerated the time in the signing-in book, and limbo-danced to his chair. Edna the secretary and Joe Roberts gave surprised looks, but the real concern was Terry Ellis, the pugnacious young man with the curly hair, snub nose, and fierce expression. He was smirking, looking far too self-satisfied for comfort. The latecomer tried to lose himself in tallying a batch of invoices sitting on his desk, but the creak heard from the door to the manager's office signalled that the moment of truth had arrived.

'This way Whitfield,' shouted Butler, returning to his office as quickly as he had emerged.

Billy respectfully obeyed.

'Shut the door behind you.'

Again he did as he was told, sitting down on the chair in front of the large desk laden with pending trays and lever arch files.

'Let me tell you about Private Johnny Corbett.'

Billy was surprised at the opening line. He had been ready for a 'What time do you call this?'

'Corbett was serving with the King's Shropshire Light Infantry at Anzio in Italy a few months ago, when he injured his foot in a landmine explosion. His fellow soldiers thought he was dead, but he wasn't. Then it was thought his right foot would have to be amputated, but it wasn't. He recovered and is alive and well today. Now... I'm sure you would agree that's what you would call a piece of good news?'

Billy was confused but answered, 'yes... I suppose so.'

'Although not good news for everyone,' said the obsequious manager, a grimace of a smile smearing his face, 'and certainly not for you.'

The young clerk's bewilderment deepened.

'I'm sorry I...'

'Don't understand? Quite... well, young Johnny Corbett used to work here before you arrived. In fact, you could say you took his job. Now, despite his recovery from the land mine incident, he has unfortunately been invalided out of the army and is now looking for a job on Civvy Street. The good news for Johnny is that I have offered him his old job back. The bad news... well I'm not sure it is bad news, but, whatever, I'm going to have to let you go.'

It took a few moments for Billy to understand what was happening. He slowly realised he was getting the sack with one week's notice, which he was not required to work. The official reason for going was to accommodate the returning soldier, but it was really all about the timekeeping. Butler assured him that his future employment prospects would not be damaged by the outcome. He handed him a letter and told him to clear his things. Billy walked slowly and disconsolately to his desk to gather up his possessions.

Joe came across.

'What's up Bill lad?'

'He's told me to go.'

'Go 'ome?'

'Yes... I've been sacked.'

Joe puffed his cheeks and blew out.

'Crikey, that's not good.'

'Are you leaving us?' said Terry from the next desk, unable to hide his contentment at the turn of events.

Joe jumped to the defence of his young friend.

'Hey carrot face! D'yer wanna another black eye?'

It wiped away the smirk in an instant.

Joe put his hand on Billy's shoulder.

'Listen Bill lad, yer better off out o' here. I'm joining up next month, and yer don't wanna be stuck with old greasy chops in charge and that pipsqueak over there doin' 'is biddin'.'

Terry flushed a little.

'Thanks Joe, I think you're right.'

Edna approached. 'I see you're off.'

'Yes.'

'Well good luck.'

She kissed him on the cheek. It was his turn to flush before beginning the lonely walk out of the office.

'And one other thing,' the secretary added, 'do yourself a favour and get a new alarm clock for your birthday.'

Billy smiled and agreed, leaving the fifth floor via the lift for the final time. Despite the shock of the morning's events, he spent the journey home feeling relaxed about telling his mum and dad, the Johnny Corbett story a great help in that sense. But he did ponder about what to do next. Maybe it was time to fulfil his dreams, or at least his practical dreams. Goalkeeping would have to wait until the war was over, but Billy Whitfield could become a draughtsman. Yes, he liked the sound of that.

CHAPTER 38

It was terrible thing to wake to, Eric alone in the billet, his first image the desperately sad sight of Ginger and Barrington's empty beds. After a wash and shave, he headed to the main building of the base to seek the latest information. There was none. The pair as prisoners of war was the best hope, the only hope. News broke that the squadron were stood down from operations for the day, ordinarily good news, but today of all days, Eric wanted to be occupied. One of the drawbacks in Bomber Command was the downtime between operations. Sometimes, resting aircrews had too much time on their hands, too much time to dwell on the difficult things. And so it proved.

He spent much of the day writing letters, one to his mum and dad, one to Len, one to Vera. In truth, he was lonely, envious of the camaraderie still intact for surviving seven man crews. His band of brothers was all over the place, Mac and Don enjoying pastures new somewhere, Joe and Arthur home on leave courtesy of a forty eight hour pass, Ginger and Barrington, well only God knew their whereabouts. He was about to take the envelopes to be posted, when he checked himself. He opened the letter to Vera and re-read it, immediately realising he was in the wrong frame of mind to write home. He tore the paper into small strips, depositing the shreds in the small metal bin near the door and then did the same with the other two envelopes. Writing would have to wait until another day.

Struggling to get Ginger and Barrington out of his head, he again went to see if there were any more developments, irrationally believing the news could be good. And there was new information. A communications centre in the UK had intercepted and decrypted a communiqué from the Luftwaffe indicating that a four engine enemy aircraft had been shot down by flak, bursting into flames at 22.15 hours on 26th March 1944, 2km north of Essen. The bomber had suffered 99% damage with six dead.

It was shattering news for Eric. Despite the possibility that one of his friends may have survived, it was an unlikely prospect given the dubious challenge that faced mid-upper and rear gunners when attempting to escape from their little turrets. Furthermore, it could be months before any real news broke about a surviving POW. He had to accept he had lost both pals. Needing some fresh air, he went outside for a smoke. A few other crew members passed and said hello. Eric ignored them, through distraction not discourtesy. He lit another cigarette, drawing and inhaling hard. This was the lowest moment of his RAF life, his lowest moment in any life, if truth be told. The trail of death and sorrow that lay behind him was mesmerising.

There was the son of his cigar-smoking landlady in Blackpool lost in an Atlantic convoy; the husband of the demure Kitty killed in a RAF training incident; the wonderful Reg Wilson from Ludlow who had left a widow and an unborn child after he 'went for a Burton' over Hamburg; the one and only Dougie McVitie the Maltese Scot; and the copious 103 and 166 squadron crew members who had paid the ultimate price in the fiery hell of the skies above Germany, culminating in the latest victims, his closest pals in the RAF, Rear Gunner Sergeant Barrington Haynes and Mid-Upper Gunner Sergeant Alec 'Ginger' Bowland... Bud Flanagan and Chesney Allen.

These thoughts suddenly gave rise to a surge of indignation within that hastily transformed into anger. He threw the rest of his cigarette to the ground, twisting and pulverising it with the sole of his boot. He needed to get out of here, to escape, to leave this sorry mess behind and live a life that was mundane, ordinary, unexciting. Where the small things in life mattered. Where there was a future. A future where he took his mum and dad for afternoon tea at Liverpool's Adelphi Hotel. A future where he and Billy went for a pint at the Boot Inn. A future where he and Vera walked a Silver Cross pram through Central Park on a sunny Saturday afternoon. Vera... lovely Vera...

Now he understood how Reg felt when they left Blackpool... the trunk call to ask Gwen the big question. Eric checked the time and closed his eyes to visualise the rail timetables. If he hurried, he could catch the train from Barnetby to Leeds, get a connection to Liverpool, and be at Vera's house before bedtime to ask for her hand in marriage. There was no time to get an official pass, but he was due leave anyway. Any awkward questions he would attribute to an administrative error.

Jumping on his bike, he rode to his billet as though on *Le Tour de France*, grabbed his travelling papers and wallet, the same wallet that Vera had sent through the post as a 'very late Christmas present', and hurried out to cycle the few miles to the station. There was no problem leaving the base, the guards waving him through, and he was in Barnetby Le Wold sooner than expected, travelling along Victoria Road past the Post Office until the train station came into sight. Beyond its red brick walls a plume of smoke wafted into the air. Eric heard the slow chug of a locomotive and prayed this was the sound of a train arriving and not one departing.

To his dismay the trail from the engine's smokestack was moving away from him, and his fears were realised when he rode through the entrance and on to the platform to see the rear of the last carriage pulling out of the station. He had missed his train, yet instead of doing the sensible thing and accepting the fact, he quickened his pedalling and chased after the departing coaches along the narrow lane that ran adjacent to the track. At one point he believed he was catching up, but the Barnetby to Leeds gathered speed, and Eric ran out of road. Breathing heavily, he came to a halt, a flood of frustration drowning out the rational conclusion that the chase was always going to fail. He jumped off his bike and held it up above his head like Hercules before slinging it down into a narrow, dry ditch. He then jumped on it like the cigarette stub earlier and similarly pounded the stricken cycle with his boots, twisting and disfiguring the spokes on the wheels and snapping one of the brake cables. There was no witness to this loss of control, this breakdown, this act of wanton violence against the inanimate, steel object. He sat down on the grass amongst the weeds and wept, 'Underneath the Arches' playing inside his head, the song he would never hear again without a flash of sadness and sorrow.

The tears dried up, but he remained on the ground staring into space. He was not sure for how long he stayed there, but a train coming from the opposite direction awakened him from his daydreams, his overriding emotion now one of remorse. He was the lucky one. He was alive. And as for the idea to head home without official permission in his current state of mind, it was foolish to say the least. He pulled the wounded bicycle out from the ditch, relieved to see it was just about roadworthy. He twisted the handlebars and seat so they were straight, reattached the chain to the front sprocket, tied the damaged brake cable to the crossbar, and then rode back along the lane, out of the station and on to the Kirmington road. Arriving at the camp gates, he was welcomed back by the guards, no questions asked, and anonymously deposited his bike in a quiet spot to be found later by a bemused member of the RAF Police. There was only one place for him to go to now.

The chapel was as quiet as yesterday, when his prayers to protect Ginger and Barrington had fallen on deaf ears. He sat on the same front seat, removed his side cap again, lowered his head and spoke silently to God, wanting to know why there was such injustice, why so many good people left this earth too early. The questions were rhetorical. He was not expecting a booming voice to shout an explanation from the heavens, but he sought an answer nonetheless. He arose from this biblical solitude and slowly made his way back to the isolation of the Nissen hut where, not for the first time, his bible was to provide much needed solace. From the trough of Barnetby Station, he had recovered his poise. Tomorrow would be a new day. He had to stay strong. Like it or not, there was still a war to be won.

CHAPTER 39

The rumour spread that the day ahead, Thursday 30th March 1944, was going to be a big one, and by early afternoon battle orders had been issued listing the names of twenty pilots in 166 Squadron selected for the raid later that evening. With Eric still unaffiliated to a particular crew, he had no idea at this point if he was flying, but as the day progressed and the pre-mission routines bustled with a level of activity rarely seen, he appeared destined for another day stood down from operations.

He was in the mess reading a newspaper, when a group of none-too-pleased airmen returned from their briefing session. Its number included Flight Sergeant 'Freddie' Fenner, the pilot from Eric's recent sorties to Frankfurt.

'Every alright Fred?'

'Not really,' he grumbled.

'What's up?'

'We're going to Nuremberg.'

'Well it's not Berlin,' said Eric, airing the 'Anywhere but Berlin' opinion commonly held by aircrew.

'It's not the place... it's the route... one virtual bloomin' straight leg.'

'What do you mean?'

'We follow a horizontal line past Liege, Cologne and Frankfurt, which are all heavily defended areas with flak, searchlights, and nearby night fighter squadrons. The route will give their ground radar plenty of time to trace the stream and then send in fighters for them to have a field day... let's hope to God there's decent cloud cover.'

Eric looked out of the window, the view a more or less clear blue sky, and muttered, 'Yes... let's hope so.'

'It's a full moon as well! Sometimes I wonder about our Commander-in-Chief.'

'I expect it'll be cancelled.'

The last few days had seen crews stood down late in the day due to adverse weather conditions.

'Maybe... but I'll tell you one thing Eric... you're a lucky blighter to be sitting this one out.'

The stance of Freddie Fenner was the norm rather than the exception, Eric inclined to agree with the sentiment. He wished his fellow airmen good luck and returned to his billet ready to write a few letters home, now that he was enjoying a much healthier frame of mind after the upset of the other day. He began writing to his mum but had only composed a few lines when he felt drowsy. The stop start nature of the week's cancelled operations had interfered with his regular sleep pattern, not least because of the amphetamine tablets taken to sustain concentration at high altitude. These 'wakey wakey' pills were less useful when trying to get some normal shut-eye at the base. Eric was soon in the land of nod.

He was woken later by a gentle knock at the door.

Sitting up quickly in bed, he shouted, 'Come in.'

It was all very civilised, such a contrast to the days of square-bashing and bawling NCOs. A WAAF stood there.

'Excuse me... Sergeant Whitfield?'

'Yes?'

'You're needed urgently in Operations. The flight engineer on Flight Lieutenant Tiler's aircraft has reported sick with jaundice, and you've been assigned to take his place.'

So much for the good fortune... he was going to Nuremberg after all.

He looked at the pathetic output from his letters home and concluded they would have to wait until tomorrow.

There was a 'meat wagon' waiting outside to speed him to the 'Para' department to collect his parachute and flying gear. After getting togged up, Eric was driven to the edge of the base in the same vehicle to join the Tiler crew on the Lancaster Mk III standing at its dispersal point. As he absorbed the awe-inspiring sight of the vast metal airframe silhouetted against a near cloudless, moonlit sky, the cold air turned his exhaled breath into small clouds of vapour. Fred Fenner's unease about a lack of cloud cover remained a distinct concern.

In fact, the first sentence from one of the ground crew who greeted him was a terse and tense, 'I'll be surprised if you fly tonight.'

Eric climbed up the small ladder and into the aircraft, clambering his way through the confined space. He greeted the navigator and wireless operator as he moved past them towards the cockpit, where he discovered an extra man aboard, a new pilot flying 'second dickie' on his first sortie. They shook hands, the trainee introducing himself as Harry Hughes. The skipper explained he would handle the take-off before passing the controls to Sergeant Hughes at cruising altitude. There was no indication about what would happen when close to the target, but that was a long way off. Nuremberg was one of the more distant cities, and even if all went to plan, the flight was likely to last over eight hours. Given their full bomb load, he was not the only flight engineer in Bomber Command that evening with anxieties over fuel.

Eric quickly defaulted to professional mode and slotted into the pre-flight check routines with ease. He did, however, keep one eye on the control tower, perhaps more in hope than expectation for a red light to indicate cancellation of the raid. But with the time at 21.45, the first Lancaster taxied its way to the end of the runway for departure. He watched as the four Merlin engines powered thirty tons of machine and munitions along the concrete strip and off the ground towards the stars in the clearest of skies. The red light had failed to appear. Eric was definitely going to Nuremberg.

Tiler was one of the more experienced pilots, though 'experience' was a relative term, the skipper still in his early twenties with only a few months under his belt. Being a flight officer acting up as a flight lieutenant, his crew would be amongst the first to leave, a factor that always enhanced the chances of survival, enemy fighters scrambling too late to catch the early bird bombers. And so at 21.53, ME638 became only the fourth of the 166 Lancasters to take off for the target. As they climbed, Eric shot a hurried backwards glance out of the Perspex canopy to see the remaining sixteen aircraft lining up in an orderly manner to ascend and join the fray.

The first part of the journey to Charleroi passed without incident, the pilot exchanging places with Sergeant Hughes as promised. The number of aircrews scheduled to leave Kirmington had indicated this was a major raid, yet Eric was still surprised at the number of bombers in the main stream. He had never seen such participation, and it added to his alarm. The cloud cover promised by the men from the Met Office was conspicuous by its absence, and there was worse, ME638 leaving a path of smoke in its wake. Eric initially believed the problem was engine trouble, and he executed a quick check on the instrument panel, but the readings were normal. He then noted other bombers in the stream painting the same white lines across the sky.

'They're bloody vapour trails,' said the Skipper, standing behind Hughes. 'We'll be sitting ducks.'

The meteorological conditions were providing the ideal environment for bomber fumes to produce contrails of condensation. The Luftwaffe, now mobilising their fighter pilots for the rich pickings in the sky above, would find hitting the target today a matter of child's play.

'Co-Pilot, descend immediately to 12,000 feet,' barked Tiler, 'we need to get rid of those trails and quick.'

'Yes Skip.'

The man at the controls took the aircraft down to the required level, a height at which they were much more vulnerable to flak, light so far on the outward journey. They were soon caught in a searchlight and hit by shrapnel from nearby explosions, the airframe shaking violently as a consequence.

The Rear Gunner came through on the intercom.

'We've still got the vapour trails Skipper.'

Despite dropping 10,000 feet, the air was still cold enough to produce the tracks of condensation.

'Thanks Rear Gunner... Co-Pilot... ascend to 21,000 feet.'

'Yes Skip.'

The Lancaster rapidly gained height to escape the anti-aircraft fire, yet there was no let-up from the danger. Within minutes the crew witnessed an RAF bomber on the horizon explode into a ball of flames, its blazing remains immediately nose-diving towards the ground. The navigator was alerted to record the loss. Almost instantly, the same thing happened, and then inexplicably another. This was carnage in the skies. Yet it didn't quite make sense. They had yet to see an enemy fighter and were out of range from the anti-aircraft guns. But then they saw it with their own eyes.

They watched with heart-racing alarm as a Messerschmitt 110 appeared in the distance, the Luftwaffe pilot manoeuvring his aircraft into a position that was directly under a Halifax to shoot down the bomber with an upward-firing gun. This was new. None of the crew in the stricken Handley Page would have seen the enemy hidden immediately below. Eric and the two pilots all looked at one another. Words were not required. One long, undeviating leg for the bomber stream from Belgium to the north of Nuremberg, a cloudless sky, vivid moonlight, vapour trails guiding the attacker, and fighter planes with the ability to shoot upward when positioned in a blind spot beneath the aircraft... Eric experienced fear in the pit of his stomach like never before, and he heard the Skipper reciting the 23rd Psalm quietly under his breath. Yet there was still some way to go to reach the target. According to the navigator, they were 30km Northwest of Koblenz, only halfway along the straight leg greeted with such dismay at the earlier briefings.

'Co-pilot, it's better if I take the contr...'

Flight Lieutenant Tiler was unable to finish his sentence because ME638 was suddenly rocked by the deafening impact of a direct hit from an enemy fighter below, the aircraft immediately lurching to one side. The engines shrieked and groaned in unison as crew and equipment were buffeted from their positions, Eric falling to the left and colliding with Harry Hughes, who manfully struggled at the controls to get the Lancaster level again. He succeeded for a few brief seconds, long enough for Eric to assimilate that the situation was hopeless.

'Starboard wing and both starboard engines on fire Skipper,' shouted Eric.

From the rapid intercom exchanges, it was clear that all crew had survived the hit. The skipper was decisive.

'Prepare to abandon aircraft... prepare to abandon aircraft.'

The stricken Lancaster was losing height, and the crew knew from training they had little time. The skipper, navigator, and wireless operator had their parachutes attached and moved to the rear of the plane to meet up with the gunners for their escape. Eric reached behind his seat to locate the parachutes for the pilot and flight engineer, clipping his own on first and Harry's second, ensuring the handle was on the right hand side. The planned escape route for them was the small hatch by the bomb aimer's prone position, the space measuring no more than 23" x 26", a difficult task at the best of times, but with a parachute attached in a fuselage being battered by the forces of nature on its inexorable fall to earth, it was nigh impossible. The noise inside the dying metal frame of the Avro was now thunderous, the engines screaming in protest as the aircraft headed towards its fate.

Harry arrived at the escape point first, glanced back at Eric, and held his thumbs aloft, Eric returning the gesture. But when the co-pilot tried to open the hatch, it was stuck. Frantically, he heaved with all his might but to no avail. Eric moved adjacent to try himself. It was no good. The strike from the enemy fighter had been from underneath, and the hit had buckled and damaged this part of the fuselage. They were not getting out of the Lancaster here.

The aircraft was getting closer and closer to its inevitable impact with the forests and picturesque scenery of the Rhine and Moselle countryside, the roar emitted by the engines, an increasingly high-pitched, complaining bellow. Scrambling back up from the bomb bay, the pair headed towards the rear of the plane in order to take the same escape route as the others. Beneath the layers of his protective clothing, Eric was sweating profusely, the inside temperature of the Avro rising with every second as fire and acrid smoke spread through the fuselage. He was now calling upon reserves of energy, reserves of determination, reserves of courage but was perilously close to running dry, and he slumped to the floor in utter despair on discovering that the exit to the rear was blocked by a fireball. They were trapped, the two men retreating back to the bomb bay. They had to try the front hatch again. It was their one and only hope.

Eric grabbed a fire axe and attempted to prize it open.

'Open you bastard! Open you bastard!' he screamed at the top of his voice, his body vibrating as much as the Lancaster as he summonsed every ounce of energy left within his body, continuing to hammer and hammer at the hatch until the last drop of his resolve faded away to be replaced by the resignation that this was the end. Harry Hughes was lying on the floor whimpering and repeating the 23rd Psalm that Flight Lieutenant Tiler had whispered a few minutes earlier. Eric sank to his knees. So this was it. Twenty years, not quite twenty one. He would live no more. Not a year more, not a month more, not a week more, not a day more, not an hour more, not a minute more. Yet a few seconds more as an incredible calm overtook him and time seemed to slow. An overpowering feeling of love was enveloping him.

He was suddenly on his Kirmington bike riding past the Post Office in Barnetby-le-Wold with the plume of smoke from the train at the station coming into view. He was just in time to make his connection back home. He was then with his mum and dad guiding them by the hand through the lobby of the Adelphi Hotel to lead them to a table where they enjoyed the luxury of an afternoon tea. He thanked them for their love, for their care, for bringing him up the right way, for imparting the right values, and for allowing him to follow his dream, even if things hadn't turned out how they might have done. He was then with Billy, brothers in arms of love and affection, walking through Central Park on the way to the Boot Inn. They had been robbed of so much time together thanks to Adolf Hitler and the war, and they would never walk together as adults. But there was still time for that pint and sitting at the bar in the pub, they drank their mild, Billy promising his brother he would always take care of Mum and Dad. And then Eric was knocking on Vera's front door. She answered, looking as beautiful as the first time he set eyes upon her at bible class, all those years ago. She invited him into the empty house. He tried to say something, something about marriage, about love, about children, about a life together, a long life, but nothing came out, his words choking. She put a finger to his lips and placed the black bible in his palm before leading him up a flight of stairs towards a door that opened out into a room full of the most intense, bright light Eric had ever seen in his short life. They kissed and held one another tightly until a peace and serenity descended, and he drifted away to a far, distant, unknown place, a place of comfort, a place of peace, a place of love.

PART THREE

QUEEN ELIZABETH

CHAPTER 40

Ted Whitfield was reading the morning's Daily Post, its date Wednesday 3rd May 1950. The back pages previewed the football fixtures for Liverpool at home to Huddersfield Town and Tranmere away at Doncaster Rovers, while the inside pages found plenty of space to discuss the big event taking place in Birkenhead later the same day. Queen Elizabeth was visiting Cammel Laird Shipyard to launch the Royal Navy's latest aircraft carrier. Everything about the ship was brand new other than its name, the Ark Royal, and its bell, rescued from the vessel sunk in the Mediterranean by a German U-Boat at the height of the Second World War.

It was the usual breakfast of porridge for Billy, and as he stared at the grey sludge in his bowl, he anticipated what lay in store today. It was reckoned that 60,000 people were attending the launch ceremony to witness the Ark Royal slide from its dry dock moorings into the murky waters of the River Mersey. Shipyard workers and two guests were entitled to attend, but as his dad was working in his latest job at Heavysege's wine and spirit merchants, his mum and her friend Lily 'Birkenhead' were to accompany him. The Royal visit had generated a great deal of excitement, especially on the part of his mother, still largely preoccupied with what hat and coat to wear. Only yesterday, Ted Whitfield had vented his feelings.

'Bloody hell Eva... it's the launch of a bloody ship not a Royal Wedding.'

'Less of the bloodies Ted.'

Some things never changed. Eva's vain attempt to curb her husband's language was a battle as forlorn as that to stop him breaking wind when bending down to grab his shoes from the bottom of the wardrobe every morning.

Billy had worked on the Ark Royal for most of his time served at Lairds. He was now twenty two and a qualified fitter, his hopes of becoming a draughtsman dissolving many years before within weeks of losing his job at GEC. His application for an apprenticeship at the shipbuilder had occurred immediately after the news came through that Eric was missing, his mum insistent he get a trade to protect him from being called up. His preference for design to utilise his drawing skills had been forlorn with no available vacancies for apprentice draughtsmen. They did, however, need fitters, and so after his dad had paid the requisite £10 upfront fee, a career was born for the young Billy Whitfield, his first day of work in the shipyard the Monday after his sixteenth birthday, a mere four weeks on from Eric's Nuremberg sortie.

'It'll be lovely to meet the Queen,' said Eva, trying on a hat in the mirror for the umpteenth time.

'Bloody hell Eva, not that old chestnut again,' Ted moaned. 'She'll be a little dot on the horizon. That's not what you call meeting someone. Bloody hell... we had this when the King opened the tunnel.'

'Oh bugger off Ted,' said Eva, using language about as agricultural as she could muster.

Billy smirked into his empty porridge bowl.

'I wonder if the King'll be there?' she pondered, removing her hat and placing it on the table.

'He won't be there,' grumbled Ted. 'He's not a well man.'

'Well, whether he's there or not, it'll be a proud moment seeing the ship that Billy built.'

'Crikey, you've been busy haven't you son? Forty thousand tons of metal. That must have taken some building on your own.'

'Come off it Ted, you know what I mean. Anyway... shouldn't you be getting to work?'

'Alright, alright, bloody hell. I'll tell you something son. It's a woman's world we live in now, a bloody woman's world.'

Eva rolled her eyes

Billy had never seen so many people in one place before. Above the crowds, the giant cranes and rigs of the shipyard hovered menacingly, their industrial grey steel exteriors blending seamlessly with the overcast and featureless skies. Out on the river, the bulk of HMS Illustrious, its officers and crew standing in perpendicular lines on the decks and the galleys, was waiting in mildly choppy waters to welcome its fellow carrier. It was a blustery day and the women with posh hats, Billy's mum and Lily included, needed one hand on their headgear to stop it flying up into the air like a balloon. Most had something ready to wave, the swathes of working men their cloth caps, the women, small flags.

'Here she is,' somebody shouted.

A great roar went up from the well-wishers, the signal for a mass of deferential cheers and flag waving. At the head of a small group of dignitaries comprising naval commanders, old men in suits, and women in wide rim sun hats, Queen Elizabeth appeared, walking elegantly along a small, cordoned-off passageway to the side of the dry dock. Everybody wanted to pay tribute to this graceful lady with the warm smile who had stood so resolutely for her country during the darkest days of the war, a constant and unwavering presence of strength, determination and hope.

'Ooh Eva, doesn't she look lovely,' said Lily, standing on her tiptoes and flourishing a cloche-style hat she had borrowed from her mother for the occasion.

'I know Lily, really lovely.'

To Billy's eyes, she was that dot in the distance his dad had talked about. She was wearing a light blue coat with something on her head that seemed to have feathers sprouting upwards, presumably not a half-plucked turkey.

That was about as much as he could see.

But the real star of today's ceremony was 36,800 tons of British steel, 804 ft long, with a 112 ft beam and 33 ft draught, the Ark Royal's enormous, unblemished structure stretching out towards the Mersey. Billy had seen the vessel come to life from tiny beginnings to the bulk of its completed state. It was not a new sight, he had become familiar with its mighty presence for some time now, but viewing it ready to slide away to begin its sea-faring career brought a new level of wonder and admiration, and he had done his bit to make it happen.

The VIPs and bigwigs journeyed to the side of the giant hull and on to an elevated platform, its wooden edging emblazoned with a golden royal crest. The Queen approached a small table with a collection of tall microphones, continuing to acknowledge her supporters with the famous, almost slow motion wave of the right hand, her other grasping a bouquet of white flowers.

The cheering subsided when she started to speak over the public address system. Everyone knew the script, but it was a tremendous thrill nonetheless to hear the surprisingly child-like voice with its gentle, slightly high-pitched timbre.

'I name this ship Ark Royal. May God protect her and all who sail in her.'

Elizabeth was passed the sacrificial bottle of champagne hanging from its decorated swing, a joker in the crowd shouting a few words of encouragement. She launched the bottle towards the bow, and the glass smashed first time, spraying its bubbling contents to coat the steel panels. A giant roar from the crowd greeted the moment and another as the Ark Royal began its slow but steady slide away from dry land to its expected long life on the ocean waves. Its predecessor, built here in 1937, had only lasted four years before its demise at the hands of the German U-boat near Gibraltar. But at the start of this new 1950s decade, the war seemed a long time ago, and there was growing optimism that such ships would be more about keeping the peace than fighting the wars.

Admiring the sleek lines of the Royal Navy's latest edition, Billy had a sudden desire to find paper and pencil to sketch the vessel, the young fitter's mind drifting back to his childhood drawing of HMS Hood, the battlecruiser that had earned him first prize in the school art competition in Bridgnorth. Bridgnorth... that sleepy Shropshire town, his home for over fifteenth months when just a lad... it had been by some distance the most formative time of his life, shaping him in so many ways. He still had moments hankering after those days, harsh and austere yet blessed with a beauty and splendour absent from the industrial towns and cities of his everyday life since. Notwithstanding the context of the war, his day-to-day existence in 1941 and 1942 had been sugar-coated with an innocence and naivety long since replaced by experiences liable to leave more of a bitter taste. He supposed it was called growing up. He hoped one day to return to Bridgnorth to relive old times and discover what happened to the farmer, the farmer's wife, the farmer's daughter, and maybe even Dick Tracey the mysterious chauffeur.

As the ship rolled away from the adoring spectators, a few crew members and shipyard workers visible on the vast deck at the stern waved back. They looked like tiny toys. The tugboats in the water parted to allow the bulk of the Ark Royal through, the crowd permitting this wonder of British engineering one final wave and hurrah. Billy took a deep breath and exhaled with deep satisfaction. There she was in all her glory... the ship that Billy built.

It was time for the crowds to disperse, Eva and Lily Birkenhead, still holding on to their hats, leaving the ceremony to get the bus home, ready to tell friends and family about the day they saw the Queen. Meanwhile, Billy headed towards the machine shop, his normal place of work, to join up with fellow shipbuilders, a group of about fifty clustered at one end of the building, the size of three football pitches. They quickly began sparring with some good natured banter.

'Has anyone seen Tommy?'

'E's out on the Ark Royal.'

'What's 'e doin' there?'

'Got caught short and went to the lav at the wrong time.'

'I thought I saw him clinging on to the port side licking off the champagne!'

The laughter was interrupted by an anxious shout in the distance.

'Here she comes!'

Queen Elizabeth was on a tour of the shipyard and about to enter the machine shop. Without any discussion or planning, Billy and his fellow workers dispersed from their huddles to form straight lines a few men deep just in time to greet the royal visitor who appeared at the door with the same group of bigwigs in tow. This was no dot on the horizon. The wife of King George VI was a matter of yards away, resplendent in kingfisher blue.

Billy had not consciously pushed himself to the front of his group, but that's where he was positioned when the Queen began her slow walk along the improvised rows of dutiful subjects, inspecting them as though a group of soldiers at a passing out parade. She was carrying a white handbag under her arm, Billy pondering as to what was inside. A lipstick? A brush? A bottle of the lavender perfume now present in the air? She was getting closer by the second, his heart beat quickening. He adjusted his slightly hunched posture, flattened his hair with both hands, straightened out his clothes, and moistened his drying mouth by running his tongue across the surface of his lips. In this sea of work-hardened, weather-beaten, and in the case of some of the older workers, drink-soaked faces, the Queen's complexion was pale and delicate. She may have lacked the silver screen beauty of a Hollywood film star, but she had the requisite grace and elegance, with a smile that radiated natural warmth and friendliness.

For a while, it seemed she wasn't going to say anything, perhaps only there to observe the men and machinery that had grafted and crafted the Audacious-class aircraft carrier freshly launched. But then she stopped, as did all the men trailing behind her. She was standing immediately in front of Billy, looking him in the eyes. The situation had become unreal. Tens of thousands of workers and their friends and families had attended today in the hope of catching a glimpse of Queen Elizabeth, and she had chosen him, William Edgar Whitfield, as the one person to engage. A garden full of butterflies fluttered in his stomach. Would she move on or ask him a question? It was the latter.

'Have you worked here long?' she said, her words perfectly modulated in that same slightly high-pitched tone heard over the public address system earlier.

It was a maths question, not really Billy's strong suit. He tried to do the arithmetic in his head and came up with the wrong answer.

'Five years' ma'am.'

It had been six.

This was not the usual stage-managed royal exchange where the interviewees had been tutored by the Monarch's charges as what to say and how to say it, yet somewhere in his head, he had heard the instruction to say ma'am as in jam.

'And what is your job?'

'I'm a fitter ma'am.'

'And do you enjoying working here?'

His answer to her third question might have been more candid.

'It's alright I suppose... though it would be a lot better if we didn't have piss-pot bosses like Mr Billy Boot.'

He wisely chose the brief option.

'Yes ma'am.'

And with that, she smiled broadly, turned, and moved away slowly along the line and out of the machine shop, leaving him to come to terms with what had just happened.

Billy had forgotten his key and so had to knock at the front door, Rex the dog first to acknowledge the sound. This was different from the norm, having good news to impart. There had been plenty of occasions in the past when he had waited on the same stone step gathering the courage to confess something or other to his mum and dad, arriving home late from a dance or having his wages docked for bad timekeeping, to name but two. Today, unequivocally, was not run of the mill. He had done something only a handful of people achieved in their life, meeting and speaking with the Queen. His mum was going to be so proud of her son.

She answered the door.

'Hello Billy.'

'Mum...'

He followed her into the house, as she carried on the small talk.

'It was such a lovely day today. Lily really enjoyed herself. And didn't the Queen look wonderful. It was so good to see her close up.'

She was teeing him up beautifully, 'close up', according to her definition a few hundred yards. He took off his coat, placed it on the hook, and moved to sit down at one end of the settee in the back room.

'Did you want a cup of tea?' she asked, as she always asked.

He usually said no, but today it was a yes. He was savouring the moment, enjoying the harbouring of his remarkable secret. It was only when they were both sitting down enjoying a gentle sip from their china cups that he chose the moment.

'Mum, you won't believe what happened today?'

A shaft of alarm penetrated her features. Billy had too much previous for her to relax at such a question, never quite able to navigate the straight line.

'What? What happened? You're not in any sort of trouble are you Billy?

371

'No, no, of course not.'

'Then what?'

'I met the Queen.'

'We all met the Queen silly, she...'

'No mum, I really met Queen Elizabeth. She visited the machine shop and stood right there in front of me then asked a few questions.'

Eva was struggling to comprehend and sensibly concluded he was playing the prankster.'

'Don't be daft,' she said dismissively, 'you shouldn't tell fibs like that...'

'Mum, I promise, I'm not telling fibs. It's the God's honest truth.'

Something in his earnest manner made her think twice.

'She really talked to you?'

'Yes.'

He told her of the bland exchanges. She didn't know what to say, incredulous that her son had truly met the Queen.

'Eric would have been so proud.'

It was a rather strange thing to say. His mum didn't mention her elder son very often, his memory fading with each passing day, but she would occasionally reintroduce him to the conversation and their lives. Having heard Billy's momentous news, a rare moment of absolute joy, the first person she wanted to tell was Eric. He glanced at his mother. Her face had taken on a drawn, faraway look, one that he had seen before... on that fateful day at the end of March 1944.

372

CHAPTER 41

Spring 1944 was underway, tomorrow the start of April, the month in which Billy would reach the age of sixteen. He was returning from the cinema after seeing Nelsen Eddy and Jeanette McDonald sing their hearts out in *New Moon*, and as he hummed the tune to 'Stout Hearted Men', he mused there was nothing like a musical to change the mood, a factor all the more welcome after recently losing his job at GEC. And so it was a confident and optimistic Billy that turned the lock in the front door to enter and walk through to the back room of the three-bedroom terraced house in Barrington Road.

He knew immediately that something was wrong, the boisterousness of the Eddy and McDonald sing-a-long dying in an instant. The room was silent... silent other than the ticking clock. His mum and his dad were sat in their respective armchairs staring ahead almost vacantly into space, and at one end of the settee, he was surprised to find Great Uncle Joe, his expression stern, serious, sombre.

'Sit down Billy,' he said kindly, patting the space next to him.

Billy did as he was asked.

'It's Eric,' said his mum, her impassive face giving nothing away.

'What about him?'

'He's missing.'

She handed Billy a small, buff-coloured piece of paper. It was a Post Office Telegram with a hand written message.

Regret to inform you that your son Sgt Eric Norman Whitfield is missing as a result of air operations on the night 30th March 1944 - stop - letter follows - stop -

pending receipt of written notification from the Air Ministry no information should be given to the press.'

There was no wailing, hysteria or drama. Yet neither was the atmosphere one of shock, the dangers of Bomber Command delivering an element of expectation and inevitability about the news. The realities of war had deadened the senses, the continuing quiet shrouding the room in a cloak of preoccupied detachment, emotions of any colour, absent. There were plenty of questions to ask, not least of all 'what does missing mean?', but nothing more was said, and the day ended with Joe going home, and the rest of the family quietly making their way to bed, hopeful of a peaceful night's sleep and an awakening from this bad dream the following morning, hopes they all knew were both forlorn and pitiful.

Two days later, the letter from the RAF arrived.

Dear Mr Whitfield,

Confirming the telegram of recent date, I regret to inform you that the RAF Casualty Officer has advised me that a report has been received from the International Red Cross Society at Geneva concerning your son, Sergeant Eric Norman Whitfield, previously reported missing on Active Service.

The report quotes German information which states that your son lost his life on March 31st 1944, but does not contain any additional particulars. The International Red Cross Society is making every effort to obtain further information, although I feel sure you will appreciate the difficulties attendant upon securing such details.

Since this information originates from enemy sources, it is necessary for the present to consider your son 'missing presumed killed' until confirmed by further evidence. However, in the absence of additional information, his death will be presumed after a lapse of six months from the date he was reported missing.

May I assure you and the members of your family of my deepest sympathy.

Yours sincerely,

Acting Wing Commander F. Powney
Squadron Commander
166 Squadron

'Missing presumed killed.'

When Billy read the letter, the word 'killed' might just as well have been written in capital letters with a double underline, such was its power to jump from the page and demand his attention. He suspected his old man thought the same, his mum, however, had focussed on a different word.

'Presumed... they've only presumed,' she said quietly. 'He might be a prisoner of war.'

She was having the conversation on her own, neither husband nor son required to make any comment. The Eva Lillian Whitfield from forty eight hours before was talking to the present day version, reviving the spent hope and faith. The exchange had an impact, his mum perking up as the day progressed. However, later in the evening, there was another hammer blow to the prospects of an unlikely happy ending. Lord Haw-Haw was broadcasting from his Hamburg base.

The Whitfield family, in common with most British households, tuned in regularly to hear 'This is Germany Calling' spoken in a deliberately hackneyed upper-class toff's accent. In the regular feature where the names of newly captured prisoners of war were read out, they were stunned to hear the crew of ME638 mentioned, all those present sitting up instinctively. This could be the moment when his mother's optimistically-charged intuition was vindicated. Lord Haw-Haw articulated the pilot's name, Flight Lieutenant Tiler as a POW. Eva's eyes widened. More names followed from the same crew, all survivors, all safe, all in the hands of the

375

enemy. But there was no Sergeant E N Whitfield listed, and when the broadcast moved on to another crew, his brother's fate was sealed. Eric had paid the ultimate price for serving his country. Billy shot a glance at his mum. She was sat back in her chair, knitting some indeterminate object, perhaps a scarf, little use to anyone with the summer months ahead, but he knew it was the act, not the item that was important. Her face betrayed no upset or resignation. It was neutral, unreadable, frozen from any reaction culled from the extremes. His dad picked up the newspaper to read. Billy was being taught an important lesson for times ahead. Life goes on.

****

The ill-fated bombing raid on Nuremberg had proved a disaster, not just at a personal level for families such as Eric's, but at a strategic level for Bomber Command. Nearly a hundred aircraft were lost on the 30th /31st March 1944, a night when the assertion of Commander-in-Chief Arthur Harris that area bombing would win the war for the Allies, like so many of his four engine bomber aircrews, was shot down in flames. The abject failure of the mission provided the signal for the Air Ministry to change strategy thereafter.

Three months on from Eric's death, the D-Day landings turned the war unequivocally in favour of the Allies, after which victory in Europe became a matter of when rather than if. Although Bomber Command played a key role in Operation Overlord, launching raids on pre-invasion targets, their part was relegated to one of support. They would not emerge from these battles as the heroes of the hour, Churchill and his Chiefs of Staff extraordinarily keen to sweep their carpet bombing strategy under the mat for fear of any war crimes retribution.

None of this was known to the families of the aircrew who had lost their lives fighting the Nazis in the conflict labelled later in the decade, the

Second World War, although a few started to wonder a thing or two. The military honours awarded to those who served in Bomber Command were minimal. Eric had posthumously earned the 1939-1945 Star, the Air Crew Europe Star, and the War Medal, but the attitude of his mum and dad to the medals was dismissive, seeing them as little more than bits of metal and ribbon. If they had been lovingly presented in a ceremony of commemoration, respect and honour, they may have felt different. Even the brief letter from King George VI at Buckingham Palace was filed away without any particular attention.

The Queen and I offer you our heartfelt sympathy in your great sorrow. We pray that your country's gratitude for a life so nobly given in its service may bring you some measure of consolation.'

And so as the politicians and leaders embraced their convenient military amnesia, the Brylcreem Boys lost their sheen. It would fall upon friends and family to ensure these brave men were never forgotten.

Yet eighteen months on from Nuremberg and nearly six months since the end of the war, Eric was rarely talked about in the Whitfield household, and if he was mentioned, it was normally in the context of something trivial or ordinary such as playing the piano or the neatness of his handwriting. Discussion beyond the mundane was effectively out of bounds. Then from nowhere, he was catapulted back centre stage.

One morning, an envelope with a Koblenz postmark landed on the mat in the hall. Billy handed it to his mum who moved her knitting to the side of the armchair and sat down to read the letter inside.

'It's in German,' she said. 'I can't understand a word.'

She passed it back to her son. It was predictably nonsense to Billy's eyes, aside from the occasional reference to Sgt E N Whitfield.

'Do you know anyone who speaks German?' he asked, turning the page as though another angle might be more illuminating.

'The Red Cross in Liverpool can...'

377

Her words trailed away. Inside the envelope, she had found a small accompanying photograph measuring about 5" x 3". Her stare was expressionless, Billy about to discover that a picture could paint a thousand words. Its impact severed all hope, however unpromising and desperate. Eric had not survived the war.

'What's the photo Mum?'

She didn't offer it him, though nor did she resist when he took it from her hand. He studied the monochrome image. Against a background of trees and woodland, two white crosses were positioned upright in the ground, wild flowers and plants threatening to overwhelm their base. One cross was marked 'Hughes 921975', the other 'Whitfield 1622364'. It was a photograph of Eric's final resting place. There was nothing more to say. The words 'presumed killed' were now simply 'killed'.

The impact of the news on his mum and dad took Billy by surprise. The sight of the grave had a strangely calming effect on his mother. She had naturally yearned for him to be alive somewhere, but after such a long passage of time, the certainty of his fate was a blessed relief. At last she knew. At last she could accept the fact. His father, however, suddenly appeared a broken man. Billy had never had an insight into his dad's thoughts about Eric. He had been a closed book. But now the pages were open, flapping in strong winds, the paragraphs a message of grief and sorrow. The Red Cross translation of the Bürgermeister's letter provided some comfort, referring to Eric's body as 'unblemished' when found, thereby refuting the more unpleasant explanations of his final moments. But for now, Ted Whitfield was grieving for his lost son.

****

A few months on and Barrington Road played host to three visitors, all attired in full RAF uniform. They were survivors from Eric's Nuremberg flight, including the pilot, Flight Lieutenant Tiler. During a polite yet uncomfortable occasion, the men spoke of their admiration for their lost colleague and recounted their time as POWs, before the conversation veered with mutual uneasiness towards the final seconds of ME638. The testimony of these crew members suggested that when they had left the aircraft through the rear, they fully expected Eric and the co-pilot to bail out of the front escape hatch in good time. The Lancaster was on fire, and the flames would have stopped them escaping through the rear, but they had enough time to leave the blazing aircraft through the exit by the bomb aimer's position. They could only speculate that the hatch was damaged and would not open.

The aircrew had a train to catch and so respectfully made their excuses and departed, Billy and his parents watching them walk down the road until they had turned the corner. The sight of young aircrew in RAF uniform disappearing from view, never to be seen again, was a more than symbolic moment.

****

The photograph from the Bürgermeister and the visit of his final crew members proved to be the turning point, the finality of the message paving the way for acceptance and therefore the true beginning of the healing process. However, there was one final trial for Billy's mum and dad, a letter arriving from the Air Ministry in September 1947.

Dear Mr Whitfield,

I am very sorry to renew your grief in the loss of your son, Sergeant Eric Norman Whitfield, but I am sure you will wish to know that the exhumations carried out by the Royal Air Force Missing Research and Enquiry Service at Weidenhahn have proved successful, and so your son has now been reverentially re-interred in Rheinberg British Military Cemetery, where he lies in Plot 10 Row A Grave 23. I should add that within his original grave, a bottle was found that contained a message written in French. Translated, it read 'This Aviator who fell at midnight on 30th March 1944 was buried by French prisoners on 1st April 1944'.

This policy has been agreed upon by His Majesty's and Dominion's Governments because it was felt that our fallen in Germany should not be left in isolated cemeteries but should rest in special War cemeteries which have been carefully chosen for the natural beauty and peace of their surroundings. The graves will be cared for in perpetuity by the British Staff of the Imperial War Graves Commission who will write to you later to consult your wishes regarding the inscription upon the headstone they will erect in your son's memory.

I do sincerely hope that this positive information about your son's last resting place will be of some slight comfort to you in your very great loss.

Yours sincerely,

G J Stephens
Group Captain
For Chief of the Air Staff

It was a grizzly business for bereaved parents to consider, the digging up of their son's remains to be transferred to a specially constructed war cemetery, and it presented a dilemma and difference of opinion.

'I think we should go and see the grave,' said Ted.

This caught Billy's mum unawares.

'Oh, I'm not sure,' she replied.

She might have added 'it won't bring him back you know,' but for the time being she said nothing further.

Billy noted his dad's persistence over the coming days, and at one point it seemed he would go on his own, but the plans never came to anything. Eric was finally laid to rest in body and in the minds of his nearest and dearest, alone, six hundred miles from home.

Plot 10.

Row A.

Grave 23.

CHAPTER 42

Billy awoke to the sounds of a key scraping in the front door lock and a bark from Rex. He had been asleep in the chair, dreaming about Eric, letters, telegrams, photographs, Bürgermeisters, RAF aircrew, and war cemeteries. He rubbed his eyes. It was 1950, and he smiled. Today he had spoken with the Queen, and not many people could say that. It had been quite an occasion, watching with burgeoning pride the launch of the Ark Royal and then having a chat with the Monarch.

The door closed. It was his dad, whose opening line was highly predictable.

'Any chance of a cup of tea?'

'Ted, you'll never guess what happened today?'

'Eh? What?'

'You'll never guess what happened today... at Lairds... with our Billy.'

'What are you talking about?'

'Tell him Billy,' said his mum excitedly.

'I met Queen Elizabeth today.'

His dad's response was as predictable as the request for a brew.

'Bloody hell, how many times do I have to tell you that seeing a little dot in the distance is not the same as meeting someone.'

Ted Whitfield's reluctance to accept the full tenure of his son's story continued, until a few days later when the doubts evaporated. Billy came rushing into the house early in the evening, breathless.

382

'Mum! Dad! I'm on at the pictures.'

'What's that?'

'I'm on the Pathé News... at the cinema... talking to the Queen.'

His parents wasted no time in rushing to see their son's moment on the silver screen at the Capitol picture house in Liscard, but their timing was not the best, arriving just in time to see a dreadful 'B' Movie with acting so wooden the film's lead might have been a wardrobe. Eventually, their patience was rewarded with the sound of a cockerel and the start of the news reel they had come to see.

QUEEN LAUNCHES ARK ROYAL

Accompanied by jaunty music, an optimistic voice-over mined diminished patriotic reserves to rekindle the belief that 'Britannia Rules the Waves' and that British workmanship remained the envy of the world. It was not a long piece, but long enough to incorporate a section where Queen Elizabeth visits the machine shop and stops for a brief conversation with one of the fitters, an attentive employee with black, swept-back hair and a fresh face. The fitter was Billy, Eva needlessly looking at her son and then at the film to verify they were one and the same.

Billy appraised the young man projected on to the giant screen in black and white. It was definitely him, but it seemed a better looking version. When gazing in the mirror, he was often disappointed with the image returned. His brother Eric had been a fine-looking child who developed into a handsome young man, but the best Billy could muster when young was an impish face, and as he embraced adulthood, he thought his eyes too small, his ears too big, and his frame too slight. In his mind it explained why he never seemed to get the girl, the twins Norma and Eileen, for example, always more taken with his friends Ronnie and Johnny than him. But maybe he was being too harsh on himself. He hadn't commanded the screen the way Gary Cooper or Jimmy Stewart did, but Billy Whitfield was no Mr Pastry. He vowed to have more confidence in how he looked. Who knows, it might change his luck with the girls.

The newsreel ended and the house lights came on, his mum and dad beaming with pride.

'You see Ted... he really did meet the Queen.'

'Bloody hell... who'd have thought it, eh son? Out of all the people there, she chose you.'

A few people came up to him, firing questions.

'Are you the chap who spoke to the Queen?'

'What did she say to you Billy?'

'Does she have blue eyes or green?'

'Did she talk about the King?'

For a short while, Billy Whitfield was a film star.

When it went quiet again, his mum asked, 'What's the main film son?'

'*A Matter of Life and Death*, the David Niven film.'

'Oh...'

His mum's mood changed.

'Come on Ted... we better get home.'

'What do you mean?'

'You stay and enjoy the film... we've got to go.'

She was already getting up to leave. Whether his dad liked it or not, he was not going to see the main feature today. Billy soon understood why.

It was exactly five years since the war ended, and to commemorate the anniversary of VE Day, the local cinema was showing the acclaimed Powell and Pressburger film. Billy sat back in his seat and watched the opening frames depict the universe, its stars, its suns and solar systems, the narrator, his voice, honeyed, calm, describing the spectacle. But when the camera zoomed in on planet earth, the action switched to night skies over Europe during the Second World War. A conversation was taking place between an American radio operator called June and Squadron Leader

384

Peter Carter, a Royal Air Force pilot at the controls of a burning Lancaster bomber. He had no parachute and therefore realised he was going to die. The parallels with Eric were stark, and Billy breathed a sigh of relief that his mum had left early. Nonetheless, he enjoyed the film, a celestial fantasy about the afterlife, the initial harrowing scenes not representative of the overall movie.

After the playing of the national anthem, Billy left the auditorium with the rest of the audience. As he walked into the foyer, he heard someone call his name.

'Billy! Billy!'

He looked around, and through the crowd spotted Maurice, a pal who worked as a projectionist at the cinema.

'Hello Maurice... how's it going?'

'Fine thanks... I've got something for you. Wait here a minute.'

With no further explanation, he disappeared through a staff only door, Billy waiting as the hordes became a trickle. Maurice eventually reappeared carrying a white envelope that he gave to his friend.

'What's this?' said Billy, a little confused.

'Have a look.'

'Alright.'

Inside was a small section of filmstrip, Maurice eager to explain.

'I've cut it from the Pathé News reel. It's you with the Queen. You should be able to get a photograph from it.'

'Thanks very much Maurice... that's very kind. My mum will be delighted.'

He shook his hand and left the picture house. It was a mild evening, the moon casting its light through a largely cloudless sky. Billy held up the filmstrip to take a closer look at the image with a little lunar help, yet his eyes did not see the Queen and the loyal subject in conversation, or the admiring, awestruck fellow workers, or the backdrop that was the shipyard's machine shop. Instead, there were the stars in the sky, the suns, the solar systems, and then a voice over the radio waves from a Lancaster Bomber, stricken, wounded, burning.

'Billy Whitfield?'

His reverie was broken by a woman's voice. He turned around to see Ethel, the lady from the ticket office.

'Yes?'

'I saw you on the news. Fancy you meeting the Queen, hey love... you're such a lucky man.'

She walked away to catch her bus home, leaving Billy alone on the pavement. His gaze returned to the heavens. He had recently turned twenty two, one year longer than Eric had managed, and yet he still had many, many years ahead of him. Ethel was so right.

Billy Whitfield was a very lucky man.

POSTSCRIPT

ERIC

Bomber Command continues to divide opinion. Some contend the Avro Lancaster won the war for Britain, and that a grave injustice was done when Sir Arthur 'Bomber' Harris failed to receive the recognition he deserved after the war for his efforts during the conflict. Others believe the area bombing strategy that killed so many ordinary Germans constituted a clear example of war crimes, an unforgivable practice that shamed Britain. Learning about the raids on Hamburg in 1943 and the firestorm that killed 45,000 inhabitants, it is difficult to deny the latter argument some credence. In most assessments of the strategy, the individual who comes out worst is that great warrior himself Winston Churchill. In 1940, he was the architect of the original idea and labelled RAF bombers as 'the means of victory'. Yet by the time of his closing speech at the end of the war, Bomber Command did not even warrant a passing mention within his victorious oratory.

But this largely misses the point. The unspoken victims of the controversy are the ordinary young men who so readily gave up their lives for King and Country. Sergeant Eric Norman Whitfield was not responsible for the strategy. He was simply doing his job, a job that required a special kind of courage, almost unfathomable in this day and age. He was one of 125,000 volunteers who served in Bomber Command during the war, from which a staggering 55,573 were killed, 8,403 wounded in action, and a further 9,838 made prisoners of war. Only one in six survived a tour of thirty operational sorties, and a scarcely believable one in forty a second tour. It was the most dangerous place for a serviceman to be in World War Two, more deadly than being an infantry officer in the First World War.

Yet it was not until 2012 that a suitable memorial was unveiled for later generations to pay their respect, and there has to be an element of shame that this required private funding. The Bomber Command Memorial in Green Park London is a fitting tribute, constructed from Portland stone and housing a wonderfully detailed bronze sculpture of a seven man aircrew that have just left their aircraft on returning from a bombing raid. It is a commemoration rather than a celebration, and however you interpret this part of history, the fallen from Eric's generation are fully deserving of such a moving remembrance.

When he died, many things died with Eric. It's not known what became of many of his friends and colleagues, including Vera and Len; though it's likely they went on to live normal, uneventful lives. As for the RAF, there were a number of surprises and poignant occurrences. Eric was deemed unlucky to be called up as a late replacement for the flight engineer with jaundice on the fateful Nuremberg mission. Yet four weeks later, the same man, fit again, was killed on a bombing raid. As for his original crew, Don, Charlie and Arthur survived the war, though both Ginger and Barrington were indeed sadly killed on that 26th March 1944 sortie to Essen. There was a happy ending for Mac, the man who struggled as their pilot. Six months after disappearing from 166 Squadron, he re-emerged having earned an officer commission. The man he could most thank for giving him the time and chance to do this, Wing Commander Fred Powney unfortunately 'bought one' over Denmark when leading from the front during the last weeks of the war.

Hailing from an era when a family of two children was unusual; there is little doubt that Eric's demise had a long lasting effect on his mum and dad. If one of (say) ten siblings, the impact of his loss may have been diminished, but he was the first born, the chosen one, the one allowed to learn piano, the one most likely to succeed. And he shared those aspirations. It was the main reason he volunteered for the RAF in the first place. In keeping with the times, Eva and Ted never really talked about it, aside from the occasional brief reminiscence or comment, in itself corroboration that they never really recovered from his loss.

The final and most difficult question to answer regarding Eric's short life relates to his death. How did he die? The testimony of the Bürgermeister that he was found unblemished does, on the face of it, appear unlikely, given that the burning, fully bombed-up aircraft was still carrying three quarters of its fuel load at the time it went down. The RAF Casualty Office has confirmed that the identification of Eric and the co-pilot was sourced via their ID tags, made from asbestos and protected from incineration. The most horrific theory imagines the trapped aviators burnt alive by the fire raging within the aircraft as mentioned by the last survivor who parachuted to safety from the Lancaster. But in that scenario, the likely cause of death would have been smoke inhalation. The Avro was a fantastic aircraft, rightly held up as one of the marvels of British Engineering from the era, yet it was not designed with safety at the forefront. There would have been many inflammable structures and pieces of equipment that would have given off toxic fumes when ablaze.

Ultimately though, the Bürgermeister's statement has to be considered legitimate. He had neither an axe to grind nor a compulsion to immunise the relatives of the dead from further suffering. His mission was to provide as much accurate information as possible. The conclusion, therefore, is that when the Lancaster made contract with the ground, the part of the aircraft housing Eric broke off and was jettisoned away from the main fuselage, thereby escaping the destruction that the fire and exploding fuel tanks would have exacted. It is the most likely explanation, and if we assume that Eric had lost consciousness before crashing due to the fumes, it is also the most palatable. For these reasons, it ought to go on record as the cause of his death.

Although from a family not especially religious, Eric was a young man who found great comfort and solace from the Bible. The version with his hand-written pages has survived, presenting clear evidence that here was someone who embraced his spiritual side, a man faithful, loyal, and dutiful, a good man with faith in the Lord and faith in the good book. A man who loved. A man who was loved. May he rest in peace.

Eric Norman Whitfield
Born: May 23rd 1923
Died: March 31st 1944

BILLY

By the end of the 1950, six months after his encounter with Queen Elizabeth at Lairds, Billy had met Joyce. Admiring the striking brunette on the dance floor of the Grosvenor Ballroom, he had tossed a coin with Ronnie Rose to see who would get the chance to ask her for the last waltz. He called heads and won. Joyce admired his clothes, Billy thankful for his mum's skills as a seamstress. In a sea of drab demob garments, his blue suit with hand stitching stood out as a cut above the rest. After the dance, he proposed to escort her home. She agreed, although this meant a bus journey to Moreton, and after a peck on the cheek outside her house, a sprint to chase down the last No.7 moving away from the bus stop on Birket Avenue. He jumped on to the moving vehicle and grabbed the handrail with seconds to spare, climbing the stairs to the top deck, where he sat down and looked out towards the night sky. He was ecstatic. Joyce Boughey was a stunner.

There were a few more dances and buses home, but one moment sealed their partnership, a partnership that has lasted over six decades. Joyce asked Billy to look after her ration card for sweets but then forgot about it. When he turned up early one evening, wearing a beautifully tailored suit and carrying the gift of one pound of assorted toffees and boiled sweets, she knew he was the man for her.

Billy Whitfield certainly did his bit to keep the surname going. He and Joyce went on to have five children, one daughter, Carol June in 1952, and four sons, Paul William in 1955, Christopher Colin - yes that Chris - in 1956, and twins David and Mark in 1961. The five children in turn produced twelve grandchildren, and now a new generation of great-grandchildren have made their way into the world.

Billy revisited Bridgnorth and Potseething Farm twice, once about twenty years ago, and the second time within the last year. On the first occasion he managed to meet up with Patricia, the daughter from the farm. She explained that by the time she had finished school and was working, her mother Rose had left Farmer George - by then completely disinterested in the farm - and returned to Newmarket. Although not explicit, there was an inference she had been accompanied by another man, presumably wearing a Dick Tracey hat and driving a sleek Jaguar.

The burden of raising a family brought Billy's promising football career to a premature end. After playing for Runcorn and South Liverpool in the Lancashire Combination, one level below the Football League, he was signed by New Brighton FC, newly relegated from the old Third Division North at the end of the 1951/52 season when failing to gain re-election. Although he continued to harbour dreams of playing in the FA Cup Final at Wembley; dreams fuelled by the occasional report that scouts from the big clubs like Aston Villa were scouring the lower leagues for new talent, the opportunity to sign for a top side remained elusive. After playing for a further couple of years, he was injured in a game against Wigan Athletic and forced to take unpaid leave from work as a consequence. With hungry mouths to feed, playing goalkeeper in the rough and tumble of non-league football was proving too much of a risk, and so he hung up his gloves and his boots to call it a day. He did make one return between the sticks in 1969 at the age of 41 for his works team, desperately short of men on the day. The side lost 0-6, though Billy had a decent game, keeping the scoreline almost respectable. Respectable, however, was not the word used to describe the next three days, when he lay comatose on the settee in a vain attempt to recover from the exertions of coming out of retirement.

On the job front, after Cammel Lairds he moved to Manganese Bronze, later Stone Manganese Marine, and remained there for the rest of his working life, finishing as an Engineering Inspector. His draughtsman aspirations were never fulfilled, but he carried on sketching, habitually impressing the men and offending the ladies with his big-nosed caricatures. He even took to painting at one stage, adept at landscapes such as the Liverpool waterfront, although his nudes' phase was far from his finest hour, many a young visitor's libido in peril when appraising the terrifying flesh hanging from the wall.

Billy was very fortunate to marry Joyce, for many reasons, not least because she was, and is, blessed with very youthful looks. This was put to most effect during the 1980s and 1990s when she was a regular contestant in the Butlin's Glamorous Grandmother Competition. She appeared on TV, in the newspapers, and on radio, the pair enjoying many cash prizes and holidays as a reward. She eventually won the competition when crowned national champion in 1992, her husband the first to admit he had done well and certainly punched above his weight.

Until her death at the age of eighty three in 1987, Billy was very close to his mum, Eva. The loss of Eric intensified the relationship between the pair, and Billy certainly lived the notion perpetuated by his dad, who died in 1969, that 'your mother will always be your best friend.'

He stayed pals with the likes of Ronnie Rose and Johnny Williams for many years, although when Johnny died in his fifties and Ronnie sadly developed dementia at an early age, Billy found himself gravitating towards the friendships that accompanied him on his nightly visit to the local pub for a pint of mild or two… or three… or maybe even four.

Now in the twilight of his days, Billy's involvement in the writing of this book has been genuinely cathartic. Revisiting in detail his time as an evacuee has helped him appreciate the significance of the experience. An experience that shaped his personality to one of self-reliance, independence, with a slight tendency to be a loner, notwithstanding the size of the Whitfield clan he has fathered. Yet even more significant has been the rediscovery of his long lost brother. Billy was only fifteen when Eric lost his life in the blazing steel tomb of his wounded Lancaster. Too emotionally immature to grieve, he unwittingly joined Winston Churchill and the strategists in failing to honour the memory of this courageous and valiant Bomber Command airman. However, he has now righted that wrong. Adolf Hitler may have torn the brothers apart over seventy years ago, but in the final analysis good always conquers evil. It is gratifying to report that Billy and Eric are brothers again, and closer than ever.

PHOTOGRAPHS

Eric 1924

Billy & Eric 1930

Billy & Eric 1929

Billy (top left) 1935

Billy 1936

397

View from Bridgnorth Hightown

Potseething Farm

Bridgnorth Castle

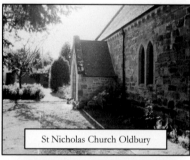

St Nicholas Church Oldbury

Billy, GEC employee

Joe & Billy in Liverpool

AC2 E N Whitfield 1942

Sgt E N Whitfield 1943

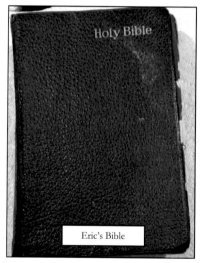

Eric's Bible

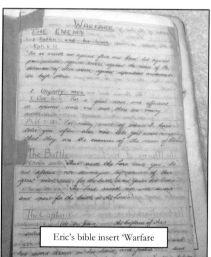

Eric's bible insert 'Warfare

Extract from Eric's RAF Personnel Records

Eric's bible insert 'G.O.S.P.E.L.'

400

WW2 Avro Lancaster four engine bomber

BUCKINGHAM PALACE

The Queen and I offer you our heartfelt sympathy in your great sorrow.

We pray that your country's gratitude for a life so nobly given in its service may bring you some measure of consolation.

George R.I.

E. Whitfield, Esq.

Telegram from the King

RAF mug shot

Eric's wallet gift from Vera

Flight Lieutenant M Hudson MA BA
AHB2A(SO2)
Air Historical Branch (RAF)
Bentley Priory Building
RAF Northolt
West End Road
Ruislip
HA4 6NG
United Kingdom

Telephone	+44 (0)20 8833 8162
Facsimile	+44 (0)20 8833 8170
E-mail: Personal	
Business	ahb.raf@btconnect.com

Ref. D/AHB(RAF)8/27
Mr W E Whitfield
██████████████

Wallasey
Wirral
██████████

4 March 2014

Dear Mr Whitfield

We have received your application for information from the RAF Casualty file relating to your late brother, Sergeant E N Whitfield, who lost his life whilst serving with the Royal Air Force in 1944. I have recalled and reviewed the relevant casualty file and the information that I have found is given below.

On the night of 30/31 March 1944 Sgt Whitfield was the Flight Engineer of Lancaster ME638 of 166 Squadron, which with 19 other aircraft from the Squadron, which was taking part in an attack on Nuremberg and failed to return. The crews from 166 squadron which did returned to RAF Kirmington reported that although the opposition from the ground defences was slight the fighter opposition was the heaviest they had yet experienced immediately they a[...] M.O.D. letter from Casualty Records [...]ircraft were engaged in comba[...] [...]r members of the crew of Lancaster ME638

Eric's initial grave in Wiedenhahn

Plot 10
Row A
Grave 23

Billy meets the Queen at the launch of the Ark Royal 1950

Billy and Rex 1947

Eva and Ted 1957

Billy and Joyce 1951

403

Top (L - R) Mark, Chris, Carol, Paul, Dave
Front (L - R) Billy, Joyce

Bomber Command Memorial and the Author

Billy & Joyce

The Author

Other books by Chris Whitfield:

The Drummer's Tale
Chimpanzees in Dungarees
Hitchhikers and Scary Bikers
Big Balls - World Cup Nations

www.chimpsindung.co.uk